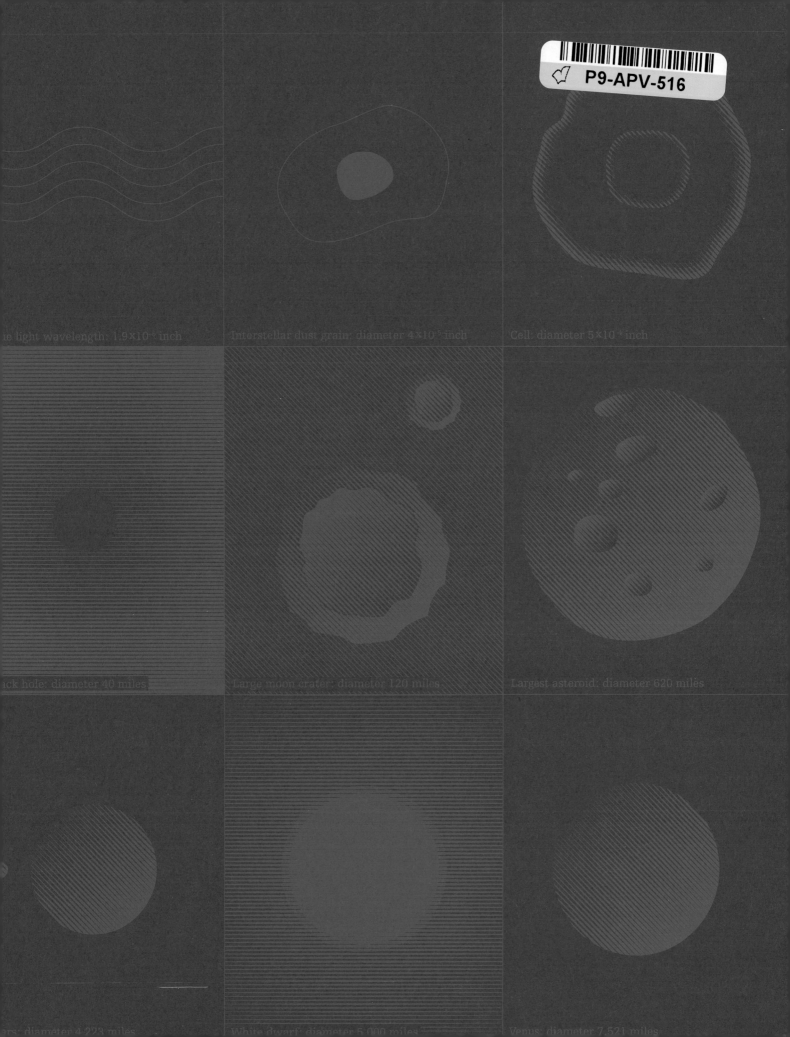

ie light wavelength: 1.9×10⁻⁵ inch

Interstellar dust grain: diameter 4×10⁻⁵ inch

Cell: diameter 5×10⁻³ inch

ick hole: diameter 40 miles

Large moon crater: diameter 120 miles

Largest asteroid: diameter 620 miles

ars: diameter 4,223 miles

White dwarf: diameter 5,000 miles

Venus: diameter 7,521 miles

ATLAS

Like air squadrons on a cosmic mission, galaxies move through space in stupendous gatherings bound together by gravity. The Local Supercluster, for example, whose principal members are depicted at near right, is dominated by the Virgo cluster *(center)*, which totals thousands of galaxies, including about 200 bright ones. Within the Local Supercluster, the Local Group *(box, far right)* is a loosely held collection of about 30 galaxies, shown here with the Milky Way galaxy at the center. Concentric circles in the box at right represent distances of 25 million light-years; those in the box at far right represent distances of about 650,000 light-years.

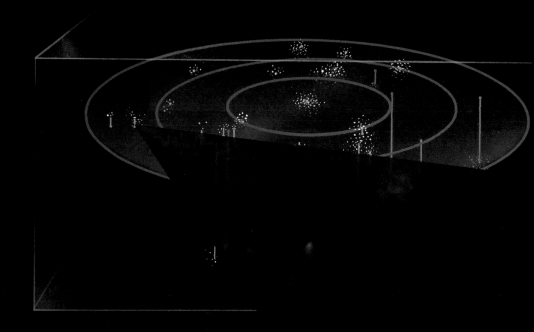

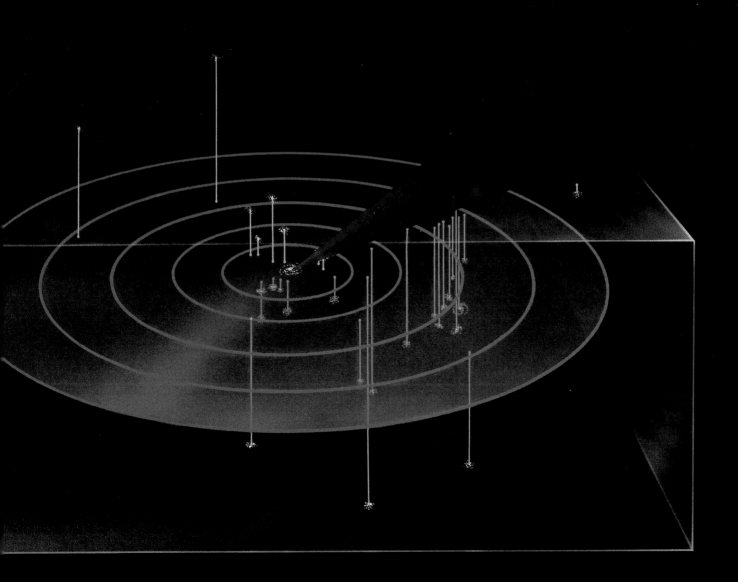

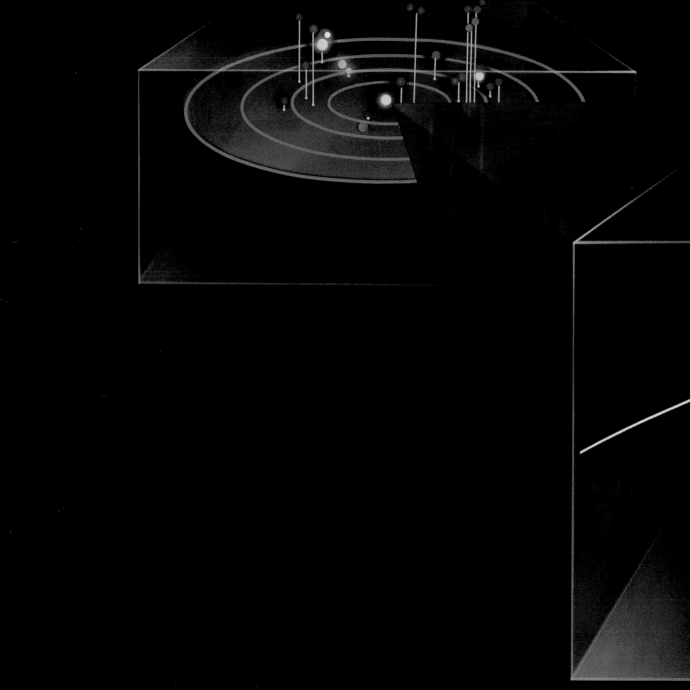

Spanning some 100,000 light-years from side to side, the Milky Way galaxy *(left, top)*—once believed to be the cosmos in its entirety—is now recognized as just one of billions of galaxies, its central bulge shining with the reddish light of older stars. Among the stars making up one of the galaxy's outlying spiral arms are the Sun and some of its nearest neighbors *(middle)*. A voyager zeroing in on that stellar grouping would find the Sun at the center of a clutch of nine planets—the Solar System that is Earth's home *(below)*.

Other Publications:
LOST CIVILIZATIONS
ECHOES OF GLORY
THE NEW FACE OF WAR
HOW THINGS WORK
WINGS OF WAR
CREATIVE EVERYDAY COOKING
COLLECTOR'S LIBRARY OF THE UNKNOWN
CLASSICS OF WORLD WAR II
TIME-LIFE LIBRARY OF CURIOUS AND UNUSUAL FACTS
AMERICAN COUNTRY
THE THIRD REICH
THE TIME-LIFE GARDENER'S GUIDE
MYSTERIES OF THE UNKNOWN
TIME FRAME
FIX IT YOURSELF
FITNESS, HEALTH & NUTRITION
SUCCESSFUL PARENTING
HEALTHY HOME COOKING
UNDERSTANDING COMPUTERS
LIBRARY OF NATIONS
THE ENCHANTED WORLD
THE KODAK LIBRARY OF CREATIVE PHOTOGRAPHY
GREAT MEALS IN MINUTES
THE CIVIL WAR
PLANET EARTH
COLLECTOR'S LIBRARY OF THE CIVIL WAR
THE EPIC OF FLIGHT
THE GOOD COOK
WORLD WAR II
HOME REPAIR AND IMPROVEMENT
THE OLD WEST

This volume is one of a series that
examines the universe in all its aspects, from
its beginnings in the Big Bang to the promise
of space exploration.

VOYAGE THROUGH THE UNIVERSE

ATLAS

BY THE EDITORS OF TIME-LIFE BOOKS
ALEXANDRIA, VIRGINIA

CONTENTS

1

10 **THE SOLAR SYSTEM**
64 THE PLANETARY DANCE

2

78 **STAR LIGHT, STAR BRIGHT**
92 THE STARRY FIRMAMENT

3

102 **GALAXIES ABOUNDING**
126 A TELESCOPE PRIMER

134 BIBLIOGRAPHY

137 INDEX

142 ACKNOWLEDGMENTS

143 PICTURE CREDITS

Circling the Sun counterclockwise in the course of a year, Earth's window on the cosmos changes each season: Constellations visible during the northern summer *(far left)* disappear in the fall; the winter sky *(below)* vanishes in the spring. Against this stellar backdrop, astronomers plot the movement of the Sun and planets along the ecliptic *(yellow band)*, the plane of Earth's orbit around the Sun.

hose who gaze at the sky from Earth have long perceived it as a celestial dome whose luminous inhabitants rise up from the eastern horizon and sink in the west. Because this heavenly panorama appears to move around Earth, the ancients believed that Earth was the stationary center of a revolving crystalline globe to which Sun, Moon, and stars were attached. Their theories were somewhat confounded, however, by five of the brightest starlike objects, which seemed to travel independently of the rest. Awed by these "planets" (Greek for "wanderers"), early societies named them in honor of their gods: Mercury, Venus, Mars, Jupiter, and Saturn.

In the second century AD, the Greek astronomer Ptolemy propounded a complicated system of circling spheres that accounted for the planets' waywardness yet preserved the geocentric, or Earth-centered, cosmos. The Ptolemaic scheme survived for more than 1,400 years, until Polish astronomer Nicolaus Copernicus published an alternative in 1543, instigating a revolution that would shake the foundations of science, theology, and philosophy. By the close of the seventeenth century, the geocentric view had given way to a heliocentric one, in which Earth was just one of several planets—eventually known to number nine—revolving around the Sun.

The heliocentric system explained many of the conundrums of celestial mechanics. For example, although constellations in the night sky seem to scroll past in a cycle that repeats every 365 days or so, it is actually Earth that moves, making its annual journey around the Sun. Each day, the planet progresses about one degree of arc along its orbit, and the stellar backdrop shifts accordingly, like the view from a slowly turning carousel. Furthermore, Earth was found not only to circle the Sun but also to spin around its own axis once every twenty-four hours as it goes, so that the Sun rises and sets at roughly twelve-hour intervals. And because this axis of rotation is tilted twenty-three and a half degrees to the plane of Earth's orbit, each hemisphere undergoes seasonal changes in the amount of sunlight it receives *(below and opposite, top).*

As for the planets, their peculiar habits were explained by the simple fact that they too orbit the Sun *(pages 14-15).* Mercury and Venus, traveling inside Earth's orbit, never stray very far from the Sun when viewed from the third planet and are visible for only a few hours after sunset or before sunrise. The outer planets, for their part, seem to undergo a kind of backward hiccup in their journey, an illusion resulting when Earth overtakes them on the inside—much as a car

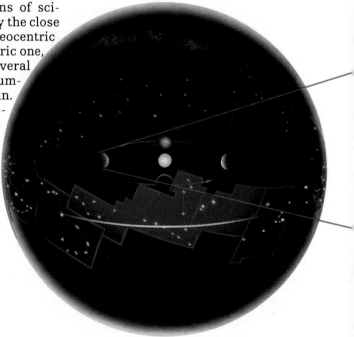

Because Earth is tilted twenty-three and a half degrees to its orbital plane *(yellow band),* the Northern and Southern Hemispheres experience opposite seasonal changes in temperature: Summer in the north is winter in the south *(near right).* The tilt also accounts for the lengthiness of summer days and the brevity of winter days, especially at high latitudes *(opposite, top and bottom).*

seems to drift backward from the viewpoint of a passing vehicle.

Yet despite the advent of a more accurate description of the Solar System, the age-old concept of Earth surrounded by a star-studded globe remains useful for mapping the movements of heavenly bodies. Such a model, based on how the heavens look from Earth, is called the celestial sphere *(below)*. Its major reference points are extensions of Earth's equator, poles, and orbital plane, or ecliptic, which, because of Earth's axial tilt, is inclined twenty-three and a half degrees to the plane of the equator. (Earth's orbital plane is called the ecliptic because eclipses occur when the Moon lines up in this plane with Earth and the Sun.) As plotted on the celestial sphere, the ecliptic represents the apparent path that the Sun traces in the course of a year. Viewed from Earth, the Sun and planets seem to move along the ecliptic against a belt of back-ground constellations called the zodiac (from the Greek for "circle of animals"). Once perceived as the dominion of the gods in their stellar incarnations, the zodiac offers a set of landmarks for skywatchers who wish to observe the nightly celestial show.

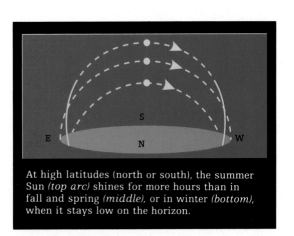

At high latitudes (north or south), the summer Sun *(top arc)* shines for more hours than in fall and spring *(middle)*, or in winter *(bottom)*, when it stays low on the horizon.

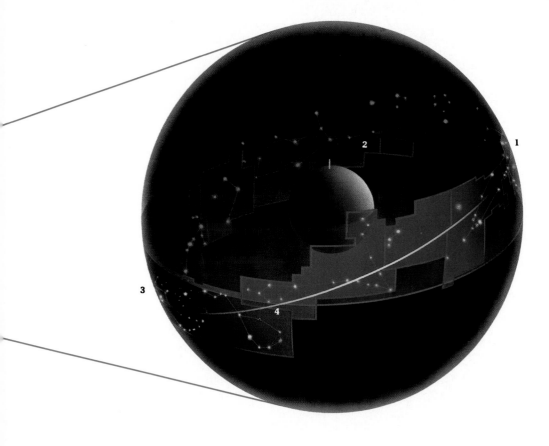

The celestial sphere. The imaginary globe encircled by the starry band of the Milky Way has Earth at the center with its axis of rotation *(blue)* oriented vertically. Extending its poles marks the north and south celestial poles; extending its equator forms the celestial equator *(purple)*, which is inclined twenty-three and a half degrees to the ecliptic *(yellow)*. Traveling along the ecliptic, the Sun and planets appear to pass through the stars that make up the constellations of the zodiac *(purple band)*. As Earth moves in its orbit at the rate of about one degree of arc per day, the Sun appears to shift along the ecliptic at the same pace. Thus, for observers at temperate and high latitudes, the Sun's daily path will change with the seasons *(above)*. In the Northern Hemisphere, the summer solstice *(1)* marks the longest day of the year, when the noonday Sun is at the highest point on the ecliptic. When the Sun crosses the celestial equator during the fall equinox *(2)*, day and night are of equal length. At winter solstice *(3)*, the shortest day of the year, the Sun is at its lowest on the ecliptic. In late March, the Sun passes through the spring equinox *(4)*, en route to another northern summer.

13

CELESTIAL LAWS AND EFFECTS

The sixteenth-century realization that all planets in the Solar System revolve around the Sun was one of astronomy's most important discoveries, for it enabled German astronomer Johannes Kepler to shed considerably more light on the general movement of celestial bodies. The first of three momentous laws that he published in the early 1600s asserted that any body in the Solar System traces an ellipse (rather than a perfect circle, as was previously believed), with the Sun at one of two foci *(below)*. Second, although a body travels faster when its path brings it closer to the Sun, it always sweeps out the same area in its orbit in the same amount of time. Third, planets orbiting near the Sun travel at faster speeds than those that orbit farther out. Some effects of these fundamentals of celestial mechanics are illustrated here.

Orbital mechanics. At right, the Sun is at one focus of the elliptical orbit of, say, a comet, and a point in space is at the other. (With nearly circular planetary orbits, the two foci virtually merge.) An imaginary line drawn through the foci establishes the major axis. One end, perihelion, is the comet's closest approach to the Sun; aphelion is the point farthest away. At perihelion, the comet travels faster than at aphelion, but—obeying Kepler's second law—it sweeps out equal areas of its orbit *(gray)* in equal periods of time.

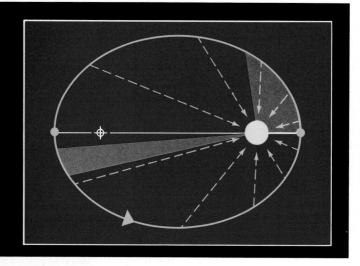

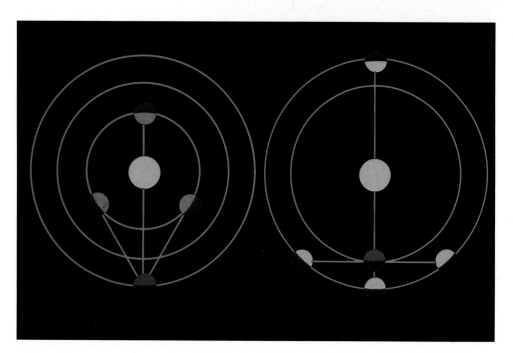

Inferior and superior orbits. The times when a planet is visible from Earth depend on whether its orbit is "inferior" or "superior"— that is, inside Earth's orbit or farther out, as exemplified by the orbits of inferior Mercury *(far left)* and superior Mars *(near left)*. For instance, the inferior planets are best seen when the angle they form with the Sun and Earth is at its widest, a position known as maximum elongation. When Mercury and Venus are behind the Sun (superior conjunction), they cannot be seen at all; when they are in front of it (inferior conjunction), the sky is generally too bright to see them. A superior planet is best seen at opposition—when the Earth lies directly between it and the Sun—rather than at its maximum elongation of ninety degrees. The outer planets are visible in the night sky for most of the year, except when they near conjunction, passing behind the Sun.

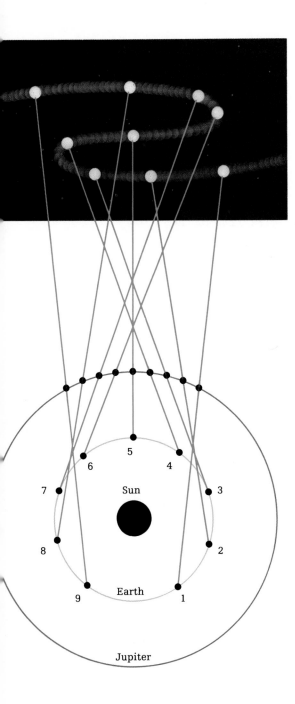

Retrograde illusion. Because the outer planets travel more slowly than Earth, they sometimes appear to reverse direction. As illustrated in the sequential diagram above, when Jupiter lies ahead of Earth *(1-4)*, it seems to move steadily from west to east. But when the planets are at opposition *(5)*, Jupiter seems to have strayed backward, and it continues to do so *(6)* until Earth has passed it *(7)*, at which point the outer planet starts moving eastward again. Jupiter traces an S-curve, never crossing its previous path, because its orbit is slightly angled to Earth's.

What is a day? On any planet in the Solar System, a day may be defined as the time between one high noon and the next, a period known as a solar day, or sol, because it is based on the Sun's position in the sky. Astronomers also define a day as the time it takes a planet to rotate once on its axis against the seemingly fixed background of distant stars, a period called the sidereal day, from the Latin for "star."

The two measures differ—to a degree that is greater on some planets than on others—because as planets rotate counterclockwise (or, in some cases, clockwise) on their axes, they also move counterclockwise along their orbits. On Mars, for example *(above)*, an observer could mark the beginning of the day when either the Sun or a vastly distant star was directly overhead *(blue line, above left)*. After one 360-degree turn, the star would again be overhead *(blue line, above)*, but because Mars had moved forward in its orbit, it would have to continue rotating before the observer would once more see the Sun at high noon *(white line, above)*. On Mars, the solar day exceeds the sidereal day by ninety seconds. On Earth, the discrepancy is four minutes. But on Mercury the difference is much more dramatic: Because the tiny body spins very slowly, while its orbital speed is the fastest in the Solar System, its solar day is three times longer than the period measured against the stellar background.

15

THE SUN'S ENTOURAGE

The nine planets, more than sixty moons, and countless asteroids that orbit the Sun do so in a relatively flat plane that echoes the Solar System's origins in a huge spinning disk of dust and gas. With the exception of Mercury and Pluto—the two smallest worlds—the planets follow nearly circular orbits only slightly inclined to the ecliptic. The composition of the Sun's planets is another reflection of the Solar System's evolution. The inner four lost most of their volatile gases to the heat blast of the nascent Sun; the outer bodies are vastly larger and gaseous, except for Pluto, whose small size and ice-covered, rocky surface lead to speculation that it is a fragment left over from the Solar System's formation or an escaped Neptunian moon.

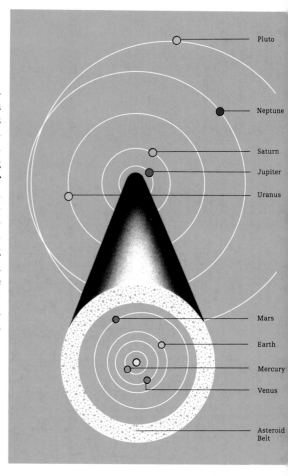

The Solar System. As seen in this overhead view *(right)*, the asteroid belt separates the inner planets from the outer ones. Most of the planets orbit in nearly circular paths, except for innermost Mercury and distant Pluto, whose eccentric track brings it inside the orbit of Neptune for a portion of its circuit.

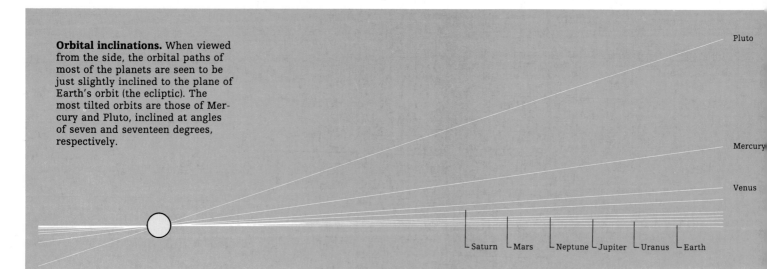

Orbital inclinations. When viewed from the side, the orbital paths of most of the planets are seen to be just slightly inclined to the plane of Earth's orbit (the ecliptic). The most tilted orbits are those of Mercury and Pluto, inclined at angles of seven and seventeen degrees, respectively.

Orbital distances. The planets' average relative distances from the Sun are depicted schematically below, starting with Mercury, a mere 36 million miles out, and ending with Pluto, 100 times as far at 3.6 billion miles.

Planetary Data	Mercury	Venus	Earth	Mars	Jupiter	Saturn	Uranus	Neptune	Pluto
Equatorial Diameter (Miles)	3,031	7,521	7,926	4,223	88,846	74,898	31,763	30,775	1,430
Mass (Trillion Trillion Pounds)	0.735	10.739	13.177	1.415	4,188.86	1,254.24	191.59	225.98	0.029
Mean Density (Earth = 1)	0.98	0.95	1.0	0.71	0.24	0.125	0.23	0.297	0.37
Gravity (Earth = 1)	0.382	0.905	1.0	0.378	2.53	1.066	0.906	1.137	0.077
Period of Rotation (Hours)	1,403.76	5,816.32	23.934	24.623	9.925	10.656	17.24	16.11	152.87
Escape Velocity (Miles per Hour)	9,619	23,265	25,055	11,185	134,222	80,533	46,978	53,689	2,337
Major Atmospheric Gas	Sodium	Carbon Dioxide	Nitrogen	Carbon Dioxide	Hydrogen	Hydrogen	Hydrogen	Hydrogen	Methane
Inclination of Equator (Degrees)	0.0	178.0	23.44	23.98	3.08	26.73	97.92	28.8	98.8
Known Moons	0	0	1	2	16	18	15	8	1
Eccentricity of Orbit	0.206	0.007	0.017	0.093	0.048	0.056	0.047	0.009	0.248
Mean Orbital Velocity (Miles per Hour)	107,136	78,372	66,636	53,964	29,232	21,564	15,228	12,132	10,620
Minimum Distance from Sun (Millions of Miles)	28.6	66.8	91.4	128.4	460.2	838.8	1,702.1	2,774.8	2,749.6
Maximum Distance from Sun (Millions of Miles)	43.4	67.7	94.5	154.8	507.1	937.6	1,870.8	2,824.3	4,582.7
Mean Distance from Sun (Millions of Miles)	36.0	67.2	93.0	141.6	483.6	888.2	1,786.4	2,798.8	3,666.2
Orbital Period (Earth Years)	0.24	0.615	1	1.88	11.86	29.46	84.01	164.79	248.6
Inclination of Orbit to Plane of Ecliptic (Degrees)	7.00	3.39	—	1.85	1.30	2.49	0.77	1.77	17.00

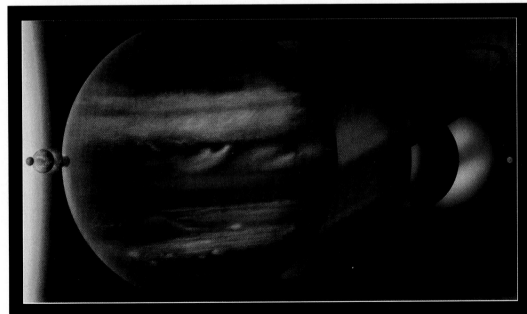

Family portrait. No two are alike among the nine complex worlds of the Solar System. Pictured to scale at left and charted by their vital statistics above, the planets vary enormously in size, composition, and character. Earth's three nearest neighbors all have densities roughly similar to that of Earth itself, but each presents a different face to the cosmos, from blistered Mercury and sulfurous Venus to the desert world Mars. In the far reaches, massive Jupiter leads a group of immense gaseous worlds —Saturn, renowned for its rings, oddly tipped-over Uranus, and the mysterious blue planet Neptune— all of which dwarf tiny Pluto, final outpost in the solar neighborhood.

ANATOMY OF A MEDIUM-SIZE STAR

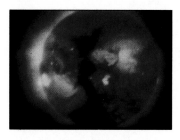

Equatorial Diameter
865,000 miles
Mass
(trillion trillion pounds)
4,353,125
Density (Earth = 1)
0.256
Period of Rotation
27 days at equator
34 days at poles
Age
4.6 billion years

Formed about 4.6 billion years ago from the gravitational collapse of a cosmic cloud of gas and dust, the Sun is a medium-size star about halfway along in its life cycle. Because it is average and so near at hand, it serves as a kind of stellar Rosetta stone, a key to understanding the composition and behavior of stars far distant in the universe.

Over the years, solar physicists have delved ever deeper into the Sun's mysteries, refining their theoretical models of the magnetism that gives rise to surface features such as sunspots and solar flares and developing new techniques for probing the star's hidden core. The core contains roughly half the Sun's mass in only one sixty-fourth of its volume, a condition that would lead to inward gravitational collapse were it not for the outward pressure exerted by the phenomenal thermonuclear heat generated there.

Every second, the powerhouse at the heart of the Sun transforms 700 million tons of hydrogen gas into 695 million tons of helium gas through the nuclear reactions depicted below. The remaining 5 million tons of matter escape as pure energy, traveling outward through successive layers and eventually shining forth into the Solar System as visible light and other forms of electromagnetic radiation. Although Earth receives less than half a billionth of the Sun's energy output each second, it is more than enough to give nourishment and power to the entire planet.

A nuclear furnace. Core temperatures of 15 million degrees Kelvin and pressures some 250 billion times that of Earth's atmosphere sustain a series of nuclear reactions that fuel the Sun and light the Solar System. Gamma ray photons produced by these reactions journey out from the core *(1)* through the radiative zone *(2)*, where collisions with densely packed atoms of hydrogen and helium gas rob them of a tiny bit of energy, transforming them into longer wavelength x-rays and, eventually, into visible light. In the convection zone *(3)*, photons are absorbed by turbulent gases that carry the solar energy on out toward the surface, or photosphere *(4)*, where it is emitted as visible light. Above the surface, the chromosphere *(5)*, or middle atmosphere, stages a host of solar features *(opposite)*, as does the corona, a region of superheated tenuous gases that begins about 1,500 miles above the photosphere and extends for millions of miles.

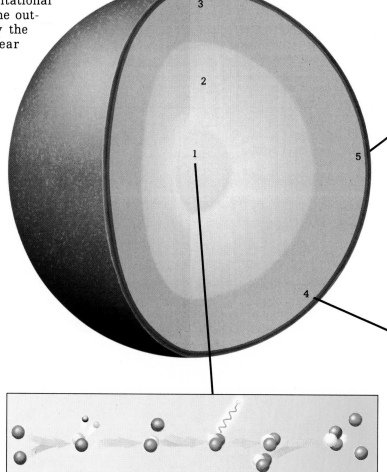

The proton-proton chain. The process that converts hydrogen to helium begins when two hydrogen nuclei, or protons *(red)*, fuse into a deuteron made up of one proton and one neutron *(white)*, releasing a positron *(black)* and a neutrino *(green)*. The deuteron then fuses with another proton to form helium-3 (two protons and one neutron), giving off energetic gamma rays *(purple)*. Two helium-3 atoms fuse to form helium-4 (two protons and two neutrons), liberating two protons to begin the cycle again.

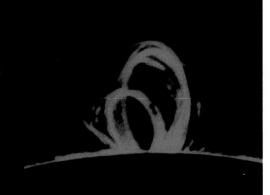

The corona. Most familiar as a luminous white halo around the Sun's disk during a total eclipse, the corona also serves as a backdrop for an explosive light show of gases called solar prominences, vast arcs originating in the chromosphere in response to solar magnetic activity. Loop prominences like the one at right take shape when hot plasma condenses and rains back along magnetic field lines into the chromosphere. So-called coronal holes (dark gap in the x-ray image at far left) are regions where magnetic field lines stretch out into space, venting the high-speed solar wind.

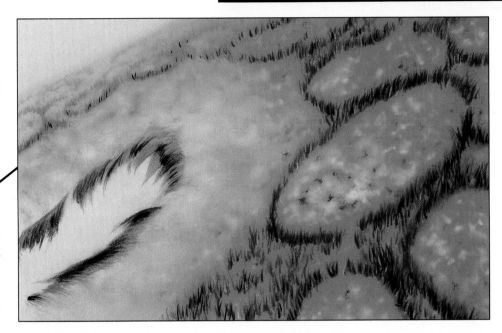

The chromosphere. Visible to the unaided eye only during a total eclipse, the chromosphere ("sphere of color") appears as a fleeting, fiery red ring around the silhouette of the Moon as it passes in front of the Sun. Because solar plasma (the collective term for ionized gases in the Sun) is much less dense here than in the Sun's lower regions, it cannot contain the Sun's powerful magnetic forces but rather is at their mercy. Spikes of chromospheric gas called spicules form fencelike borders around supergranular cells as much as 20,000 miles across *(near left)*. Areas of intense magnetic activity are often marked by fibrils *(far left)*, streams of gas, each typically 7,000 miles long and 450 to 1,300 miles wide. Although each fibril lasts only about ten to twenty minutes, the overall formation may persist for several hours.

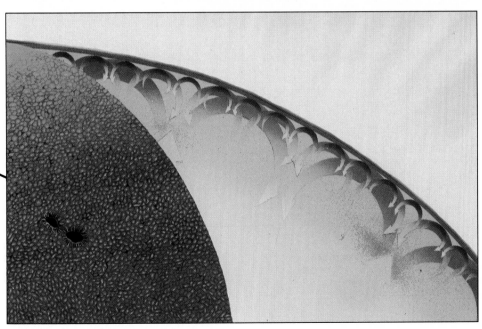

The photosphere. Referred to as the Sun's surface because it is the region most easily perceived from Earth, the photosphere ("sphere of light") is a 200-mile-deep region whose gases glow at about 6,000 degrees Kelvin—bright enough, usually, to outshine the layers above it. Energy generated at the core travels through the radiative zone and is carried to the photosphere by means of turbulent currents in the convection zone *(near left)*, whose circulating flows of hot and cooler gas reach the base of the photosphere to give it its granular appearance. The granules, each about 600 miles in diameter, appear and disappear in about fifteen minutes. Sunspots *(dark blotches)*—areas sometimes larger than Earth where concentrations of the Sun's magnetic field lines have broken through the surface—appear dark only because they are cooler than the surrounding material.

THE SUN'S MAGNETIC INFLUENCE

At every moment, two solar forces—magnetism and the coronal plasma—struggle for dominance in the Sun's corona. Within 250,000 miles of the solar surface, the Sun's magnetic field lines *(below)* are strong enough to confine the coronal plasma, a tenuous gas of superheated charged particles. At higher altitudes, the forces of magnetism are not strong enough to resist the pressure of the expanding plasma, which blows the looped field lines far out into space.

Depending on where and how the solar wind escapes from the corona, it may jet forth in high-speed, low-density streams *(near right)* or somewhat denser, less forceful "helmet streamers" *(far right)*. A more spectacular phenomenon is the coronal mass ejection *(right, middle)*, violent eruptions that can accelerate charged particles to 2.7 million miles per hour. As the solar wind rushes outward at an average speed of a million miles per hour, it sweeps into interplanetary space, dragging the Sun's magnetic field lines with it to form the interplanetary magnetic field *(opposite, bottom)*.

Near Earth, the solar wind makes its presence known when it breaches the planet's magnetosphere, producing powerful electric currents and geomagnetic storms that interrupt radio communications. The interaction also gives rise to the dancing lights of the auroral displays.

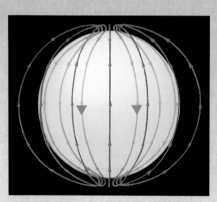

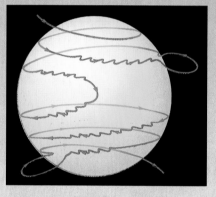

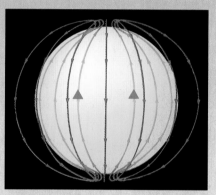

At the start of an eleven-year cycle of solar activity, the Sun's magnetic field lines are evenly dispersed from one pole to the other. In this example, the lines run from north to south, and a compass on the Sun would point to the north pole. Because the field lines are so orderly, magnetic activity is at a minimum, as are sunspots and other surface features.

The Sun's faster rotation at the equator than at the poles pulls the field lines out of their vertical orientation. (For clarity, one line represents the multitude that permeate the Sun.) As the lines wrap horizontally, those in the northern hemisphere will have a magnetic direction opposite that of lines in the south. Churning gases twist the lines further until bundles known as flux tubes pop through the photosphere, giving rise to sunspots at high latitudes. At the peak of the cycle, when the lines are very tangled, new sunspots erupt nearer the equator.

Eventually, cyclonic motions in the solar gases cause a reconfiguration of the field lines that will bring the cycle to an end. Sunspots subside as the field lines revert to a smoother, less tangled distribution. At the end of the cycle, the magnetic poles are reversed: A compass on the Sun would point to the south.

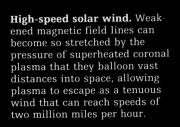

High-speed solar wind. Weakened magnetic field lines can become so stretched by the pressure of superheated coronal plasma that they balloon vast distances into space, allowing plasma to escape as a tenuous wind that can reach speeds of two million miles per hour.

Explosive solar wind. Resulting from huge magnetic disturbances, a violent emission known as a coronal mass ejection spews about one to ten billion tons of matter into space. These plasma bubbles, threaded by magnetic field lines that pinch off from the Sun, explode from the corona at speeds that can exceed two million miles per hour.

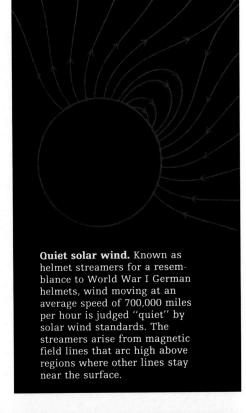

Quiet solar wind. Known as helmet streamers for a resemblance to World War I German helmets, wind moving at an average speed of 700,000 miles per hour is judged "quiet" by solar wind standards. The streamers arise from magnetic field lines that arc high above regions where other lines stay near the surface.

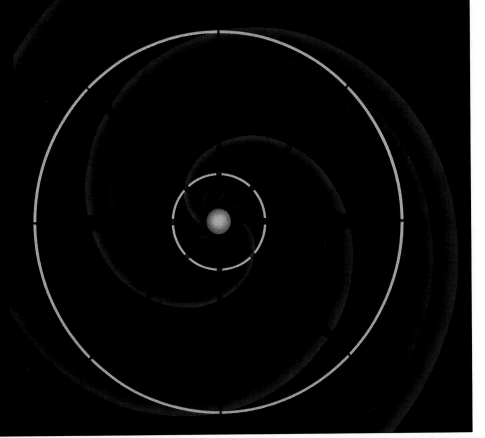

The interplanetary field. As the outrushing solar wind drags the Sun's magnetic field lines *(purple)* into interplanetary space, the lines get stretched out and weakened. Then, because of the Sun's rotation, the lines become twisted until the interplanetary field takes on the spiral shape of a nautilus shell. The solar wind itself, meanwhile, radiates from the Sun in all directions *(red arrows)*, following a straight line relative to the spiraling field. At Earth's orbit *(inner white circle)* the spiral field forms a 45-degree angle to the solar wind; by Jupiter's orbit *(outer white circle)* the field is nearly perpendicular.

MERCURY: PLANET OF EXTREMES

Equatorial Diameter
3,031 miles
Mass
(trillion trillion pounds)
0.735
Density (Earth = 1)
0.98
Gravity (Earth = 1)
0.382
Orbital Period
0.24 Earth years
Known Moons
0
**Mean Distance
from Sun**
36 million miles
Period of Rotation
1,403.76 hours

As the innermost planet in the Solar System, Mercury, named for the Roman messenger god, circles so near the Sun that its pattern of visibility *(diagram, bottom)* led ancient sky watchers to believe it was two bodies: an evening and a morning "star."

This proximity to the Sun has had profound effects on Mercury's evolution. Although the planet completes one orbit in eighty-eight Earth days—fastest in the Solar System—scientists theorize that tidal forces induced by the Sun's gravity have gradually slowed the world's rotation. Today, Mercury takes nearly fifty-nine Earth days to spin once on its axis against the background stars (a sidereal day), and it completes only three sidereal days in two orbits. This 3:2 spin-orbit ratio, unique in the Solar System, has unusual consequences. At certain locations on Mercury observers could see a double sunrise *(opposite)*; at

other locations they could witness extended noons and midnights. Combined with the planet's temperature extremes *(below)*, these anomalies produce, in effect, hot and cold spots on Mercury's surface.

According to theory, when the Sun was young, a blast of solar wind stripped Mercury and other nearby planets of whatever atmospheres they had developed. Venus and Earth were later able to reconstitute relatively dense atmospheric coverings, but Mercury has remained essentially unprotected from the Sun's radiation—and from the violent bombardment of comets and meteoroids that has left its surface as barren and cratered as the Moon's *(pages 24-25)*. Virtually a vacuum compared to the density of Earth's airy blanket, the atmosphere is too thin to scatter much light or transmit sound, leaving the Mercurian sky black above a silent landscape.

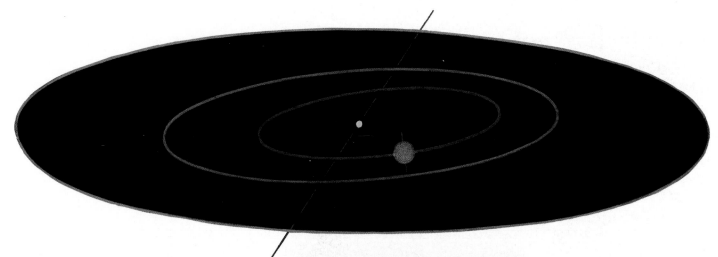

Orbital characteristics. The path Mercury travels *(gray orbit, above)* tilts at a seven-degree angle to the ecliptic, the plane of Earth's orbit *(blue)*. It is also the second most eccentric planetary orbit, after Pluto's, bringing Mercury within roughly 28.6 million miles of the Sun at perihelion, its closest point, and out to 43.4 million miles at aphelion, its farthest point—a difference of nearly 15 million miles. (For Earth, in contrast, the difference is only about 3 million miles.) These orbital extremes, combined with Mercury's slow axial rotation rate, cause the planet to suffer the greatest temperature fluctuations in the Solar System: from −300 degrees Fahrenheit during its long night to 800 degrees Fahrenheit during the day.

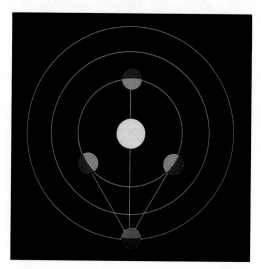

Visibility. Its Sun-hugging orbit makes Mercury difficult to spot from Earth except at maximum elongation, when the angle it forms with the Sun and Earth is at its widest *(left, bottom)*. An earthbound observer can see Mercury for one and a half hours before sunrise (when the planet is to the right of the Sun from Earth's view) or for an hour and a half after sunset (when it is to the left); later at night, the observer is turned away from the planet, and in full daylight, Mercury travels in the glare of the Sun.

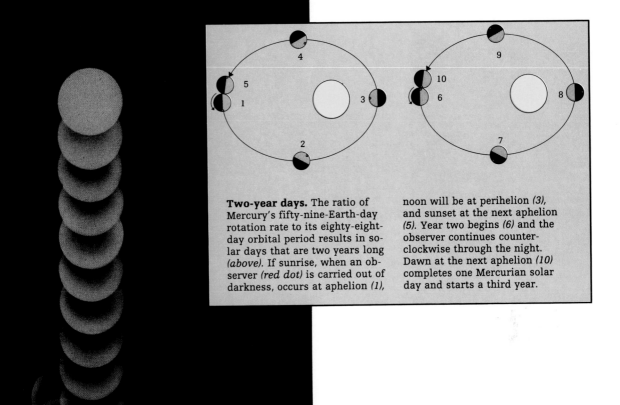

Two-year days. The ratio of Mercury's fifty-nine-Earth-day rotation rate to its eighty-eight-day orbital period results in solar days that are two years long *(above)*. If sunrise, when an observer *(red dot)* is carried out of darkness, occurs at aphelion *(1)*, noon will be at perihelion *(3)*, and sunset at the next aphelion *(5)*. Year two begins *(6)* and the observer continues counter-clockwise through the night. Dawn at the next aphelion *(10)* completes one Mercurian solar day and starts a third year.

Double sunrise. Great orbital speed and a tortoiselike rate of rotation result in an unusual relationship between Mercury's days and years *(top right)* and produce illusions of abnormal solar behavior, such as the double sunrise depicted above. As illustrated in the overhead view at right of Mercury approaching perihelion, an observer *(red dot)* sees the Sun rise for the first time *(1)* as the planet's counterclockwise spin moves the observer out of darkness. The Sun's gravitational tug accelerates the planet as it nears perihelion *(2-4)* until Mercury's orbital speed surpasses its axial spin rate; as the observer drops back into darkness *(5)*, the Sun dips below the horizon *(above)*. When Mercury travels past perihelion toward aphelion *(6-8)*, the backward tug of the Sun slows its orbital speed, bringing the observer once more across the terminator, or day-night line *(9)*, to view a second dawn.

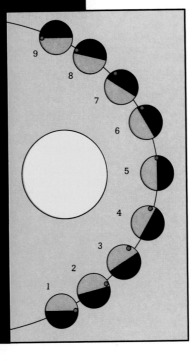

STUDY OF A CRATERED REALM

Earth-based studies long ago put Mercury's density at 98 percent that of Earth, leading to speculation that the tiny planet has a massive iron core—a theory supported by *Mariner 10*'s discovery in 1974 of Mercury's magnetic field *(opposite, bottom)*. Analysis of images transmitted by *Mariner 10* persuades many scientists that Mercury's surface is, on average, far older than that of any other terrestrial world. Spared the eroding effects of atmosphere and water, the surface holds clues to the forces and events that shaped the planet, including comet and meteoroid bombardment that left Mercury heavily cratered. Relatively uncratered sections are believed to be flood basalts, perhaps deposited by lava that welled up through fissures remaining from the planet's formative period or reopened by impacts. Other phenomena include looming cliffs, or scarps, as much as 2 miles high and more than 300 miles in extent, called lobate scarps because they outline giant lobes. By studying photographs of Mercury's varied terrains, scientists can pin down relative ages of features *(opposite)*.

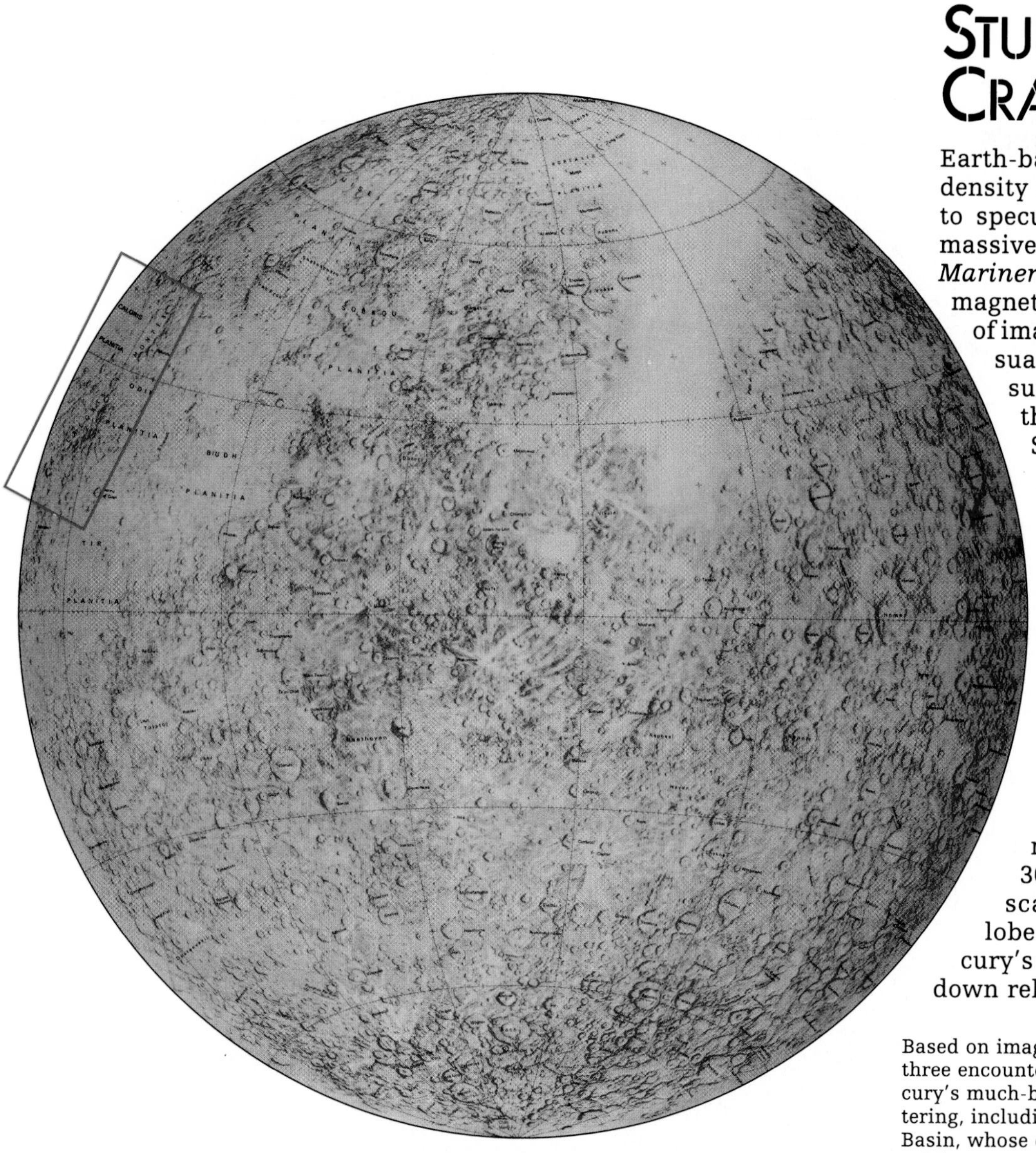

Based on images made by *Mariner 10* during three encounters, the map above reveals Mercury's much-battered face. Areas of heavy cratering, including the 800-mile-wide Caloris Basin, whose eastern edge is contained in the red box at upper left, are interspersed with relatively smooth areas, called planitiae.

Crater structure. As shown here, impact craters display a range of interior structures. Craters larger than fifty-five miles in diameter *(top)* often have a ring of central peaks, flat floors, and an outer ring of mountains. Those from six to fifty-five miles wide *(middle)* have one or more central peaks, flat floors, and terraced walls. Steep walls and bowl-shaped bottoms characterize simple craters less than six miles in diameter *(bottom)*.

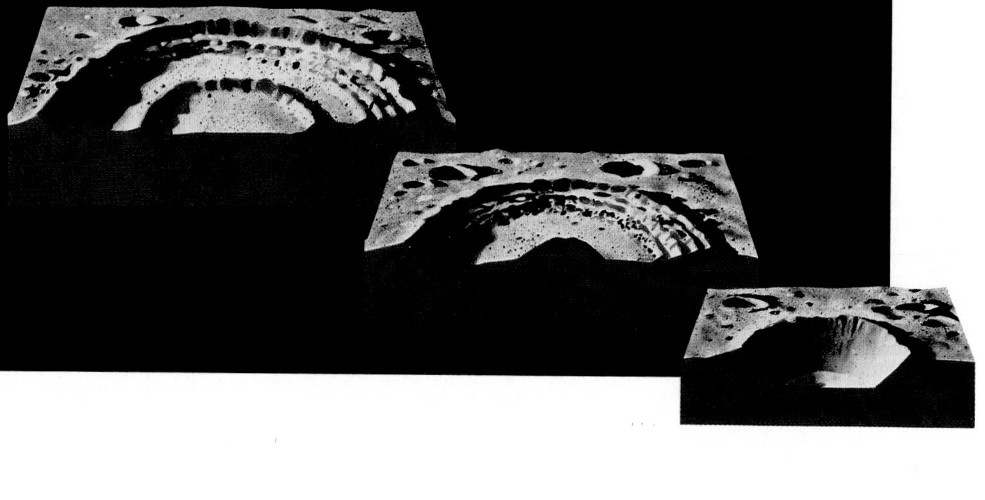

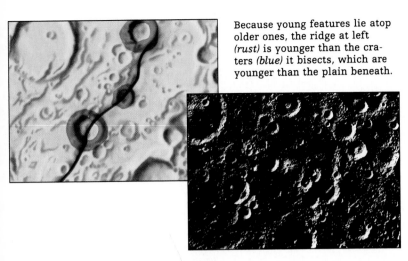

Because young features lie atop older ones, the ridge at left *(rust)* is younger than the craters *(blue)* it bisects, which are younger than the plain beneath.

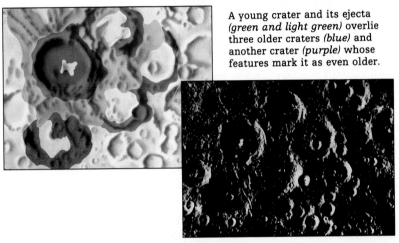

A young crater and its ejecta *(green and light green)* overlie three older craters *(blue)* and another crater *(purple)* whose features mark it as even older.

Anatomy. Mercury's high density and the existence of its magnetosphere suggest that the planet possesses a large, partially molten iron core *(orange)*. As the newly formed planet cooled, the mantle *(yellow)* and part of the core solidified, causing the planet to shrink and buckling sections of the crust *(brown)*. Protruding edges of upthrust sections of crust produce towering ridges called lobate scarps.

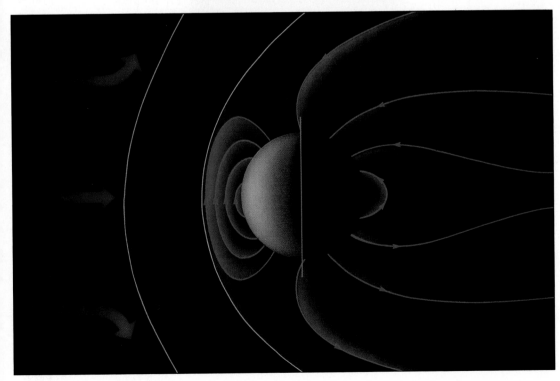

Magnetosphere. Until *Mariner 10*'s instruments detected the presence of a magnetic field around Mercury, prevailing theory held that such magnetospheres *(left)*—envelopes that deflect the charged particles of the solar wind—were generated only by a rapidly spinning planet with a partially molten metal core; Mercury's fifty-nine-day rotation seemed far too slow. Whatever its source, Mercury's magnetic field is only about one one-hundred-fiftieth as strong as Earth's. As a result, the solar wind, which is at its most dense so close to the Sun, can at times ram Mercury's magnetosphere almost to the planet's surface.

VENUS: AN INHOSPITABLE TWIN

Equatorial Diameter
7,521 miles
Mass
(trillion trillion pounds)
10.739
Density (Earth = 1)
0.95
Gravity (Earth = 1)
0.905
Orbital Period
0.615 Earth years
Known Moons
0
**Mean Distance
from Sun**
67.2 million miles
Period of Rotation
5,816.32 hours

One of the factors that make Venus the bright jewel of the morning and evening skies is its dense covering of highly reflective clouds. But this veil also renders the planet's surface invisible to optical astronomers. With the advent of radar instruments, however, and especially since spaceborne probes have carried instruments to the planet's very door, scientists have gained tantalizing glimpses of the Venusian topography *(pages 28-29)*.

Although nearly equal to Earth in size and density, Venus has evolved into a planetary inferno. Some scientists theorize that Earth's twin may have had liquid water at some point in its past, but lost it in part because of its proximity to the Sun.

The combination of high surface temperatures and lack of large bodies of water, which on Earth play a role in dissolving such volcanic gases as carbon dioxide and sulfur dioxide, resulted in increasing concentrations of those gases in the Venusian atmosphere, forming thick sulfuric acid clouds. Only the absence of vigorous Earth-type weather in the lower atmosphere prevents the clouds from delivering a corrosive downpour rather than an acidic drizzle. Carbon dioxide and sulfuric acid, which tend to prevent the escape of heat that emanates from the planet, are also responsible for the so-called greenhouse effect *(right, bottom)* that has turned the planet's surface into an oven.

Orbital oddities. With a rotational period of 243 days and an orbital period of 225 days, Venus, like Mercury, is a planet whose day is longer than its year. The diagram at right, which shows Venus at approximately twenty-eight-day intervals, uses a flag planted at the north pole to demonstrate how the planet completes an orbit around the Sun before it can spin once on its axis. An additional effect of this sluggish rotation rate is that Venus shows much the same face to Earth at all times. The planet also displays phases, like the Moon. Finally, Venus is one of three planets (Uranus and Pluto are the others) that rotate from east to west, a phenomenon known as retrograde spin.

Morning star, evening star. Like Mercury, Venus is usually only visible from Earth just before sunrise or just after sunset, depending on the time of year. But because it is farther from the Sun than Mercury, its maximum elongation is wider, so that it is visible for longer—three and a half hours at a time, compared with Mercury's one and a half.

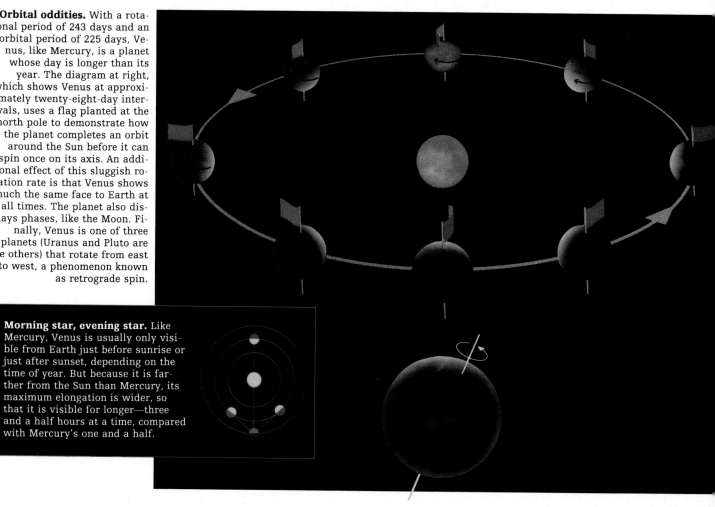

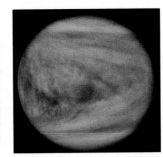

Cloud patterns. Temperature differences between Venus's night and day sides produce a difference in atmospheric pressure that in turn generates 250-mile-per-hour winds, whipping the topmost layer of clouds all the way around the planet in four days—sixty times faster than Venus itself rotates. As seen in the series of ultraviolet images above, taken over the course of two days, the clouds streaming from east to west form bands around the poles, as well as a Y-shaped feature at low to middle latitudes.

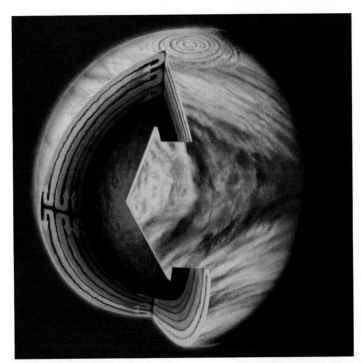

Complex currents. Scientists speculate that below the topmost clouds additional layers circulate in alternating cells at right angles to the overlying east-west winds. Clouds at the equator, which heat up more quickly than those at the poles, rise and travel poleward, where they cool and sink, and then return to the equator. In the next layer down, gas dragged along by friction from the flowing clouds moves in the opposite direction, a phenomenon that may operate in reverse one layer lower still. Where the circulation patterns meet at the poles, swirling vortices form.

A nightmare greenhouse. Although only two to three percent of the sunlight *(yellow)* that arrives at Venus actually penetrates the layer of sulfuric acid clouds *(yellow balls)* and reaches the ground, it is enough to make Venus's surface the hottest in the Solar System. Warmed by the sunlight, the surface radiates infrared energy *(red)* back toward space. But carbon dioxide *(purple balls)* at the cloud layer and below hampers the efficient outward radiation of infrared, thereby maintaining surface temperatures of about 900 degrees Fahrenheit, hot enough to melt lead.

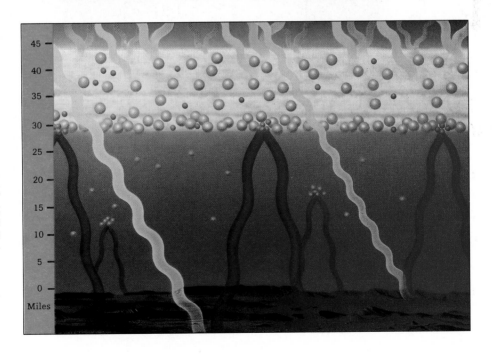

SURVEYING THE SURFACE

Channels. Possibly scored by slow-moving lava from a nearby volcano, a channel snakes its way along a chasm named Vires-akka Chasma. The channel ranges in width between 300 feet and 2.4 miles, and extends in this image for about 72 miles. Scientists theorize that volcanism may still play a leading role in shaping Venus's landscape.

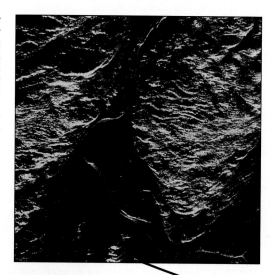

The topographic globe shown below was produced from data collected by the Pioneer Venus Orbiter, a spacecraft launched in 1978. By beaming long-wavelength radio waves through the clouds and recording how long they took to bounce back from the surface, the orbiter mapped 92 percent of the planet, excluding the north pole. Purple represents the lowest elevations and red the highest. The planet's two "continents," Ishtar Terra in the north and Aphrodite Terra in the south, are marked in yellow. The closeup images are from *Magellan,* a probe launched in May 1989. Equipped with radar instruments that can pick out features only 270 yards across, *Magellan* has mapped more than 80 percent of the planet.

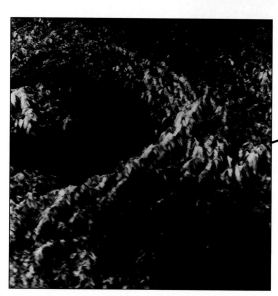

Impact craters. Similar to those found on the Moon, Venusian craters like the twenty-mile-wide Golubkina crater feature steep terraced walls and a prominent central peak. Unlike their lunar counterparts, however, those on Venus all have diameters larger than three miles, because only large meteorites can penetrate the thick atmosphere without breaking up into a shower of debris.

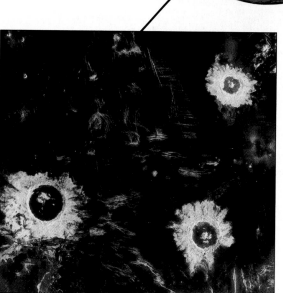

Plains and peaks. This image, of an area in the Lavinia region, shows a broad expanse of fractured plains peppered with small hills that may be volcanic peaks. Three impact craters, ranging in diameter from approximately twenty to thirty miles, wear circular skirts of radar-bright ejecta.

Mountains. On the eastern flank of the Freyja mountain range lies an unusual dome of rock about seventy-five miles across. The dome appears to be sagging under its own weight, which generates crisscrossing fractures. Scientists are not sure of the mechanisms driving mountain building on the planet, but structural similarities between the Freyja range and some terrestrial mountains suggest that those on Venus might also be the result of interactions between moving tectonic plates.

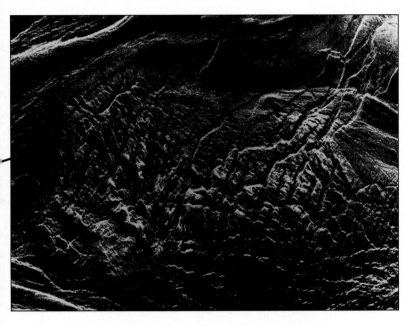

Volcanoes. Radar-bright rivers of hardened lava similar to flows from earthly volcanoes stretch some 72 miles down the side of Sif Mons, a 1.2-mile-high peak in Eisila Regio in Venus's northern hemisphere.

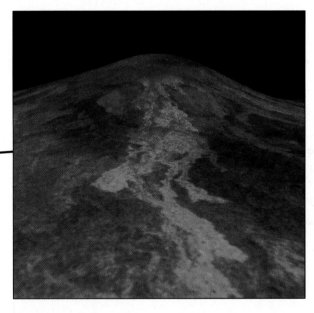

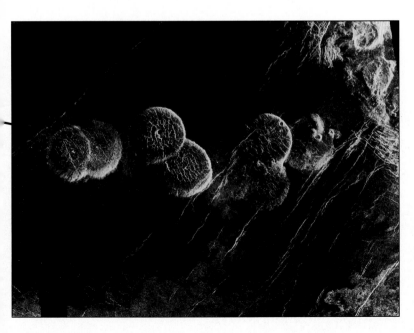

Domed hills. Dotting the eastern edge of a highland known as Alpha Regio are seven domed hills that average fifteen miles across. The hills are believed to be volcanic in origin, created by nearly symmetric eruptions of very thick lava.

Equatorial Diameter
7,926 miles
Mass
(trillion trillion pounds)
13.177
Density (Earth = 1)
1
Gravity (Earth = 1)
1
Orbital Period
1 Earth year
Known Moons
1
**Mean Distance
from Sun**
93 million miles
Period of Rotation
23.934 hours

EARTH: A LIVING WORLD

To an astronomer on Venus or Mars, Earth—the only planet in the Solar System known to have large bodies of liquid water—would appear as a blue globe with a constantly shifting cover of white clouds, a feature of the terrestrial atmosphere that helps shield the surface from most of the Sun's lethal radiation but also lets surface heat escape into space. These twin oceans of water and air are partly a consequence of Earth's location neither too near nor too far from the Sun. Together they transport warmth from the equator toward the poles and draw cool air and water from the poles toward the equator *(opposite).*

Without this heat exchange, equatorial regions would be much hotter and polar regions much colder than they are. Most of the exchange occurs within a few miles of sea level. Solar energy stored in the top layer of the sea warms the air from below, either directly, through contact, or indirectly, through evaporation. Water vapor condensing on dust and other particles gradually accumulates into the clouds that give Earth its changing blue-and-white face.

Earth's magnetosphere. Extending thousands of miles into space, Earth's magnetic field is by far the largest among the inner terrestrial planets. Unlike the weaker shield of Mercury, the third planet's magnetosphere keeps the solar wind at bay, as judged by the leading edge of the magnetosphere and the planet itself.

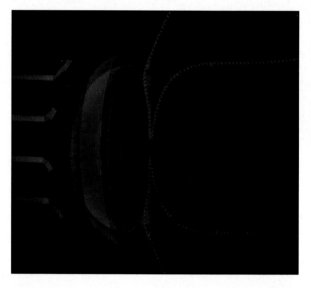

The aurorae. Charged particles that penetrate the magnetosphere at Earth's poles collide with gas atoms in the atmosphere, generating shimmery displays called aurorae *(left)*—or the northern and southern lights.

Ocean of air. Earth's many-layered atmosphere extends some 300 miles above sea level and blocks most of the Sun's radiation, permitting mainly visible light and some infrared to reach the surface. Incoming solar energy first encounters the thermosphere, where atomic oxygen and nitrogen absorb deadly gamma and x-rays. Most of the remaining radiation passes through the relatively thin mesosphere to the stratosphere, where ozone soaks up most harmful ultraviolet rays. At 10 miles above sea level, the troposphere, the stage for most weather, absorbs much of the infrared and scatters blue wavelengths to color the sky.

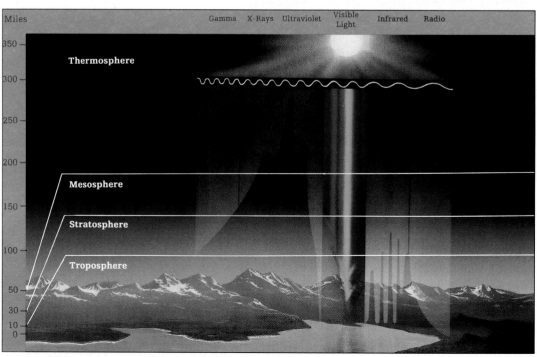

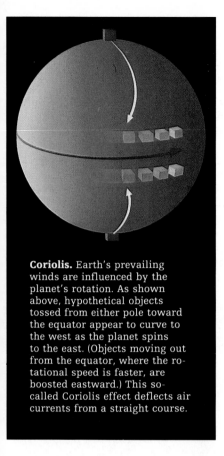

Coriolis. Earth's prevailing winds are influenced by the planet's rotation. As shown above, hypothetical objects tossed from either pole toward the equator appear to curve to the west as the planet spins to the east. (Objects moving out from the equator, where the rotational speed is faster, are boosted eastward.) This so-called Coriolis effect deflects air currents from a straight course.

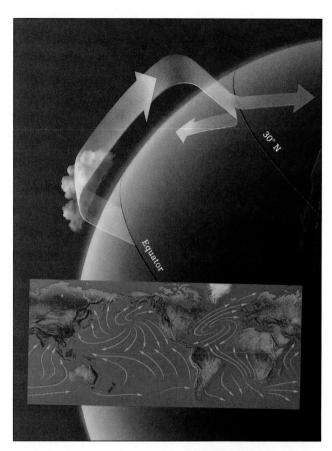

Air currents. Because equatorial waters are warmer than oceans at higher latitudes, the atmosphere around the globe roils with convection currents *(left)*. Ocean-heated air at the equator rises and drifts toward the cold polar regions. Around 30 degrees latitude in the Northern Hemisphere, the air cools and descends, dividing into two currents: mild trade breezes that circulate back toward the equator, and more variable northbound winds with embedded eddies and swirls. A mirror image of the process occurs in the Southern Hemisphere. Landmasses, which both warm up and cool down more quickly than oceans, also affect air flow. As currents move from sea to land and encounter large temperature differences, they bend or even reverse their direction. The combination of thermal effects and planetary rotation produces twisted air currents that radiate from the central oceans. The map at left shows typical currents during July; because of the annual cycle of solar heating, wind patterns change from month to month.

Ocean currents. Persistent winds drive the major systems of surface currents that circulate heat around Earth's oceans. Shaped by friction between air and sea and by the planet's rotation, four of the systems swirl in rings, or gyres, in the northern and southern Pacific and Atlantic oceans. Because of Earth's spin, which pushes the central point of the gyre off center to the west, water moving along the western limb is squeezed into narrow, fast currents such as the Gulf Stream and the Kuroshio (Japanese for "black tide"). Currents on the east are broad and slow-moving as they transport chilled water back to its tropical heat source. The Antarctic Circumpolar Current, unrestricted by land masses, circles the globe rather than spinning in a gyre, its force helping to conduct the southern ring systems.

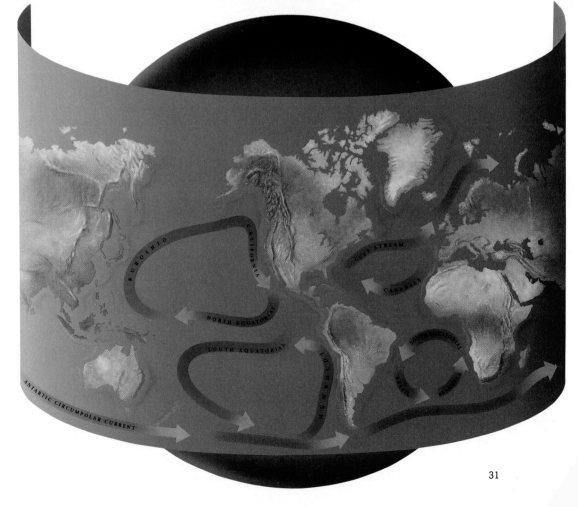

THE PLANET'S CHANGING FACE

Immutable as it may seem to its inhabitants, Earth's surface is an ever-changing reflection of its restless interior. Driven by convection currents in a layer of hot rock in the mantle, large plates of the crust, which carry the seafloor and the continents, slowly wander over the globe, establishing new configurations, heaving up mountain ranges, and sliding into deep ocean trenches as they crunch together and split apart.

As plates collide and separate, climates change, and species migrate, evolve, or die out. Indeed, all players in the system that fosters life on the third planet—land, water, atmosphere, and living organisms themselves—are in constant flux as they respond to and influence each other in an eternal struggle for equilibrium.

Signs of life. The false-color image at right offers a glimpse of Earth's blanket of vegetation. The map shows concentrations of chlorophyll, which green plants use to produce carbohydrates. On land, the areas with the highest concentrations, shown in darkest green, are rain forests. Lighter greens indicate decreasing densities of vegetation, with pale yellow representing barren deserts, polar regions, and high mountains. At sea, shallow waters teem with marine plants, depicted in red and orange; yellow, green, and blue areas are less fertile; and shades of purple indicate the least productive midocean zones. (Near the poles, regions in black are sea ice; those in the Pacific were not monitored.)

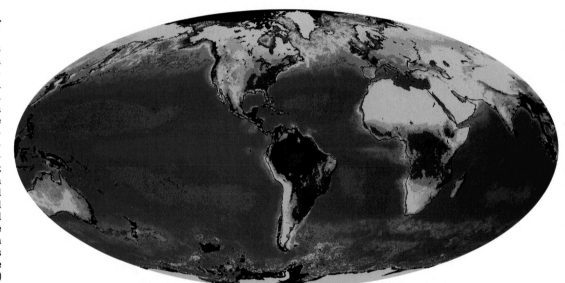

Midocean ridge. A mountain range more than 30,000 miles long *(left)* winds through the oceans like the seam on a baseball, dividing the planet into nine major slabs, or tectonic plates, and several minor ones *(inset)*. The midocean ridge is a crack in the crust that lets hot material driven by convection currents in the mantle well up, pushing older parts of the seafloor away in opposite directions. When the spreading seafloor collides with the thicker continental crust, it is forced down and back into the mantle in ocean trenches—steadily recycling the surface.

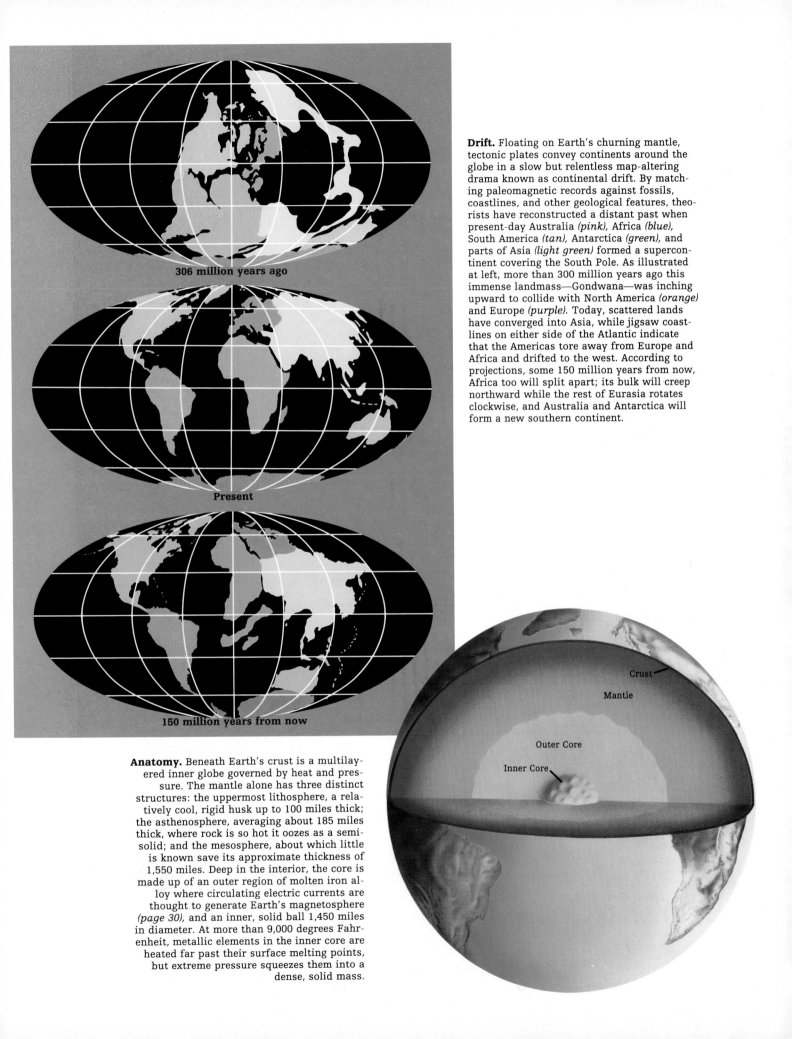

306 million years ago

Present

150 million years from now

Drift. Floating on Earth's churning mantle, tectonic plates convey continents around the globe in a slow but relentless map-altering drama known as continental drift. By matching paleomagnetic records against fossils, coastlines, and other geological features, theorists have reconstructed a distant past when present-day Australia *(pink)*, Africa *(blue)*, South America *(tan)*, Antarctica *(green)*, and parts of Asia *(light green)* formed a supercontinent covering the South Pole. As illustrated at left, more than 300 million years ago this immense landmass—Gondwana—was inching upward to collide with North America *(orange)* and Europe *(purple)*. Today, scattered lands have converged into Asia, while jigsaw coastlines on either side of the Atlantic indicate that the Americas tore away from Europe and Africa and drifted to the west. According to projections, some 150 million years from now, Africa too will split apart; its bulk will creep northward while the rest of Eurasia rotates clockwise, and Australia and Antarctica will form a new southern continent.

Anatomy. Beneath Earth's crust is a multilayered inner globe governed by heat and pressure. The mantle alone has three distinct structures: the uppermost lithosphere, a relatively cool, rigid husk up to 100 miles thick; the asthenosphere, averaging about 185 miles thick, where rock is so hot it oozes as a semisolid; and the mesosphere, about which little is known save its approximate thickness of 1,550 miles. Deep in the interior, the core is made up of an outer region of molten iron alloy where circulating electric currents are thought to generate Earth's magnetosphere *(page 30)*, and an inner, solid ball 1,450 miles in diameter. At more than 9,000 degrees Fahrenheit, metallic elements in the inner core are heated far past their surface melting points, but extreme pressure squeezes them into a dense, solid mass.

Crust

Mantle

Outer Core

Inner Core

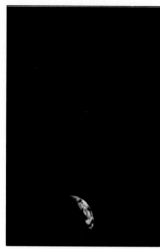

Equatorial Diameter
2,160 miles
Mass
(trillion trillion pounds)
0.162
Density (Earth = 1)
0.605
Gravity (Earth = 1)
0.165
Orbital Period
27.32 Earth days
**Mean Distance
from Earth**
238,860 miles
Period of Rotation
27.32 Earth days

THE MOON: AN INTIMATE PARTNER

The Moon, one of the largest satellites in the Solar System, was most likely formed from the debris of a collision between a very young Earth and a Mars-size fragment left over from the Solar System's formation. In spite of this common ancestry, though, Earth and Moon are in every sense worlds apart. The parent planet is a dynamic, living sphere, geologically active and constantly changing. In contrast, its satellite is completely barren, with no water or atmosphere, and geologically dead, little altered for the last 3.1 billion years.

Nonetheless, the Moon has tremendous influence over its partner. Circling Earth at an average distance of about 234,000 miles, the Moon exerts a gravitational pull that distorts the planet, most noticeably its oceans, and affects its motion in a way that might help trigger ice ages *(right)*. Conversely, Earth's larger gravitational power has slowed the Moon's spin to the point that its rotational period is exactly as long as its orbital period; as a result, earthbound observers see the same lunar hemisphere at all times. With its regular orbit and phases, the Moon served as the basis for the first calendars. Early astronomers were so well versed in its motions that they could predict when the Sun would darken during an eclipse. Once considered portentous, even ominous, events, lunar phases and eclipses are now recognized as consequences of the Moon's shifting position in a rhythmic orbital dance with Earth and the Sun *(below)*.

Phases. Emerging from the dark new moon, Earth's satellite passes through waxing crescent, first quarter, waxing gibbous, and full moon, followed by waning gibbous, third quarter, and waning crescent—before the Moon disappears again.

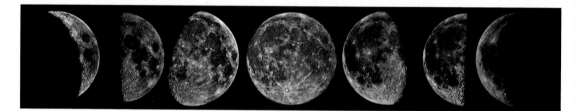

Orbital mechanics. As shown at right *(inset)*, half the Moon's surface is always illuminated by the Sun, no matter where the satellite is in its orbit around Earth. But because the angle formed by Moon, planet, and Sun changes as the Moon circles *(large diagram)*, so does the amount visible from Earth. Dark new moons and bright full moons occur when the three bodies are roughly lined up—a configuration that would always produce an eclipse if not for the slight inclination of the Moon's orbit *(pink)* to that of Earth's circuit around the Sun. Where the two planes intersect, they form a line known as the line of nodes *(dashed line)*. As depicted in the top right and lower left examples, an eclipse can occur only if the Sun and Moon are on or very near the line of nodes at full moon (for a lunar eclipse) or new moon (for a solar eclipse). When the Moon is above or below the ecliptic, the result is an ordinary new or full moon.

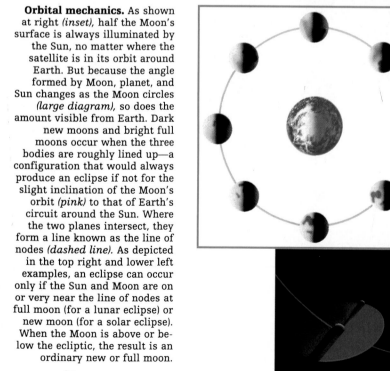

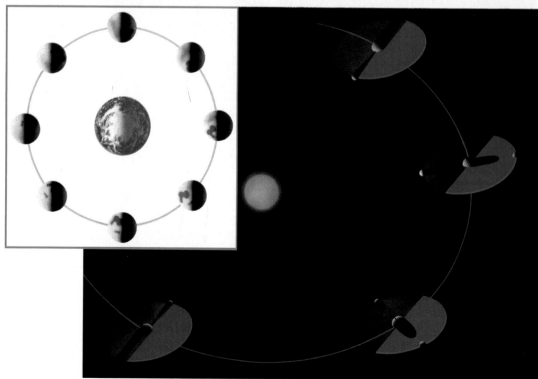

Tides. Ocean tides on Earth are one of the most visible effects of the Moon's gravitational influence. As the Moon exerts a tug on its primary, water on Earth's facing side bulges toward the satellite in a high tide. On the far side of the planet, where the Moon's gravitational pull is weakest, oceans are pulled less than the Earth's center, resulting in another high tide as the water is, in effect, left behind. Although the Sun is too distant to play a principal role in the tidal interactions of the Earth-Moon system, its gravity can augment or dampen the effects of the Moon on Earth, as shown at left. When the two bodies are aligned with the Sun, as in the top and bottom scenarios, the added pull from the Sun causes especially high tides called spring tides. When the three bodies form a right angle *(middle)*, solar gravity competes with that of the Moon, resulting in neap tides—high tides that are lower than normal. Gravitational forces exerted by the Moon and Sun on Earth also compete in such a way that they gradually change the orientation of the planet's rotational axis, causing it to describe a cone in space over a period of about 26,000 years *(above, right)*. In addition to altering Earth's view on the cosmos, this phenomenon, called precession, may contribute to long cycles of global cooling and warming.

The far side. The so-called dark side of the Moon is a region of light-colored terrain covered with craters left by heavy meteoritic impacts. The lack of signs of crustal fracturing common to the near side, along with elevations as much as six miles higher, suggests that the far side's crust is thicker.

The near side. This familiar face features dark maria—plains of lava that seeped up when the crust was fractured by huge meteorites. Mountains surrounding the mare basins are the rims of large impact craters. After the lava cooled, smaller impacts dug out craters, splashing material outward as rays.

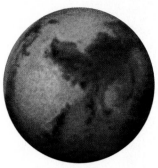

Equatorial Diameter
4,223 miles
Mass
(trillion trillion pounds)
1.415
Density (Earth = 1)
0.71
Gravity (Earth = 1)
0.378
Orbital Period
1.88 Earth years
Known Moons
2
**Mean Distance
from Sun**
141.6 million miles
Period of Rotation
24.623 hours

MARS: THE RED PLANET

Mars—named for the Roman god of war because of its distinctive red hue—is orbited by two moons, Phobos and Deimos *(opposite)*, namesakes of the deity's attendants. Although the satellites bear no resemblance to Earth's moon, the fourth planet itself is in some ways remarkably similar to the third. It is located about one and a half times Earth's distance from the Sun, and measures half Earth's diameter and one-tenth its mass—practically identical, in astronomical terms. Mars also has an atmosphere, albeit a tenuous one, made up of 95 percent carbon dioxide, with a smattering of nitrogen, argon, and oxygen. Even its days, just over twenty-four hours long, are nearly the same length as Earth's, and because its rotational axis is tilted 24 degrees to the plane of the ecliptic, Mars, too, experiences winter, spring, summer, and fall *(below)*.

During the nineteenth century, viewers observing through telescopes noted that icecaps at the poles and dark greenish patches at various places seemed to shrink and grow in seasonal cycles. Others interpreted lines across the surface as a network of canals. Together, these features led many to speculate that Mars, like Earth, held water, vegetation, and intelligent life.

Exploration and experiment in the twentieth century have since dashed almost all hope of discovering life on Mars, however. Beginning in the 1960s, the United States and the Soviet Union sent a swarm of spacecraft, named Mars, Mariner, and Viking, to profile the planet. Photographs of dried riverbeds and soil analysis by the Viking landers did yield overwhelming evidence of a wet past, and data on polar icecaps and indications of subterranean permafrost attest to the presence of water in frozen form. But generally, the red planet—so colored by oxidized iron dust—is a barren world, its shifting, seemingly verdant patches merely the veiling and unveiling of its face by dust linked to seasonal storms.

Martian seasons. Because Mars's orbit is more eccentric than Earth's, its northern and southern hemispheres experience seasons of markedly different length and intensity, as shown at right. The southern summer occurs when Mars is at perihelion *(near right)*, some 26 million miles closer to the Sun than it is at aphelion *(far right)*.

The southern summer is thus both hotter and briefer than the northern season, and its winter longer and colder. These patterns affect the polar icecaps and stir up dust storms that can enshroud the planet.

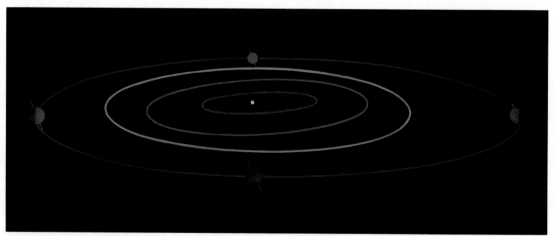

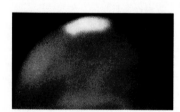

In summer, the north polar cap is mainly water ice, dirtied by dust. In winter, when carbon dioxide freezes out of the atmosphere, the cap expands to about 65 degrees north latitude. Because northern summer occurs at aphelion, the cap melts less than does the southern one.

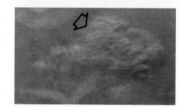

Summer dust storms like this 200-mile-wide fury in the southern hemisphere's Argyre Basin sometimes sweep the globe, reshaping the dark splotches visible from Earth and depositing dust in the northern icecap during its winter freeze.

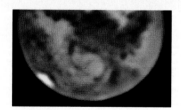

The south pole's relatively dust-free icecap of frozen carbon dioxide undergoes enormous seasonal fluctuations, swelling to 60 degrees south latitude during that hemisphere's lengthy winter and shrinking below 80 degrees south latitude during the brief summer.

In this closeup of the south polar region in summer, the cap is near its minimum—about 250 miles in diameter. Swirling winds, which vary with the seasons, produce the spiral pattern. The absence of dust in winter, when the cap is forming, leaves the cap's surface clean.

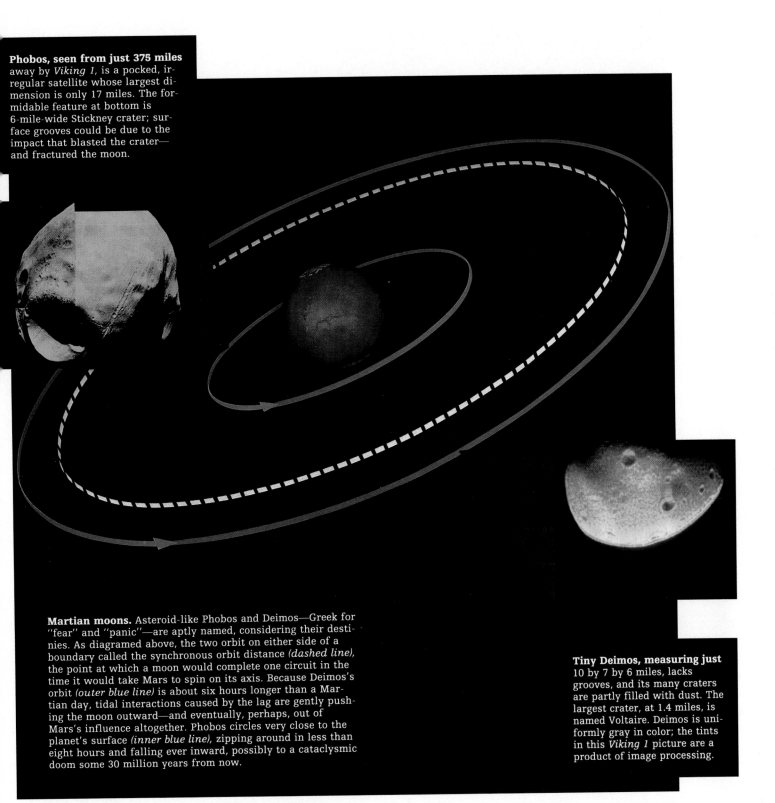

Phobos, seen from just 375 miles away by *Viking 1*, is a pocked, irregular satellite whose largest dimension is only 17 miles. The formidable feature at bottom is 6-mile-wide Stickney crater; surface grooves could be due to the impact that blasted the crater—and fractured the moon.

Martian moons. Asteroid-like Phobos and Deimos—Greek for "fear" and "panic"—are aptly named, considering their destinies. As diagramed above, the two orbit on either side of a boundary called the synchronous orbit distance *(dashed line)*, the point at which a moon would complete one circuit in the time it would take Mars to spin on its axis. Because Deimos's orbit *(outer blue line)* is about six hours longer than a Martian day, tidal interactions caused by the lag are gently pushing the moon outward—and eventually, perhaps, out of Mars's influence altogether. Phobos circles very close to the planet's surface *(inner blue line)*, zipping around in less than eight hours and falling ever inward, possibly to a cataclysmic doom some 30 million years from now.

Tiny Deimos, measuring just 10 by 7 by 6 miles, lacks grooves, and its many craters are partly filled with dust. The largest crater, at 1.4 miles, is named Voltaire. Deimos is uniformly gray in color; the tints in this *Viking 1* picture are a product of image processing.

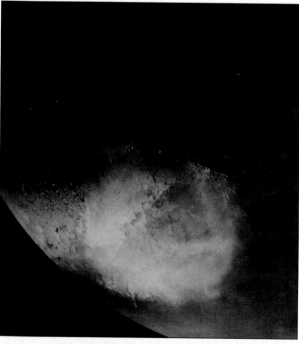

A Geologic Wonder

Home of the highest peak, the deepest canyon, and the widest impact basin in the Solar System, Mars is a world of geologic superlatives. Its volcanoes were pumping lava as recently as a billion years ago, building structures like Olympus Mons—nearly three times the height of Mount Everest—and spilling across a substantial portion of the Martian surface. For unknown reasons, smooth plains (indicative of relatively recent resurfacing by volcanic activity) are concentrated in the northern hemisphere; the south holds ancient, heavily cratered highlands. Between the two runs a global escarpment that includes Valles Marineris, a canyon that would stretch from New York to California.

Most of the information about the planet's geology comes from the flight of *Mariner 9*, which photographed the entire surface during 1971 and 1972, and two Viking missions whose orbiters and landers operated between 1976 and 1980. Maps assembled from their data *(below)* reveal a vast network of riverbeds and channels—testimony to the water that once flowed over what is now a rusty desert world.

Sinuous channels wind for several hundred miles across the slope of Elysium Mons, a volcano whose heat probably melted frozen ground water reservoirs, unleashing floods that carved these riverbeds some four billion years ago.

Blanketed with frost during winter, Hellas Basin is the largest impact site in the Solar System, with a span of more than 1,000 miles. Also the lowest point on Mars, Hellas sinks about 2.5 miles below average ground level.

Eastern hemisphere

Soaring 82,000 feet—more than 15 miles— from a base 340 miles wide, shield volcano Olympus Mons is the regent of Solar System mountains. This overhead image is a composite of several taken by the Viking orbiters.

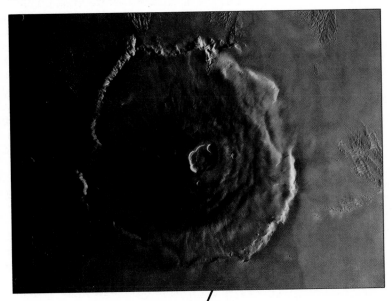

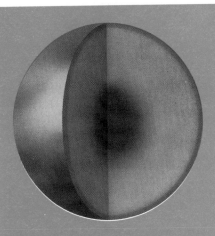

Mars is a stratified ball much like Earth, with a crust, a mantle, and a core. Scientists think that the rigid top layer averages about 20 miles in depth, and the mantle may extend another 1,500 miles. These layers are cooler and less convective than Earth's, so the surface is not churned by plate tectonics. The metallic core, about 1,200 miles across, may be entirely solid, which would account for the absence of a magnetic field to shield the planet from the sterilizing effects of the solar wind.

Western hemisphere

Slicing through 2,500 miles of equatorial terrain, the immense canyon complex named Valles Marineris, for its *Mariner 9* discovery, cuts a groove 4.3 miles deep at points. The image shown here is a Viking orbiter photomosaic.

39

JUPITER: A MINI-SOLAR SYSTEM

Equatorial Diameter
88,846 miles
Mass
(trillion trillion pounds)
4,188.86
Density (Earth = 1)
0.24
Gravity (Earth = 1)
2.53
Orbital Period
11.86 Earth years
Known Moons
16
**Mean Distance
from Sun**
483.6 million miles
Period of Rotation
9.925 hours

The largest of the Sun's planetary brood, Jupiter is nearly massive enough to have been a star in its own right. With a mass 318 times Earth's and a composition almost identical to the Sun's, the planet would have ignited had it been only 80 times bigger—a pittance on the cosmic scale.

Jupiter is the first in a series of gaseous worlds that are vastly different from the rocky bodies closer to the Sun, a distinction echoed in the Jovian system. Of its sixteen known moons, the four largest, called the Galileans for the Italian astronomer who discovered them in 1610, formed in much the same way as the planets, with those farther out being larger and less dense than their inside neighbors *(right)*. The remaining dozen moons *(below)* are tiny and resemble asteroids; all are twentieth-century finds except Amalthea *(opposite)*. Of these, the three latest—and Jupiter's ring system—were discovered during the 1970s, when the Pioneer and Voyager space probes produced a wealth of clues to the workings of the Jovian arena, including the photographs shown here.

Beyond the asteroid belt. The asteroid belt, a ring of boulders and dust that may be a failed planet *(pages 60-61)*, separates the four terrestrial worlds from Jupiter. The fifth planet in the Solar System travels an orbit inclined just 1.3 degrees to the ecliptic, rotating on an axis tilted 3.08 degrees from the perpendicular.

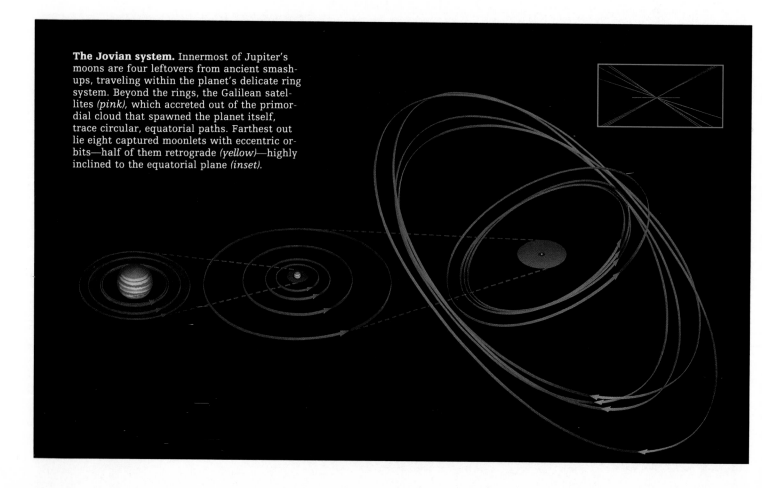

The Jovian system. Innermost of Jupiter's moons are four leftovers from ancient smash-ups, traveling within the planet's delicate ring system. Beyond the rings, the Galilean satellites *(pink)*, which accreted out of the primordial cloud that spawned the planet itself, trace circular, equatorial paths. Farthest out lie eight captured moonlets with eccentric orbits—half of them retrograde *(yellow)*—highly inclined to the equatorial plane *(inset)*.

Io. The innermost Galilean moon is a dry, rocky ball heated internally by wrenching tidal forces. As a result, it is the most volcanically active body in the Solar System, venting sulfur and sulfur dioxide as much as 200 miles high, blanketing the surface with a thick sulfurous cover and forming a torus of charged particles, or plasma, along the moon's orbital path.

Europa. Slightly smaller than Io with a diameter of 2,000 miles, the second Galilean is the brightest object in the Sun's domain, the result of a glaze of water ice over its rocky bulk. Lines reminiscent of the "canals" on Mars crisscross the billiard-ball-smooth surface, possible fractures in the ice where dark material wells up from below.

Ganymede. The Solar System's largest satellite, some 3,300 miles in diameter and thought to be about half water by weight, is covered with craters, basins, and grooves. The dark areas—including prominent Galileo Regio—have weathered the most and are older than the light-colored regions, which show more recent tectonic activity in parallel ridges and troughs.

Callisto. The most distant of the Galileans and the least dense, 2,980-mile-wide Callisto is the most heavily cratered object ever seen. With little or no geologic activity to spew forth fresh covering, the dark, icy surface is extremely aged, bearing the scars of billions of years of meteoritic impacts.

Amalthea. This tiny moonlet, which measures just 96 by 168 miles, travels close to Jupiter's surface within the planet's ring system *(below)*. The largest of four ring satellites—and, in 1892, the fifth of Jupiter's moons to be discovered—Amalthea appears red in this Voyager image because it is bombarded with sulfur from Io's torus.

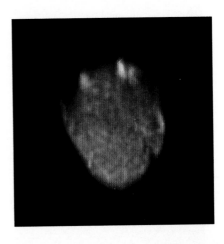

The ring system. Invisible from Earth, Jupiter's ring system was first detected by *Voyager 1* in 1979. This photograph, taken from a distance of 900,000 miles, shows the faint system as a single ring *(light green)* protruding from Jupiter's limb, with the planet casting a shadow over the ring as it arcs behind. Later analysis revealed three components circling roughly 17,000 to 88,000 miles above the cloud tops. Because the dusty specks that make up the system are eventually drawn into Jupiter's atmosphere, scientists theorize that new particles to replenish the bands may be generated by erosion of the ring moonlets.

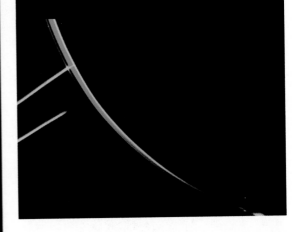

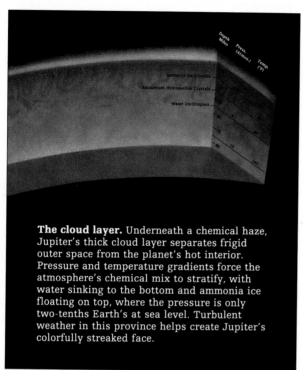

The cloud layer. Underneath a chemical haze, Jupiter's thick cloud layer separates frigid outer space from the planet's hot interior. Pressure and temperature gradients force the atmosphere's chemical mix to stratify, with water sinking to the bottom and ammonia ice floating on top, where the pressure is only two-tenths Earth's at sea level. Turbulent weather in this province helps create Jupiter's colorfully streaked face.

PORTRAIT OF A FAILED STAR

Like the Sun, Jupiter is a gaseous ball composed almost entirely of hydrogen and helium. A somewhat flattened orb without a solid surface, it is covered by an opaque blanket of clouds that gives way to denser fluid layers of increasing temperatures and pressures *(right)*. Powerful currents in the layers combine with Jupiter's dizzying spin rate of less than ten hours to produce violent weather and other fascinating phenomena. The planet's striped appearance, for example, is caused by convecting regions of light and dark clouds that are stretched in an extreme enactment of the Coriolis effect *(below)*. And originating deep in the interior, where electrically conductive liquid metallic hydrogen is whirled by Jupiter's rotation, a huge magnetic field—the largest single feature in the Solar System—envelops the globe *(opposite, bottom)*.

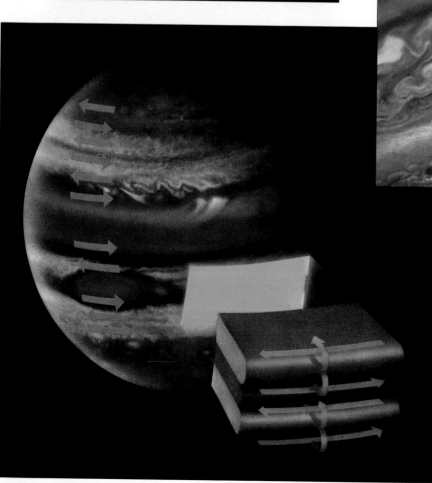

Currents and patterns. Light-colored zones in Jupiter's atmosphere consist of hot rising gas, which cools and subsides in adjacent dark belts before warming and rising again. Spinning at breakneck speed, the planet generates continuous east-west flows *(left, blue arrows)* that stretch these vertical convection currents *(orange arrows)* into stripes that wrap the globe. Jupiter is swept by about a dozen prevailing winds, blowing 200 to 330 miles per hour, and atmospheric eddies, some large enough to swallow an Earth-size body or two. Variously colored ovals, like the Great Red Spot *(above)*, are high- and low-pressure storms that form at different depths in the atmosphere, lasting anywhere from a few days to centuries. The spectacular red spot, three times Earth's diameter, has been observed since the mid-1600s.

The core. Some 44,000 miles below the cloud tops, a tiny but massive core containing the planet's allotment of iron and silicates seethes at 55,000 degrees Fahrenheit; scientists do not know if the core is liquid or solid. Around this dense center lies a 25,000-mile-thick layer of liquid metallic hydrogen, an exotic form of the element rendered electrically conductive by extreme heat and pressure. Overlying this layer is a region 13,000 miles deep of molecular hydrogen and helium, which change from liquid to gas farther out. Jupiter radiates twice as much heat, in the form of infrared energy *(arrows)*, as it receives from the Sun.

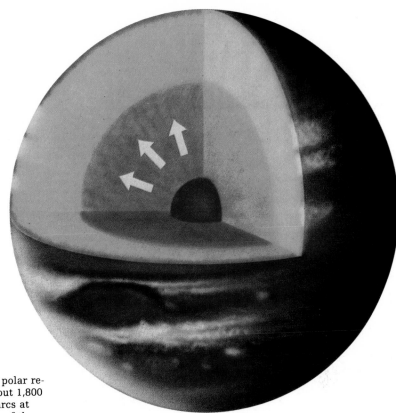

Light show. In Jupiter's polar regions, aurorae flicker about 1,800 miles above the clouds (arcs at top), as charged particles of the solar wind interact with atmospheric gases. This *Voyager 1* photograph also caught flashes of lightning (bright patches below center), testifying to the violence of Jovian weather patterns.

Magnetosphere. A dramatic consequence of Jupiter's interior ocean of liquid metallic hydrogen is a magnetic field thousands of times the strength of Earth's. As illustrated at right, the magnetosphere is compressed on its sunward side by the solar wind and streams outward from behind in a magnetotail that nearly reaches the orbit of Saturn. Although most of the solar wind is deflected by Jupiter's vast field *(arrows)*, small amounts of charged particles do penetrate and become trapped in belts of radiation. Some of these particles mingle with material in the torus of plasma in Io's orbit, then leak out and spread into a thin, electrically conductive plasma sheet *(pink)*.

Equatorial Diameter
74,898 miles
Mass
(trillion trillion
pounds)
1,254.24
Density (Earth = 1)
0.125
Gravity (Earth = 1)
1.066
Orbital Period
29.46 Earth years
Known Moons
18
**Mean Distance
from Sun**
888.2 million miles
Period of Rotation
10.656 hours

SATURN: THE RING WORLD

Saturn is not the only planet in the Solar System with rings, but its broad, banded collection is by far the most dramatic. They were first spotted in 1609 by Galileo, who thought they were a pair of planets or moons on either side of Saturn, in part because of the poor resolution of his telescope but also because the orientation of the rings as viewed from Earth changes in the course of Saturn's circuit of the Sun *(below)*. The rings are made up of innumerable small particles, orbiting the planet in distinct segments and reaching more than 248,600 miles into space *(opposite)*. Despite their extent, the rings are so thin that they virtually disappear from view when seen edge-on.

Also in attendance around Saturn are at least eighteen moons, more than any other planet possesses. Titan, at 3,200 miles wide, is the Solar System's second-largest moon, with an atmosphere made up primarily of nitrogen and a significant percentage of methane—somewhat resembling the atmospheric chemistry of an ancient Earth. The smaller satellites seem to play a complex role in maintaining the ring system. One theory is that debris expelled when the moons are struck by meteoroids is a source of new particles to replenish the system. And the gravitational interaction between the moons and individual particles helps define ring boundaries.

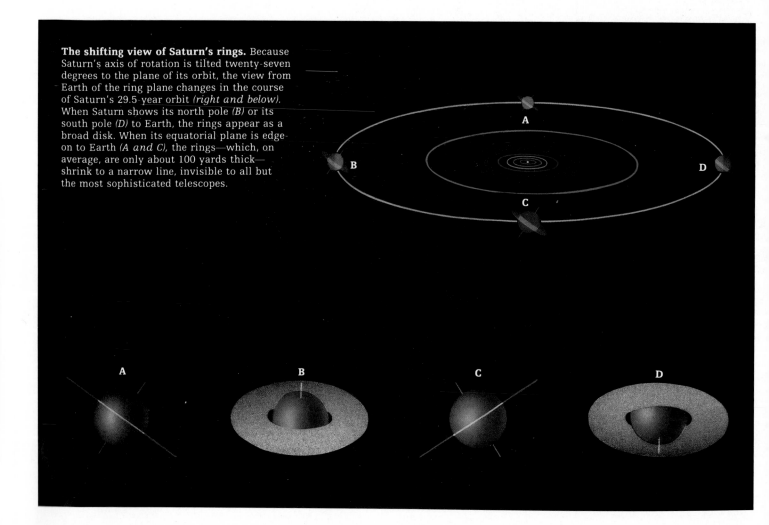

The shifting view of Saturn's rings. Because Saturn's axis of rotation is tilted twenty-seven degrees to the plane of its orbit, the view from Earth of the ring plane changes in the course of Saturn's 29.5-year orbit *(right and below)*. When Saturn shows its north pole *(B)* or its south pole *(D)* to Earth, the rings appear as a broad disk. When its equatorial plane is edge-on to Earth *(A and C)*, the rings—which, on average, are only about 100 yards thick—shrink to a narrow line, invisible to all but the most sophisticated telescopes.

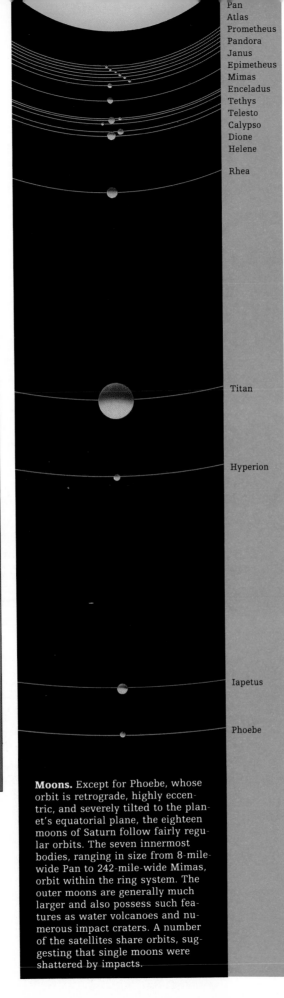

Pan
Atlas
Prometheus
Pandora
Janus
Epimetheus
Mimas
Enceladus
Tethys
Telesto
Calypso
Dione
Helene

Rhea

Titan

Hyperion

Iapetus

Phoebe

A ring roster. Saturn's rings are divided into seven major segments labeled A through G, in order of discovery. Starting just above the planet's atmosphere and reaching nearly 75,000 miles into space, they range in appearance from the broad, dense A, B, and C rings originally spotted by Galileo to the wispy F and G rings that were not discovered until the *Pioneer 11* and Voyager flybys. Although none of the probes detected individual particles, the data they collected indicates that most fragments are no larger than a few yards across, each containing water ice interspersed with small amounts of rock and minerals.

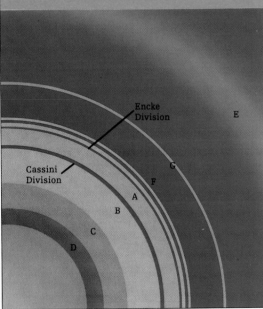

Encke
Division

E

Cassini
Division

G

F

A

B

C

D

Moons. Except for Phoebe, whose orbit is retrograde, highly eccentric, and severely tilted to the planet's equatorial plane, the eighteen moons of Saturn follow fairly regular orbits. The seven innermost bodies, ranging in size from 8-mile-wide Pan to 242-mile-wide Mimas, orbit within the ring system. The outer moons are generally much larger and also possess such features as water volcanoes and numerous impact craters. A number of the satellites share orbits, suggesting that single moons were shattered by impacts.

Titan. The dense atmosphere on Saturn's planet-size satellite glows yellow-blue in the color-enhanced *Voyager 1* photo above. Composed mostly of nitrogen and methane, the atmosphere also contains complex organic compounds such as hydrogen cyanide and cyanogen that may have been created by photochemical reactions with sunlight. As the particles grow larger, they could condense and fall to the surface to form hydrocarbon oceans, piling up complex organic molecules similar to those that led to the evolution of life on Earth.

45

OF ATMOSPHERE AND ANATOMY

Atmospheric bands. Saturn's atmosphere—made up of hydrogen with traces of methane and ammonia—is striped with a series of bands that travel mostly eastward across the planet at speeds up to 900 miles per hour. Like similar markings on Jupiter, the bands are the result of strong circulation patterns.

Like its larger neighbor, Jupiter, Saturn is composed predominantly of hydrogen and helium, chief ingredients of the nebula that gave birth to the Solar System, and may possess a rocky core. Because the planet also has an extremely fast rotational period—10.656 hours—this gaseous ball tends to bulge at the equator and flatten out at the poles, as does Jupiter. But the two differ significantly in density. Saturn is about half as dense as Jupiter and much less dense than even water: If Saturn could be put into a large enough ocean, it would float.

For reasons that are not entirely clear, the ringed planet emits 2.8 times as much energy as it receives from the Sun, which implies that it has an internal energy source. According to the prevailing theory, the energy comes from heat released as helium atoms condense into droplets and sink into the planet's interior, a hypothesis that also explains the observed scarcity of helium in Saturn's upper atmosphere.

The Great White Spot. In this series of pictures, taken by the Hubble Space Telescope over ten hours on November 17, 1990, a large white band travels eastward across Saturn's equatorial region until it breaks up. The band began two months earlier as an oval spot, which scientists think was an upwelling of ammonia ice particles that rose above the rest of the cloud layer, only to be dissipated by atmospheric winds. Like a similar feature that has been seen about every thirty years since 1876, the spot may be a repeating phenomenon generated by seasonal solar heating.

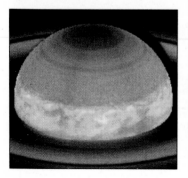
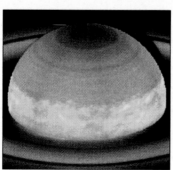
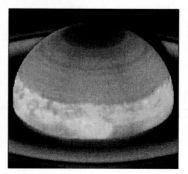
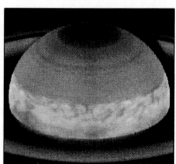

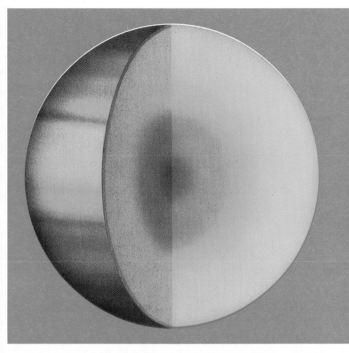

Inside the planet. Saturn has no surface to speak of, only increasingly dense layers of gas surrounding a solid, rocky core *(red)* some 15,000 miles in diameter. The core, like the planet's outer moons, consists of silicate rock and iron, as well as water, ammonia, and methane ices. Outside the core lies an 11,000-mile-thick layer of so-called metallic hydrogen *(orange):* hydrogen molecules that have been stripped of their electrons by the intense pressure in the planet's interior. Surrounding this layer is a layer of molecular hydrogen *(yellow)* that extends 19,000 miles to just below the planet's cloud tops, which account, roughly, for Saturn's outermost 40 miles.

The magnetosphere. Generated by electric currents within the layer of metallic hydrogen, Saturn's magnetic field behaves as though the planet contained a large bar magnet. Lines of magnetic force emanate from Saturn's north magnetic pole—located only seven-tenths of a degree from the planet's geographic north pole—and loop around to the south magnetic pole *(inset, below).* Depending on the pressure of the solar wind, the bow shock, or leading edge of the magnetosphere *(green),* stands off from the surface at distances that range from eighteen to twenty-five planetary radii.

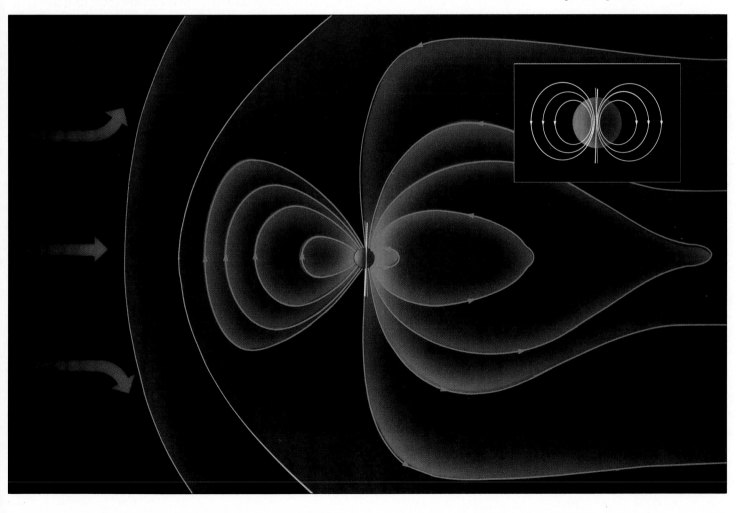

URANUS: PLANET UPENDED

Equatorial Diameter
31,763 miles
Mass
(trillion trillion pounds)
191.59
Density (Earth = 1)
0.23
Gravity (Earth = 1)
0.906
Orbital Period
84.01 Earth years
Known Moons
15
**Mean Distance
from Sun**
1,786.4 million miles
Period of Rotation
17.24 hours

Although ancient observers had readily noted the celestial journeys of the six inner planets, Uranus, named for the Roman god who was the father of Saturn and the grandfather of Jupiter, escaped detection until the advent of relatively powerful telescopes. On March 13, 1781, English astronomer and master telescope maker William Herschel found what he at first took to be a star, or perhaps a comet, until the plotting of the object's orbit persuaded him that he had actually discovered a seventh planet.

Unlike the Sun's other planets, which spin more or less upright, like tops, as they circle the Sun, Uranus rolls around with its axis of rotation nearly parallel to its orbital plane *(below)*. Scientists speculate that early in the planet's history, an Earth-size object, traveling at roughly 40,000 miles per hour, smashed into Uranus and knocked it over. The blow might have caused the planet to slough off a vast disk of hot gas that eventually coalesced into the family of fifteen assorted moons *(opposite)* that orbit Uranus in the plane of its equator.

Before the visit by *Voyager 2* in January 1986, astronomers knew of only the five largest satellites—Miranda, Ariel, Umbriel, Titania, and Oberon—and expected them to exhibit little in the way of surface features aside from impact craters. But Voyager revealed these bodies to be remarkably individual in appearance. Titania, for instance, although similar to Oberon in size and in showing flooded areas that signified a volcanic past, displayed huge, winding valleys hundreds of miles long, possibly formed when interior water froze, expanded, and cracked the thin crust. The most dramatic surface, however, belonged to Miranda, smallest of the five. Covered with ridges, craters, canyons, and a huge chevron-shaped formation, Miranda seemed to bear mute witness to a cataclysmic history.

In addition to its complement of satellites, Uranus is equipped with a system of rings. Unlike Saturn's easily visible broad bands, however, the Uranian rings are so narrow—less than eight miles across, in most cases—that they were not discovered during earth-based observations until 1977. The rings' narrowness and a surprising lack of dust in the inner rings suggest that they may be a temporary phenomenon.

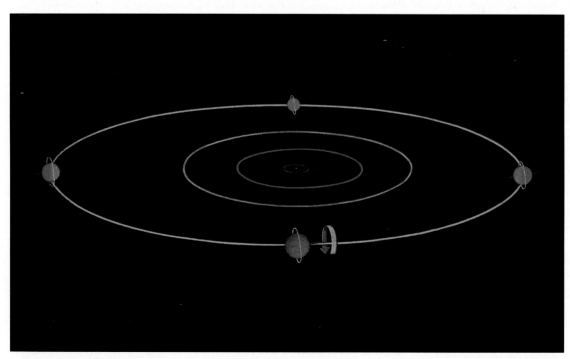

A severely tilting planet. The nearly 98-degree inclination of Uranus's equator to its orbital plane, the most pronounced in the Solar System, means that, in the course of its eighty-four-Earth-year journey around the Sun, its polar regions take turns pointing at the Sun, thereby enduring nights and days lasting forty-two years each.

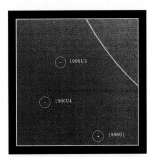

Three of the shards found by *Voyager 2* are captured in one photograph. Like their misshapen cohorts, the moons are believed to be made up of water ice.

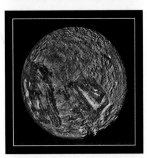

Miranda, 300 miles wide, is one of the most geologically complicated bodies in the Solar System. It may have been shattered and reassembled as many as five times—producing towering cliffs and vast plains scored with ridges and grooves.

Ariel is the brightest Uranian satellite. Its surface, reflecting 40 percent of the light that strikes it, appears to have been coated many times with fresh water ice, the result of ice volcanism that also produced faults and ridges and smoothed over valley floors.

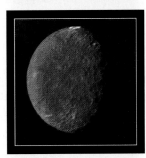

Umbriel, uniformly dark and cratered, displays no signs of geologic activity, but does possess one unexplained feature—a bright crater nearly seventy miles wide that was nicknamed the "fluorescent Cheerio."

Titania, nearly a thousand miles across, is the largest of the moons. Rift valleys extend for several hundred miles, and the satellite's surface has been re-covered by a dark material, possibly methane or water ice.

Outermost Oberon is marked by heavy cratering. Dark spots are crater floors that may have been filled by ice-rock slush erupting from its interior.

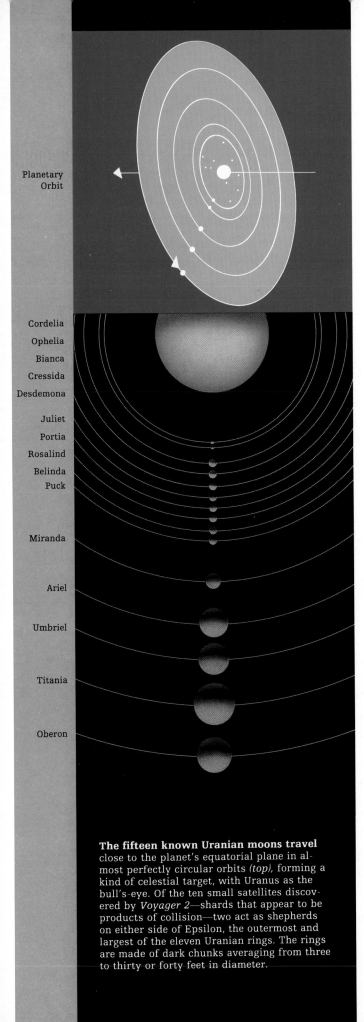

Planetary Orbit

Cordelia
Ophelia
Bianca
Cressida
Desdemona

Juliet
Portia
Rosalind
Belinda
Puck

Miranda

Ariel

Umbriel

Titania

Oberon

The fifteen known Uranian moons travel close to the planet's equatorial plane in almost perfectly circular orbits *(top)*, forming a kind of celestial target, with Uranus as the bull's-eye. Of the ten small satellites discovered by *Voyager 2*—shards that appear to be products of collision—two act as shepherds on either side of Epsilon, the outermost and largest of the eleven Uranian rings. The rings are made of dark chunks averaging from three to thirty or forty feet in diameter.

BENEATH THE METHANE HAZE

A masking haze of methane ice crystals and other particles kept Uranus largely hidden until the encounter with *Voyager 2.* Beneath the methane veil, the probe's instruments found, were bright wisps of cloud whipped along by east and west winds flowing in bands with speeds nearing 350 miles per hour. The winds seem to act as a thermostat, maintaining a planetwide temperature that varies no more than a few degrees between the equator and either pole.

Perhaps the most intriguing of *Voyager 2*'s findings, however, was that Uranus's magnetic field is radically tilted to its rotational axis *(opposite, bottom),* a characteristic shared only by Neptune. Scientists have suggested that the darkness of the Uranian rings and small moons may be the burnt residue produced when methane on the surface of the moons and ring particles is bombarded by high-energy charged particles trapped in the magnetosphere.

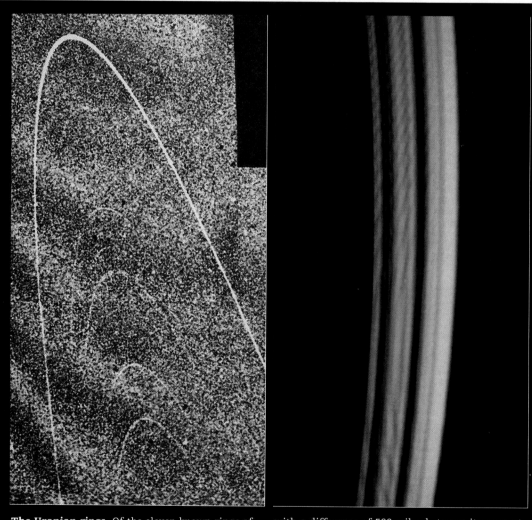

The Uranian rings. Of the eleven known rings of Uranus—so dark and narrow as to be nearly invisible—six are somewhat inclined to the planet's equator and have slightly eccentric orbits. The outermost and most eccentric is Epsilon *(left top),* with a difference of 500 miles between its nearest and farthest approach to the planet. Inboard of Epsilon is the Delta ring, shown above in a false-color image developed from data recorded by Voyager as a star passed behind the ring.

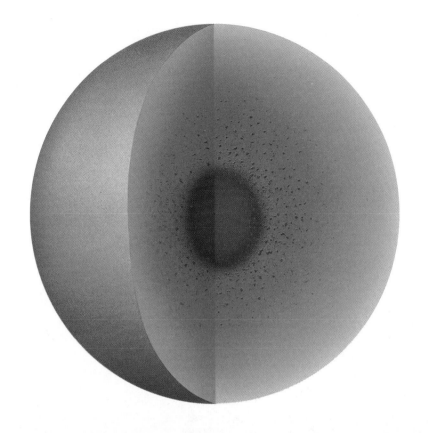

Beneath the veil. Abundant hydrogen and some helium and methane cap the Uranian atmosphere, representing 11 percent of the planet's mass, where temperatures are −350 degrees Fahrenheit. The methane, by absorbing the Sun's red wavelengths, gives Uranus its characteristic blue-green color. Below the atmosphere may be a water-methane-ammonia ocean containing 65 percent of Uranus's mass. As shown in the model of the planet at left, this ocean may surround an Earth-size core that scientists theorize is made up of magnesium, silicates, and iron, at temperatures that may reach 12,600 degrees. Despite these temperatures and for reasons unknown, Uranus—unlike the other gaseous planets, which radiate more heat through radioactive decay than they absorb from the Sun—returns hardly any heat to the Solar System.

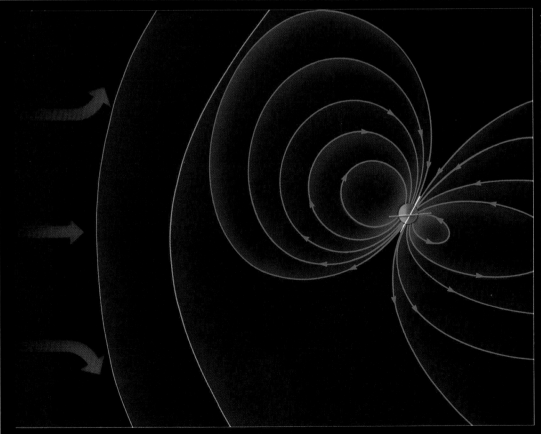

A skewed magnetic field. In marked contrast to the near-perfect alignment of the rotational and magnetic axes of other planets with magnetic fields, the two axes on Uranus are offset by about 60 degrees. Some scientists speculate that the field is generated not from the core, as is the case with terrestrial planets, for example, but from the mantle.

The displacement of the magnetic axis causes the Uranian magnetosphere to expand and contract as the axis varies in its alignment with the solar wind *(pink arrows)*, which sometimes smashes the magnetosphere to within 370,000 miles of the planet. Finally, as a consequence of Uranus's keeled-over rotational orientation to the plane of its orbit, the interaction of the magnetosphere and charged solar particles generates auroral activity at the planet's equator rather than at its poles.

Equatorial Diameter
30,775 miles
Mass
(trillion trillion pounds)
225.98
Density (Earth = 1)
0.297
Gravity (Earth = 1)
1.137
Orbital Period
164.79 Earth years
Known Moons
8
**Mean Distance
from Sun**
2,798.8 million miles
Period of Rotation
16.11 hours

NEPTUNE: THE LAST STOP

In 1846, Neptune was found almost precisely where two young scientists—John Couch Adams of England and Urbain Leverrier of France—had independently predicted it should be, based on anomalies in the orbit of Uranus. Nearly 150 years later, the eighth planet was the last world visited by *Voyager 2,* which flew by in August 1989.

The probe discovered six new moons, raising the total of known Neptunian satellites to eight, and relayed to Earth a wealth of information about the planet's turbulent atmosphere. Voyager also shed some light on Neptune's ring system, showing that what appeared in earthbound telescopes to be a series of incomplete rings, or ring arcs, are actually dense segments of the outermost of four filaments girding the planet. Although the outer ring's arclike concentrations remain unexplained, scientists are hopeful that the answer lies in further analysis of Voyager data.

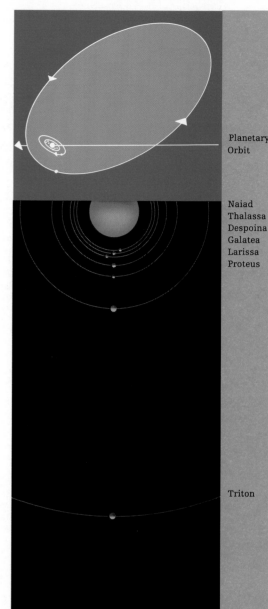

Planetary
Orbit

Naiad
Thalassa
Despoina
Galatea
Larissa
Proteus

Triton

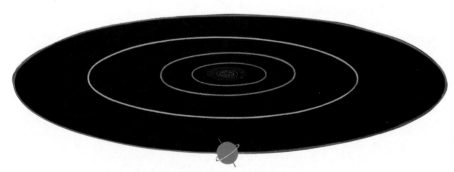

A mild-mannered orbit. Neptune's nearly circular path around the Sun is by far the least eccentric in the outer Solar System and is also inclined to the ecliptic only about 1.8 degrees. The planet itself rotates at an angle of 28.8 degrees to its orbital plane, only 5.4 degrees more than Earth.

Moons. The six innermost moons, all discovered by *Voyager 2* in 1989, follow nearly circular orbits *(top, inner circle)* around Neptune's equator, and only Naiad's tilts significantly—4.7 degrees to the planet's equatorial plane. In contrast, the outermost moons, Triton and Nereid, possess two of the strangest orbits in the Solar System. Triton is the only major moon to orbit its planet backwards, and as a result, the moon is slowly spiraling inward; eventually it will succumb to the planet's tidal forces and disintegrate. Nereid's path, although only modestly tilted compared with Triton's, is the most eccentric among the Solar System's planets and known moons.

Nereid

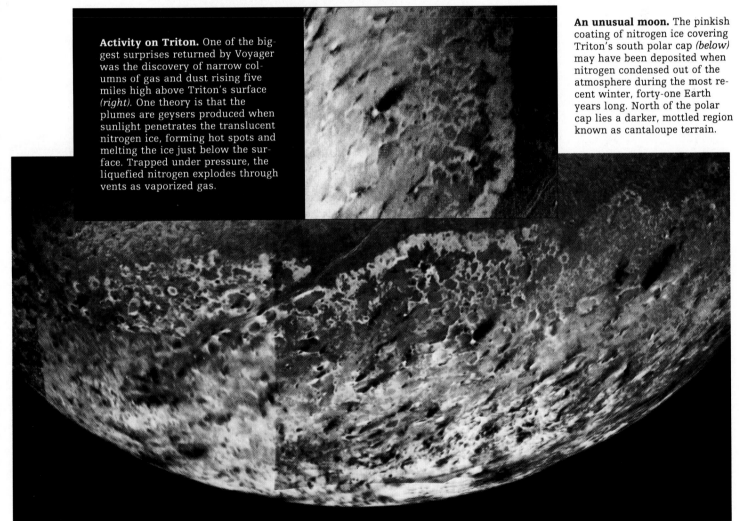

Rings and arcs. Neptune has a series of three narrow rings and one broad band that are so faint that *Voyager 2* could detect them only by overexposing the planet's image. The outermost ring contains three bright arcs *(left),* one of which is shown in closeup in the inset. Some astronomers originally suspected that the arcs were maintained by the gravitational influence of one of the small moons found by Voyager, but none proved to be correctly situated to account for the phenomenon.

Activity on Triton. One of the biggest surprises returned by Voyager was the discovery of narrow columns of gas and dust rising five miles high above Triton's surface *(right).* One theory is that the plumes are geysers produced when sunlight penetrates the translucent nitrogen ice, forming hot spots and melting the ice just below the surface. Trapped under pressure, the liquefied nitrogen explodes through vents as vaporized gas.

An unusual moon. The pinkish coating of nitrogen ice covering Triton's south polar cap *(below)* may have been deposited when nitrogen condensed out of the atmosphere during the most recent winter, forty-one Earth years long. North of the polar cap lies a darker, mottled region known as cantaloupe terrain.

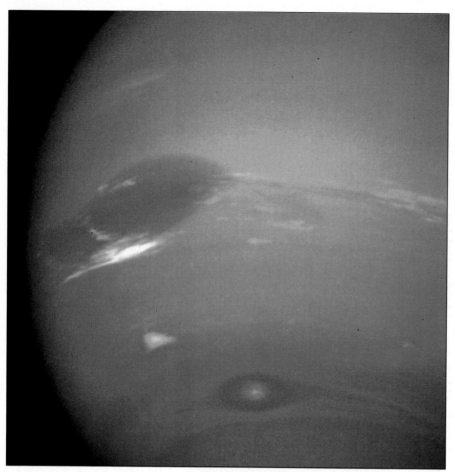

CLOSEUP OF THE BLUE PLANET

Composed of the same elements that make up the atmospheres of the other three gaseous planets, Neptune's atmosphere, like that of Uranus, contains less hydrogen than those of Jupiter and Saturn. Instead, it holds more of other gases such as helium, which accounts for 25 percent of its mass, and methane, which makes up a relatively high one percent. As is the case with Uranus, methane effectively absorbs red light and reflects only blue light, thereby producing Neptune's hue.

Although the planet lacks the color variations characteristic of Jupiter, the two share some striking similarities. Neptune's Great Dark Spot *(left)*, discovered by *Voyager 2*, was given that name for its remarkable resemblance to Jupiter's Great Red Spot; the sizes of the two storm systems in proportion to their respective planets are nearly identical, as are their locations and behavior. Other atmospheric phenomena, such as high cirrus clouds *(below)* and winds that blow at speeds of 1,200 miles per hour—the fastest in the Solar System—suggest that Neptune is a very violent place.

The atmosphere. Neptune's Great Dark Spot *(above)*, a long-lived storm system the size of Earth, lies about twenty degrees south of the equator. The cloud cover that shrouds most of the planet is absent inside this swirling vortex, offering astronomers a deeper view into the planet's atmosphere. South of the Great Dark Spot lies the Small Dark Spot, which appears to be a spout through which methane from lower levels bubbles to the top and condenses into clouds. Between the two dark spots is the Scooter, a smaller cloud, possibly formed of methane ice, that rides an eastward wind, one of the few bands of atmosphere that blow in the same direction that the planet rotates.

Cirrus. Floating thirty miles above the methane cloud deck, a series of narrow, wispy clouds of methane ice cast shadows on the layer below. Neptune is the only planet besides Earth and Mars known to possess such cirrus features.

Clouds around the Dark Spot. *Voyager 2*'s reconnaissance of Neptune revealed that the Great Dark Spot is also flanked by high, cirrus-type clouds. The clouds appear to form as methane gas is prevented from entering the Dark Spot by its high atmospheric pressure and instead is forced to rise to higher altitudes, where it condenses as clouds.

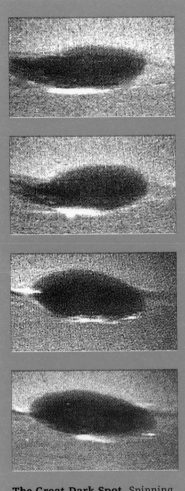

The Great Dark Spot. Spinning counterclockwise, the Great Dark Spot takes about sixteen days to rotate once around its own axis. As seen in the series of photos above, the spot varies in shape in the course of its rotation.

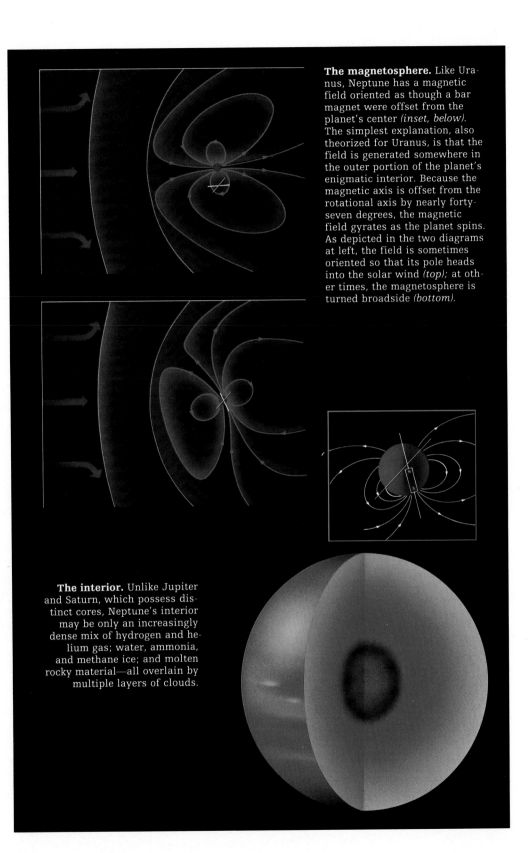

The magnetosphere. Like Uranus, Neptune has a magnetic field oriented as though a bar magnet were offset from the planet's center *(inset, below)*. The simplest explanation, also theorized for Uranus, is that the field is generated somewhere in the outer portion of the planet's enigmatic interior. Because the magnetic axis is offset from the rotational axis by nearly forty-seven degrees, the magnetic field gyrates as the planet spins. As depicted in the two diagrams at left, the field is sometimes oriented so that its pole heads into the solar wind *(top);* at other times, the magnetosphere is turned broadside *(bottom).*

The interior. Unlike Jupiter and Saturn, which possess distinct cores, Neptune's interior may be only an increasingly dense mix of hydrogen and helium gas; water, ammonia, and methane ice; and molten rocky material—all overlain by multiple layers of clouds.

PLUTO: THE LONELY OUTPOST

Equatorial Diameter
1,430 miles
Mass
(trillion trillion pounds)
0.029
Density (Earth = 1)
0.37
Gravity (Earth = 1)
0.077
Orbital Period
248.6 Earth years
Known Moons
1
**Mean Distance
from Sun**
3,666.2 million miles
Period of Rotation
152.87 hours

Orbiting some 3.6 billion miles from the Sun, Pluto is bathed by a light so faint that its surface temperature never rises above −369 degrees Fahrenheit. The dim body was detected in 1930 by Clyde Tombaugh, a young assistant at the Lowell Observatory, who spotted a tiny blip after poring over scores of photographic plates. Tombaugh used a device called a blink comparator, which alternates the operator's view between two photographic plates taken a few days apart. As the operator looks from one plate to the other, the distant stars remain still, but the change in position of nearer bodies such as planets or asteroids produces a noticeable "blink." The discovery capped a lengthy hunt by several teams of astronomers who were searching for the cause of apparent anomalies in the orbits of Uranus and Neptune.

Once found, distant Pluto gave away little about itself other than its position. Then, in 1978, James Christy of the United States Naval Observatory discovered a moon, subsequently named Charon, orbiting Pluto. The moon's orbital interactions with its parent planet allowed scientists to determine the mass of the system as well as the fact that Pluto is tilted nearly on its side, much like Uranus.

The timing of Christy's discovery was serendipitous, for astronomers quickly realized that Charon's orbit would soon be edge-on as seen from Earth. Such an alignment, which happens only twice in every 248-year Plutonian orbit, would result in mutual eclipses of moon and planet. The occultations, occurring every 3.2 days between late 1984 and late 1990, yielded vital data on the size and density of each body, and revealed that the moon's surface is predominately water ice.

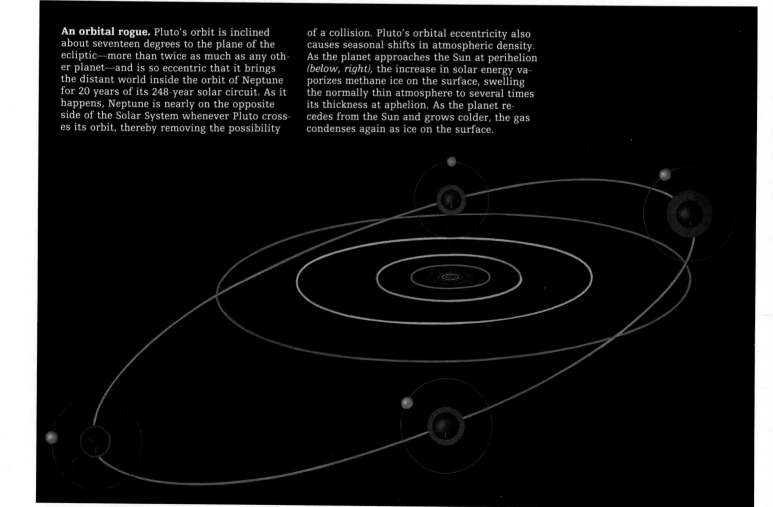

An orbital rogue. Pluto's orbit is inclined about seventeen degrees to the plane of the ecliptic—more than twice as much as any other planet—and is so eccentric that it brings the distant world inside the orbit of Neptune for 20 years of its 248-year solar circuit. As it happens, Neptune is nearly on the opposite side of the Solar System whenever Pluto crosses its orbit, thereby removing the possibility of a collision. Pluto's orbital eccentricity also causes seasonal shifts in atmospheric density. As the planet approaches the Sun at perihelion *(below, right)*, the increase in solar energy vaporizes methane ice on the surface, swelling the normally thin atmosphere to several times its thickness at aphelion. As the planet recedes from the Sun and grows colder, the gas condenses again as ice on the surface.

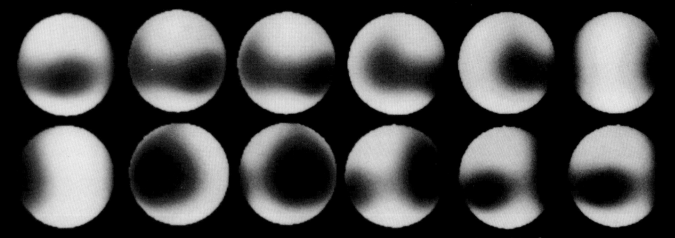

Surface variations. In this computer-generated model of Pluto's surface through a 153-hour Plutonian day, both poles stand out brightly, the result, scientists think, of a thick coating of highly reflective methane ice. The equatorial region apparently consists of a mixture of ice and darker material. Within the equatorial band a small, bright region is probably also methane ice; a larger, very dark area may be a gap in the planet's methane crust.

The interior. Pluto's relatively high density suggests that beneath its light crust of methane ice lies a substantial amount of rock. In one model of the planet's interior, the crust *(light blue)*, perhaps only a few miles thick, surrounds a mantle about 150 miles deep, composed mainly of water ice *(dark blue)*. The mantle, in turn, overlies a solid, rocky core *(gray)* 1,000 miles or so across. The decay of radioactive elements shortly after the planet's formation may have supplied the heat that allowed the heavier rock to sink to the center, while the lighter ices rose to the surface.

The search for the tenth planet. Long before the discovery of Charon permitted an accurate calculation of Pluto's mass, astronomers realized that the planet could not account for the orbital discrepancies noted for Uranus and Neptune. Believing the culprit could still be at large, Vesto Slipher, the head of Lowell Observatory, assigned Clyde Tombaugh to continue the search for a tenth planet. Tombaugh complied, spending more than a decade in the pursuit, but his efforts were in vain.

Most scientists now believe that this planet does not exist, and that the problems with the Uranian and Neptunian orbits may simply be the results of faulty measurements. However, a small number remain unconvinced. Armed with computers and sophisticated imaging equipment unavailable in Tombaugh's day, they continue to scour the sky for "Planet X," as the body is known. Said Tombaugh in 1988 about the tenacious trackers: "I wish 'em luck. They're in for a lot of hard work."

Comet Halley, 1910. With color-enhancement, this photograph, made during the spectacular 1910 appearance of the Solar System's most famous periodic visitor, reveals the comet's coma *(white)* and plasma tail *(blue)*. Although Halley's 1986 passage was a visual disappointment to earthbound observers, a fleet of space probes sent back data that yielded some intriguing clues to conditions in the early Solar System.

COMETS: CELESTIAL VAGABONDS

In ancient times, people viewed comets as omens of one sort or another. The Greeks regarded them as portents of doom, and the Chinese called them "broom stars" because comets were thought to bring in the new as they swept out the old. Then, in the 1680s, British astronomer Edmond Halley analyzed observations of a comet that had appeared in 1682 and concluded that its orbit was identical to those of bodies that were spotted in 1531 and 1607. Strongly suspecting that the three objects were actually the same one returning at roughly seventy-five-year intervals, he later predicted that it would next appear in late 1758 or early 1759. The comet that now bears Halley's name has come back on schedule four times since his prediction, each return attended by great public anticipation and fanfare.

According to a theory postulated in 1950 by astronomer Jan Oort of the Netherlands, comets originate in a vast cloud of icy and dusty bodies *(below)*, some of which follow looping paths around the Sun that could reach almost halfway to the nearest star and take 5 or 10 million years to travel once. Only the tiniest fraction of the comets in the Oort cloud, as the multitude is now known, have visited the inner Solar System in the nearly four centuries since the advent of the telescope. But whether they take three years or 5 million on their solar journey, comets spend the majority of their time far from the Sun's warmth. Preserved by the cold of deep space, they are thus believed to be primordial remnants of the solar nebula.

Comet origins. Astronomers theorize that the Oort cloud *(right)*, reservoir of the comets that periodically blaze through the inner Solar System, is a football-shaped envelope defined by the orbits of trillions of icy bodies, most circling the Sun at distances of about 50,000 astronomical units. Close gravitational encounters with passing stars or dense gas clouds sometimes throw these remnants of the Solar System's formation back in toward the Sun, where they are pulled into orbits with periods ranging from 3 to many millions of years. Depicted below are the orbits of a multitude of relatively short period comets—those with orbital periods of less than 200 years—that are considered part of Jupiter's cometary entourage because the farthest point in their orbits lies near the orbit of Jupiter.

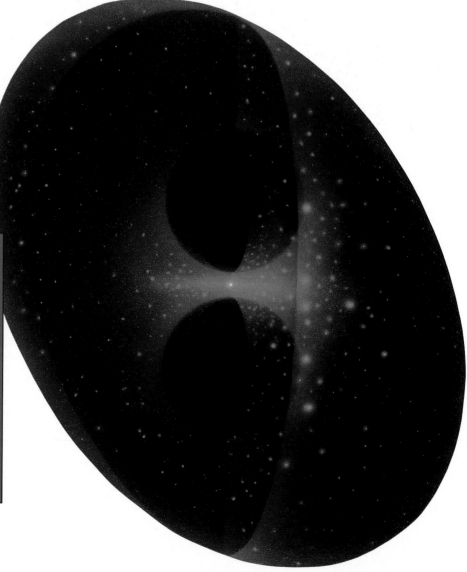

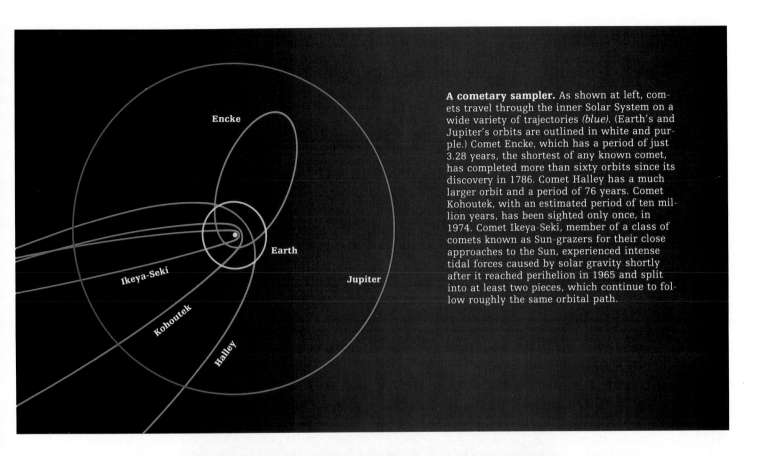

A cometary sampler. As shown at left, comets travel through the inner Solar System on a wide variety of trajectories *(blue)*. (Earth's and Jupiter's orbits are outlined in white and purple.) Comet Encke, which has a period of just 3.28 years, the shortest of any known comet, has completed more than sixty orbits since its discovery in 1786. Comet Halley has a much larger orbit and a period of 76 years. Comet Kohoutek, with an estimated period of ten million years, has been sighted only once, in 1974. Comet Ikeya-Seki, member of a class of comets known as Sun-grazers for their close approaches to the Sun, experienced intense tidal forces caused by solar gravity shortly after it reached perihelion in 1965 and split into at least two pieces, which continue to follow roughly the same orbital path.

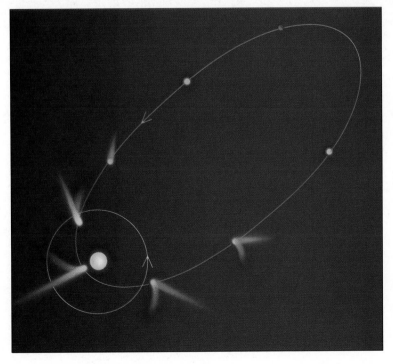

Multiple tails. When they are far from the Sun, comets are essentially naked balls of ice and dust. But as they pass Jupiter's orbit on the inbound leg of their circuit, the Sun's heat begins to vaporize surface ices, creating a gaseous halo, or coma, around the cometary nucleus. When the comet is within about two astronomical units of the Sun, charged particles in the coma are driven away by the solar wind, forming the so-called plasma tail. Because the solar wind emanates from the Sun in all directions, the plasma tail always points radially away from the Sun, often extending for tens of millions of miles. As the comet approaches perihelion, a second, less prominent tail appears. Called the dust tail, this appendage arises from dust particles that are pushed outward by photons of sunlight, curving away from the direction of the comet's travel.

Asteroids: Minor Planets

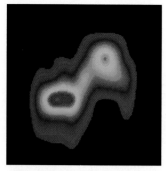

Two for one. The unusual double-lobed asteroid shown above in this false-color radar image consists of two half-mile-wide boulders whose mutual gravity drew them together. The asteroid—dubbed 1989PB—spins end over end once every few hours and circles the Sun every 400 days at an average orbital distance of 99 million miles.

Remnants of the Solar System's formation, asteroids are chunks of rock that orbit the Sun primarily in a band between Mars and Jupiter, planetesimals that never coalesced into a planet because of Jupiter's gravitational influence. Over the millennia, random gravitational encounters have tossed a great number of these fragments out of the system's bounds. Those that remain—4.6 billion years later—have a total mass of only about .04 percent that of Earth.

These so-called minor planets range from less than 50 to about 600 miles in diameter and all together may number in the millions. A portion of them swarm outside the so-called main asteroid belt, traveling regular orbits along Jupiter's path; others follow more eccentric routes that can fly outward as far as Uranus's neighborhood or swing inside toward Earth, sometimes crossing its orbit *(opposite, bottom right)*.

Asteroids are difficult to spot because of their small size. Scientists discovered the first, Ceres, as recently as 1801—and mistook the twinkling object for an eighth planet. When a second was detected in 1802, Ceres's status was revised and the bodies were named asteroids, meaning "starlike." Only eight more were sighted by 1851, but with improvements in astrophotography late in the nineteenth century and the advent of sophisticated telescopes in the twentieth, astronomers have identified about 5,000 with well-determined orbits.

Composition. Gleaning the chemical composition of asteroids from their spectra, astronomers group most asteroids into one of three main categories: S, for silicaceous; M, for metallic; and C, for carbonaceous. S asteroids such as Flora *(bottom left)*, which account for 15 percent of the main belt population, are thought by most scientists to consist of an iron-nickel core surrounded by a silicon alloy called olivine. Another 10 percent are type M, like ruddy Psyche *(bottom center)*, many of which are thought to be composed primarily of iron and nickel. C asteroids, of which Ceres *(center)* is the largest, make up the remaining 75 percent; resembling primitive types of meteorites, they are believed to be carbon rich.

Kirkwood gaps. The 150-million-mile-wide main asteroid belt, depicted at left, is marked by gaps at certain distances from the Sun where relatively few asteroids make their rounds. Called Kirkwood gaps for the nineteenth-century mathematician who identified them, these near-vacant tracks occur where orbital periods are simple fractions of Jupiter's. As a result, asteroids that inhabit these zones receive periodic gravitational tugs from the giant planet, always at the same point in their orbit, that throw them into new paths.

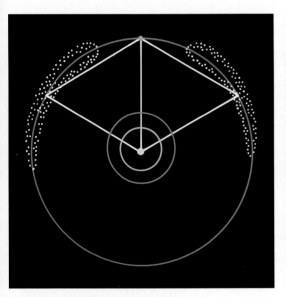

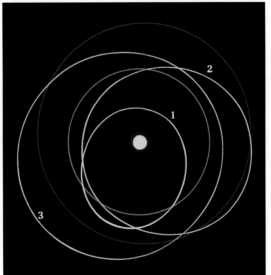

Greeks and Trojans. Astronomers estimate that Jupiter shares its orbit with as many as 2,000 large asteroids more than ten miles in diameter. Of 200 or so that have been identified, two-thirds orbit about sixty degrees ahead of the planet and the rest about sixty degrees behind. The leading contingent is collectively called the Greeks, while those that follow are known as Trojans. Each group is centered on a gravitationally stable point, that is, the vertex of an equilateral triangle with the Sun and Jupiter at the other two vertices.

Earth approachers. Three families of asteroids, each named after the first of its type discovered, travel highly elliptical orbits that either come close to or actually cross Earth's path. The Atens, represented by Ra-Shalom *(1)*, pass just outside Earth's circuit *(blue)* at their farthest from the Sun. Geographos *(2)* is an Apollo asteroid, arcing inside Earth's orbit at perihelion and outside the orbit of Mars *(red)* at aphelion. Typifying the Amors is Eros *(3)*, which crosses Mars's orbit but fails to reach Earth's.

METEORITES: COSMIC DEBRIS

Stray bodies from interplanetary space, ranging in size from dust particles to asteroid-size boulders, rocket through Earth's atmosphere untold millions of times every day. A meteor, sometimes called a shooting or falling star, is a streak of light produced by a piece of rock or metal—often cometary debris about the size of a grain of sand—as it skids across the sky. Hurtling perhaps twenty-five miles per second, the fragment is heated to incandescence by friction before it vaporizes. Meteors occur both as single, random events known as sporadic meteors and in showers, exciting group displays that occur annually *(opposite)*.

While these fragments remain in space, they are known as meteoroids; those that survive passage through the atmosphere and hit the ground become meteorites. These cosmic missiles add 100 to 1,000 tons of material to Earth's surface each day, much of it as tiny micrometeoroids too small to create a discernible flash. Larger samples that have been gathered are mostly asteroid or comet chips classed as one of three types—stones, irons, and stony-iron blends *(left)*. The stones are difficult to find partly because they are usually small but also because they resemble terrestrial rocks and rarely stand out from the surrounding terrain. Occasionally in Earth's history, however, a meteorite of immense proportions has crashed to the surface, exploding and leaving the ominous signature of an impact crater *(opposite, bottom)*.

The largest intact meteorite ever found—named Hoba—was discovered on a farm in Namibia in 1920. Weighing sixty-six tons and measuring nine by nine by three feet, the iron chunk has never been moved from its landing site. Had it been any larger, it probably would have broken apart during its passage through Earth's atmosphere.

Stones. This stony meteorite, named Clovis, spent hundreds of years underground before its discovery in 1961 in Curry County, New Mexico. Its dome shape was probably sculpted during a fiery descent through Earth's atmosphere. Stones, which account for 92 percent of all meteorite falls, are hard to find because they are composed mainly of silicate minerals, like terrestrial rock.

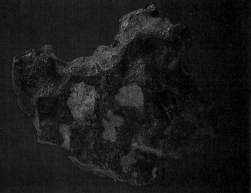

Irons. Consisting mostly of iron-nickel alloys, irons make up about 7 percent of the meteorite population. The Waingaromia iron *(right)* belongs to the most common subgroup—the octahedrites—which, when polished and etched with acid, reveal a pattern of interlocking lines not found in terrestrial iron. Because irons withstand weathering better than stones and are easier to recognize, they dominate meteorite collections.

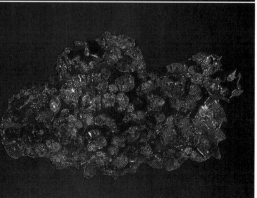

Stony-irons. These rarest of meteorites are roughly half-and-half mixtures of silicates and iron-nickel alloys. Pictured here is one named Krasnojarsk, the first of its kind to be discovered, with nuggets of the mineral olivine sparkling amid the metal alloy that surrounds them. Other stony-irons may contain different silicates, but the proportions of stone and iron are always about equal.

Meteors—fleeting tracks of light drawn by tiny meteoroids burning up in Earth's atmosphere—are visible on any clear dark night at almost any time of the year. During certain periods, however, they flash in relative abundance. On these special occasions, called meteor showers, "shooting stars" flare in profusion, often as many as fifty an hour, all seeming to come from a particular place in the sky. A number of major showers occur annually, each named for the constellation from which the meteors appear to be streaming. The Perseids, for example, radiate every August from a spot in Perseus; and the first shower of the year, the Quadrantids, emanates from what was once the constellation Quadrans, which has since been divided into Boötes, Hercules, and Draco.

These natural fireworks occur with predictable regularity when Earth, orbiting the Sun, passes through the debris-strewn path of a comet. The Orionids decorate the sky when the planet intersects the orbit of the best-known comet of all, Halley. Showers can last anywhere from less than a day to two weeks or so, with the number of meteors per hour steadily increasing, peaking, and then tapering off as the planet moves out of the comet's dusty trail. Five of the most popular showers are highlighted at right, with their approximate durations, their peak days, and the average number of meteors visible on those days, as well as star charts of the background constellations where they can be found.

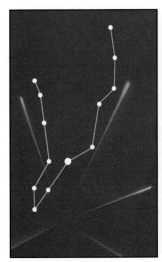

Perseids
August 12 (9 days)
50 meteors per hour

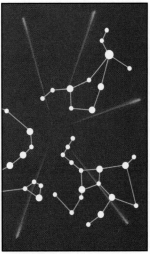

Quadrantids
January 4 (2 days)
40+ meteors per hour

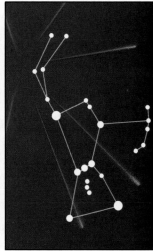

Orionids
October 21 (4 days)
25 meteors per hour

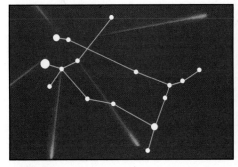

Geminids
December 13 (5 days)
50 meteors per hour

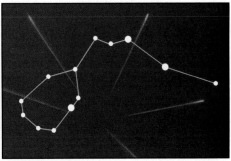

Delta Aquarids
July 28 (14 days)
20 meteors per hour

These four craters, part of a cluster of twelve near Henbury Station, Australia, are the calling cards left by an enormous meteoroid that broke up before slamming to the ground some 4,000 years ago. About 120 impact sites around the world bear witness to Earth's vulnerability to these battering forces. Although most meteorites are of a size to pose no threat, scientists speculate that once every 100 million years or so, an object several miles in diameter may collide with the third planet, wreaking the devastation of several billion atom bombs. The dinosaurs—and countless other life forms—may have perished during such a calamity some 65 million years ago.

63

THE PLANETARY DANCE

Like some code written in the heavens, the passage of the planets along a lane through the stars has teased and fascinated sky watchers ever since humans gained the power to wonder. Five thousand years ago, Mesopotamian astronomers began mapping planetary movements in terms of a sequence of a dozen background groups of stars—a locating system whose essential features are still in use today. The ancients saw magic in the patterned motions, but the planetary pageant was gradually explained by the structure of the Solar System and the movements of Earth itself. Today, the factors that shape the spectacle of the night sky are known in such detail that every perceived motion of planet or star can be predicted far into the future. For the amateur astronomer, celestial forecasts are available in almanacs, calendars, and other easy-to-use guides.

In observational terms, the night sky can be pictured as a star-flecked sphere surrounding the solar family at an indefinite distance. At the center of this celestial sphere, all of the planets except wayward Pluto (too faint to be seen with most amateur telescopes, in any event) orbit their parent star in a plane that varies from the plane of Earth's orbit by only a few degrees, ranging from .8 degree for Uranus to 7 degrees for Mercury. As a result of the flattened arrangement, the planets' apparent motions are narrowly confined: As viewed from Earth, they meander through a band of stars called the zodiac, shown at right and explained on pages 66-67. Earth's orbital plane, projected onto the celestial sphere, defines a kind of centerline for the zodiac *(yellow line)*. Known as the ecliptic because solar and lunar eclipses occur when Earth, Moon, and Sun align on this plane, it is also the apparent path traced against the background stars by the Sun in the course of a year.

Many other factors lend variety to the planetary dance. As explained on pages 70-73, the position of Mercury and Venus inside Earth's orbit causes them to stay close to the Sun and endows them with phases like the Moon's. The slower revolution of the outer planets makes them appear to reverse course when Earth speeds past. The elliptical shape of orbits sometimes brings planets relatively close to Earth for good viewing and sometimes carries them far away. Most marked of all, the tilt of Earth on its axis induces the whole planetary pageant to shift about in the sky as the seasons change. That the ancients found it all mystifying and marvelous seems only natural.

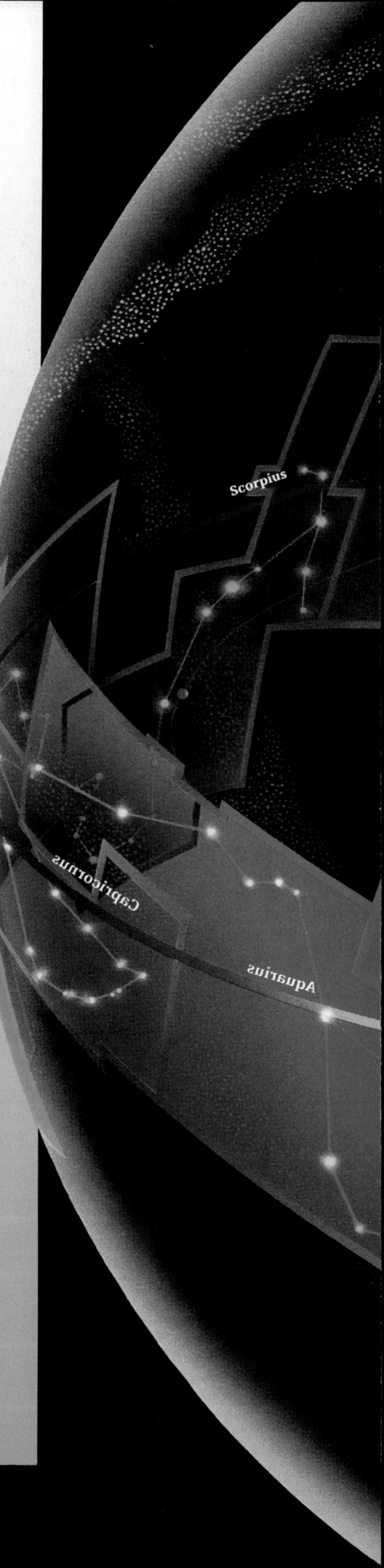

Scorpius

Capricornus

Aquarius

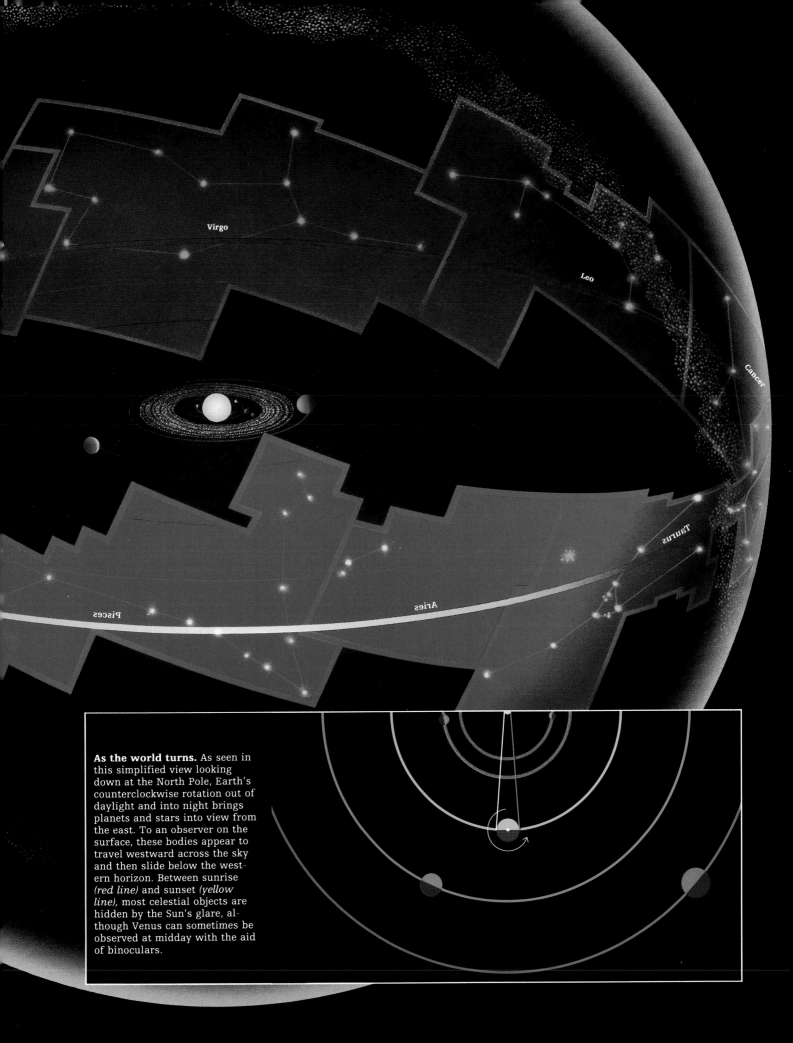

Virgo

Leo

Cancer

Taurus

Aries

Pisces

As the world turns. As seen in this simplified view looking down at the North Pole, Earth's counterclockwise rotation out of daylight and into night brings planets and stars into view from the east. To an observer on the surface, these bodies appear to travel westward across the sky and then slide below the western horizon. Between sunrise *(red line)* and sunset *(yellow line),* most celestial objects are hidden by the Sun's glare, although Venus can sometimes be observed at midday with the aid of binoculars.

Leo, the Lion. A bright constellation, Leo contains one star—blue Regulus—that is luminous enough to be mistaken for a planet.

Gemini, the Twins. The heads of the twins are marked by the stars Pollux, slightly more orange, and Castor, the more northerly.

Aries, the Ram. Located above the ecliptic, Aries is formed by three primary stars, which mark the horns of the ram.

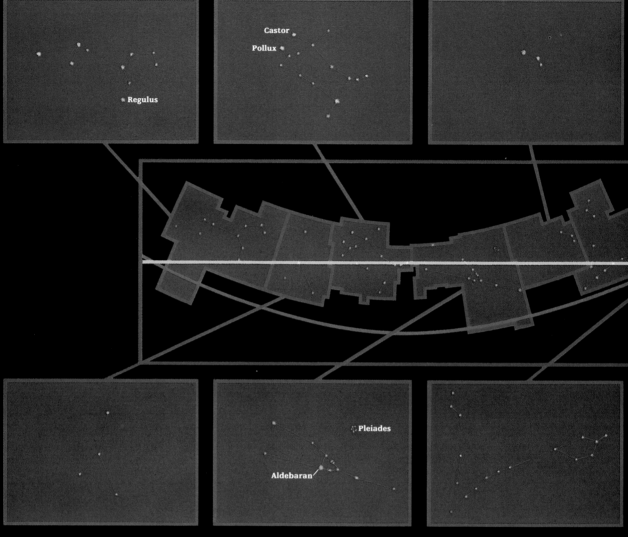

Cancer, the Crab. Visible only under the best conditions, Cancer is so faint that a bright object spotted here is probably a planet.

Taurus, the Bull. A V-shape of stars called the Hyades marks the face of the bull. The bright star Aldebaran forms a glaring red eye.

Pisces, the Fishes. A stretched-out constellation imagined as two fish at the ends of linked strings, dim Pisces is visible only in a dark sky.

Pathway through the Stars

Because the members of the Sun's family orbit in a relatively flat plane, the paths of the planets as seen from Earth fall in a band of sky that is not quite sixteen degrees wide. Ancient astrologer-priests divided this band into twelve "signs"—one for each of the twelve full moons that occur during the course of the year. (The Moon itself moves within the band, as well, since its orbital plane differs from Earth's by only five degrees.) The Greeks opted for an eleven-part division and associated each of their zones with star-pictures of animals, people, or figures that were half-animal and half-human. They named the whole sequence of constellations the zodiac, meaning "circle of animals." The Romans restored the total to twelve, cutting off one of Scorpius's claws to form Libra, the only inanimate constellation in the zodiac. Although the Greco-Roman system still prevails, modern astronomers have eliminated any ambiguities

Aquarius, the Water Carrier. A large, dim constellation, Aquarius straddles the ecliptic and lies just below the celestial equator.

Sagittarius, the Archer. Also located below the celestial equator, this constellation lies in the direction of the Milky Way's center.

Virgo, the Maiden. This long and mostly dim constellation holds one bright star, Spica—easily confused with a planet.

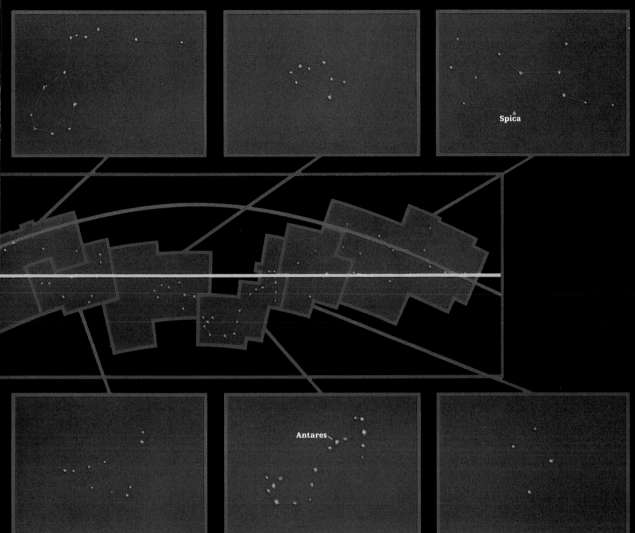

Capricornus, the Goat. A faint constellation lying athwart the ecliptic, Capricornus is usually pictured with a fish's tail.

Scorpius, the Scorpion. Positioned mostly below the ecliptic, Scorpius holds Antares, a bright red star whose name means "rival of Mars."

Libra, the Scales. Once part of Scorpius, dim Libra contains the Northern and Southern Claws, two of the Scales' brightest stars.

of location by giving the constellations precise boundaries, forming a sort of continuous patchwork of stellar real estate, depicted in the maplike illustration above. The celestial equator, a projection of Earth's equator onto the celestial sphere, appears as a sinuous purple line that crosses the middle of the zodiac. Generally, constellations that lie below the equator are more easily seen from the Southern Hemisphere. If the stars were visible in daylight, the Sun would be seen to follow the zodiac eastward as the year proceeds, its track scribing the ecliptic *(yellow line)*. At one point in the annual journey, when crossing from Scorpius to Sagittarius, the Sun strays outside the zodiacal boundaries. Unofficially, the gap is filled by a thirteenth constellation—Ophiuchus, the Serpent Holder. Because so much of Scorpius lies below the ecliptic, the Sun actually spends more time in this supplementary precinct than in Scorpius.

LATITUDE AND SEASON

Looking up at the night sky from any point on the surface of Earth, an observer sees half of the imaginary celestial sphere *(below)* whose poles and equator *(purple line)* are extensions of Earth's own. In the illustration, the observer is situated at forty degrees north latitude. The celestial objects seen and their trajectories vary with the season *(opposite)*.

A common way to describe the local position of a celestial object is by its altitude and its azimuth. In the illustration below, the directions north, east, south, and west are indicated respectively by a pine tree, a church, a water tower, and a house. Because the observer is in the Northern Hemisphere, the planets will lie to the south. They will rise in the east and set in the west as Earth turns eastward, always traveling close to the Earth-Sun plane, or ecliptic *(yellow line)*. The position of the ecliptic in the sky will shift with the seasons because of the twenty-three-and-a-half-degree tilt of Earth on its axis. In winter, for example, when the Northern Hemisphere leans away from the Sun, the Sun's path across the daytime sky is at its lowest for the year; at night, the position of the ecliptic—and that of the planets—will be highest. In summer, the opposite occurs.

The local position of any celestial object, such as the Moon—which, like the planets, travels close to the ecliptic—may be described by its altitude, or angle above the horizon, and azimuth, the horizontal angle measured clockwise from due north. These measurements change during the night as Earth rotates.

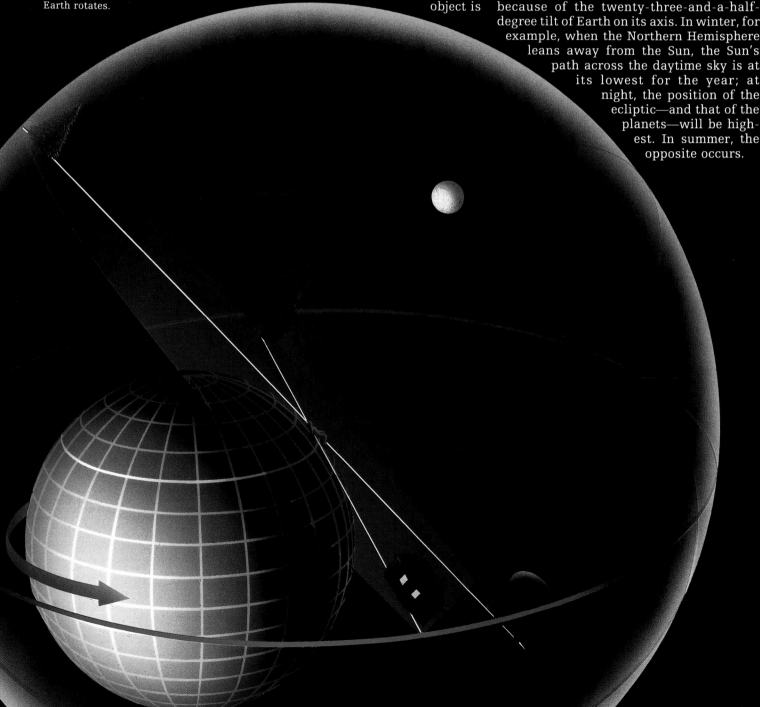

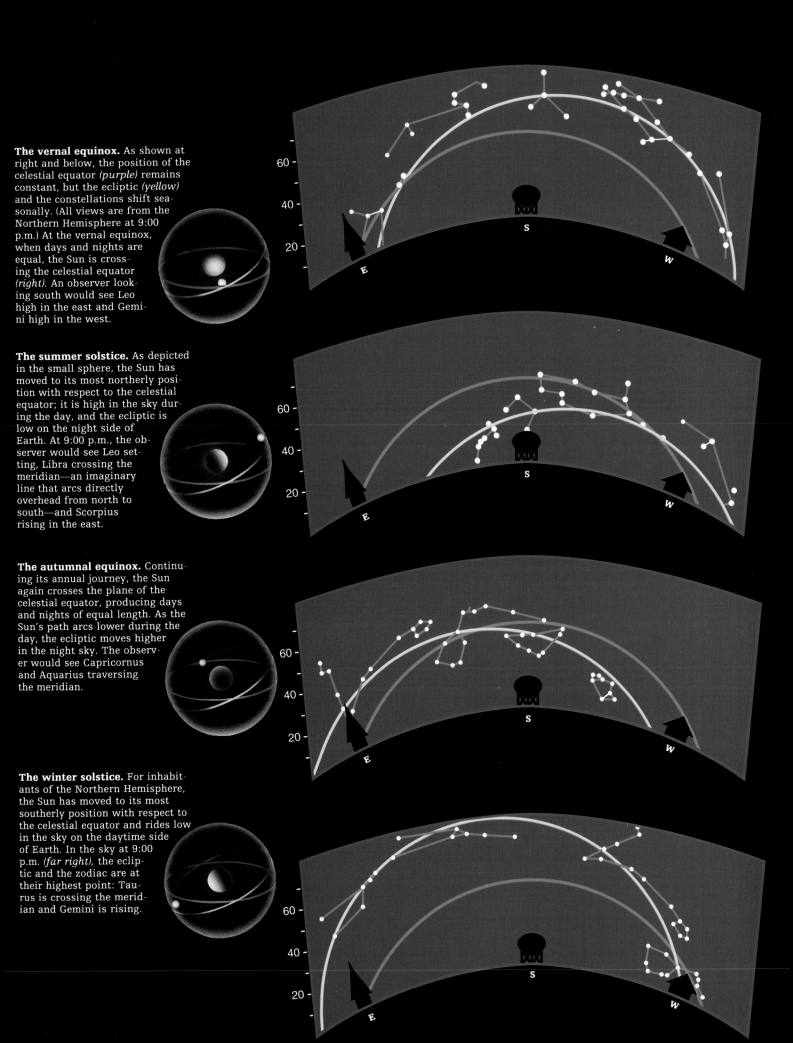

The vernal equinox. As shown at right and below, the position of the celestial equator *(purple)* remains constant, but the ecliptic *(yellow)* and the constellations shift seasonally. (All views are from the Northern Hemisphere at 9:00 p.m.) At the vernal equinox, when days and nights are equal, the Sun is crossing the celestial equator *(right).* An observer looking south would see Leo high in the east and Gemini high in the west.

The summer solstice. As depicted in the small sphere, the Sun has moved to its most northerly position with respect to the celestial equator; it is high in the sky during the day, and the ecliptic is low on the night side of Earth. At 9:00 p.m., the observer would see Leo setting, Libra crossing the meridian—an imaginary line that arcs directly overhead from north to south—and Scorpius rising in the east.

The autumnal equinox. Continuing its annual journey, the Sun again crosses the plane of the celestial equator, producing days and nights of equal length. As the Sun's path arcs lower during the day, the ecliptic moves higher in the night sky. The observer would see Capricornus and Aquarius traversing the meridian.

The winter solstice. For inhabitants of the Northern Hemisphere, the Sun has moved to its most southerly position with respect to the celestial equator and rides low in the sky on the daytime side of Earth. In the sky at 9:00 p.m. *(far right),* the ecliptic and the zodiac are at their highest point: Taurus is crossing the meridian and Gemini is rising.

FLEETING, ELUSIVE MERCURY

Mercury is a reluctant subject. Because it orbits closer to the Sun than does Earth, it can be seen only by looking sunward, which means it is usually lost in the Sun's glare. From the Northern Hemisphere especially, the tilt and eccentricity of Mercury's orbit also conspire against good viewing. When the planet swings farthest out from the Sun from Earth's perspective—called maximum elongation—and should thus be easiest to see, it barely rises above the horizon, offsetting the observer's advantage.

The planet begins to appear in the evening sky (evening apparition) when it emerges from behind the Sun *(first orbital diagram, below)* and is approaching a position known as maximum eastern elongation *(second diagram)*, during which it lags to the east behind the setting Sun and may be viewed for about one and a half hours after sunset. During maximum western elongation *(third diagram)*, it rises one and a half hours before the Sun, after which it appears in the predawn sky (morning apparition) for a few weeks *(fourth diagram)* before it disappears behind the Sun again.

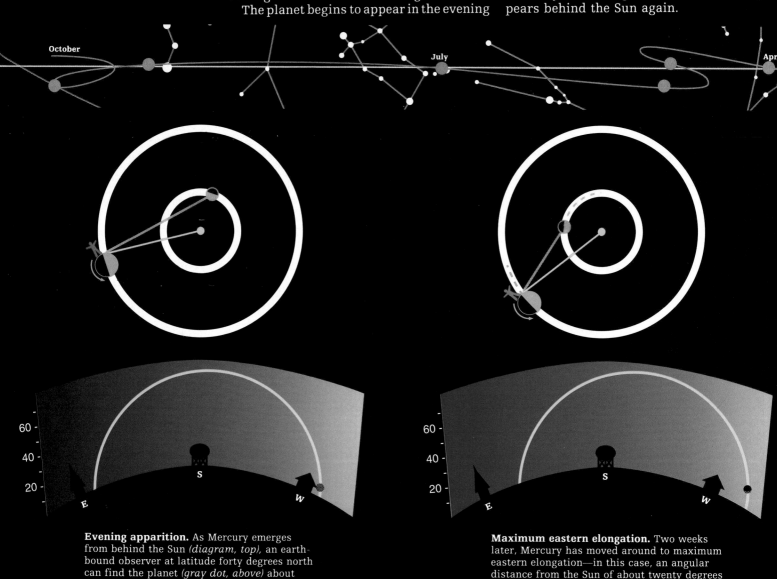

Evening apparition. As Mercury emerges from behind the Sun *(diagram, top)*, an earth-bound observer at latitude forty degrees north can find the planet *(gray dot, above)* about seven degrees above the horizon as the sky darkens, about half an hour after sunset. (The yellow line is the ecliptic, which Mercury follows as it trails the Sun through the sky.)

Maximum eastern elongation. Two weeks later, Mercury has moved around to maximum eastern elongation—in this case, an angular distance from the Sun of about twenty degrees as viewed from Earth. The planet is now almost fifteen degrees above the horizon *(gray dot, above, right)* for its best possible viewing in the evening sky.

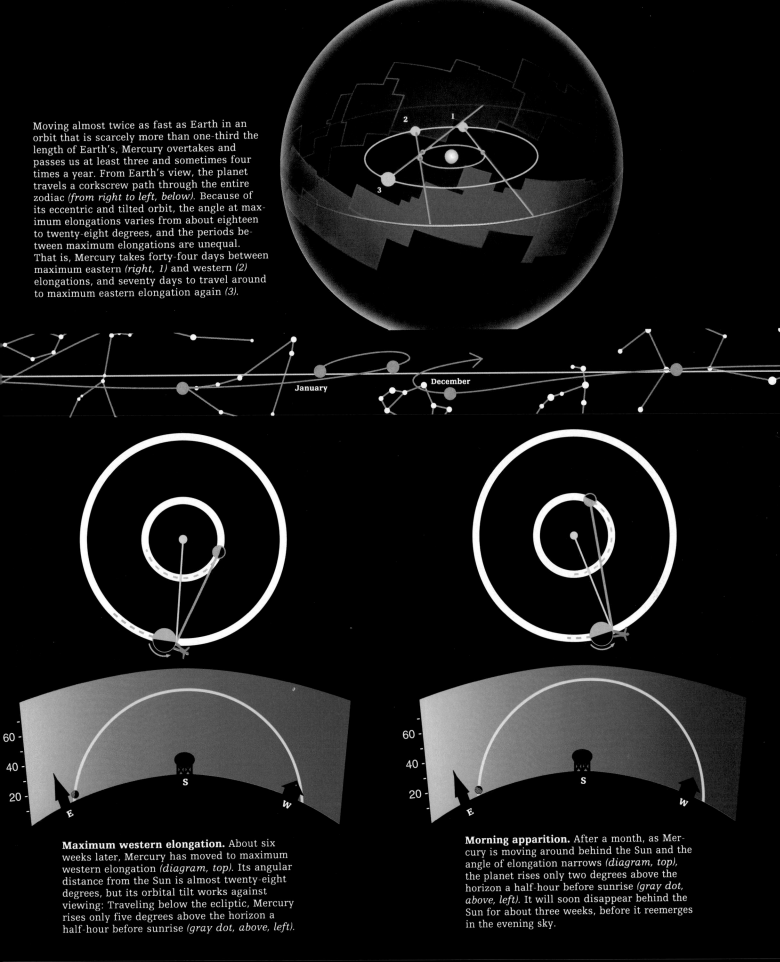

Moving almost twice as fast as Earth in an orbit that is scarcely more than one-third the length of Earth's, Mercury overtakes and passes us at least three and sometimes four times a year. From Earth's view, the planet travels a corkscrew path through the entire zodiac *(from right to left, below)*. Because of its eccentric and tilted orbit, the angle at maximum elongations varies from about eighteen to twenty-eight degrees, and the periods between maximum elongations are unequal. That is, Mercury takes forty-four days between maximum eastern *(right, 1)* and western *(2)* elongations, and seventy days to travel around to maximum eastern elongation again *(3)*.

January

December

Maximum western elongation. About six weeks later, Mercury has moved to maximum western elongation *(diagram, top)*. Its angular distance from the Sun is almost twenty-eight degrees, but its orbital tilt works against viewing: Traveling below the ecliptic, Mercury rises only five degrees above the horizon a half-hour before sunrise *(gray dot, above, left)*.

Morning apparition. After a month, as Mercury is moving around behind the Sun and the angle of elongation narrows *(diagram, top)*, the planet rises only two degrees above the horizon a half-hour before sunrise *(gray dot, above, left)*. It will soon disappear behind the Sun for about three weeks, before it reemerges in the evening sky.

SIGHTS ON BRILLIANT VENUS

Covered with a veil of reflective clouds, Venus outshines every celestial object except the Sun, the Moon, and special events like very bright meteors, comets, and supernovae. Thus, although the planet's orbital plane is inclined about three degrees to the ecliptic, the tilt does not significantly affect Venus's visibility because it is so bright.

A nearly circular orbit with a radius of 67 million miles swings the planet out to about forty-six degrees from the Sun, roughly twice as far as Mercury, enabling it to be seen with the naked eye for as much as three and a half hours before sunrise or after sunset. With optical aid, Venus can be observed even at midday. Because its orbit takes 225 days, Venus changes from morning to evening sky only once a year. Orbiting inside Earth's path, it displays phases as do the Moon and, less discernibly, Mercury. For five weeks before and after passing inferior conjunction, the orbital point closest to Earth, Venus is at its brightest and appears as a crescent.

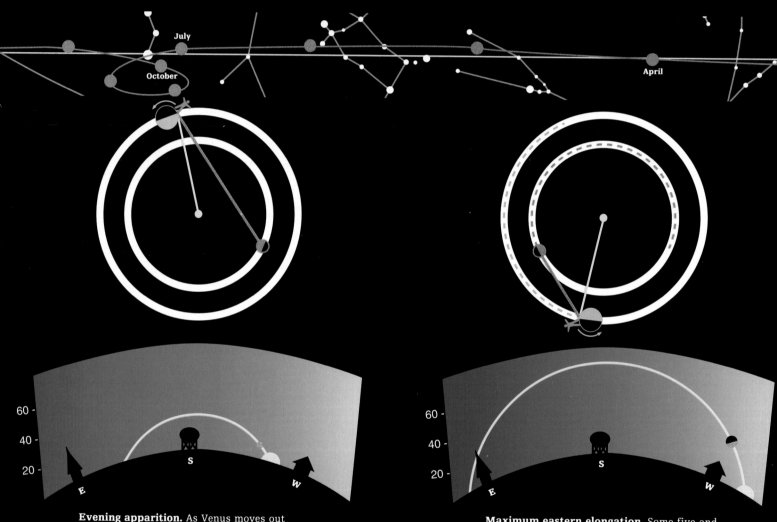

Evening apparition. As Venus moves out from behind the Sun and begins to swing around toward Earth *(diagram, top)*, a Northern Hemisphere observer facing south at sunset can find it ten degrees above the southwestern horizon *(above, right)*. Each night until maximum elongation, it will appear higher and higher in the twilight sky.

Maximum eastern elongation. Some five and a half months later, the angular distance between the Sun and the planet has widened to about forty-six degrees. Venus will appear about forty-six degrees above the horizon just at sunset and sink to thirty degrees altitude *(above, right)* as the sky grows dark, before setting more than three hours after the Sun.

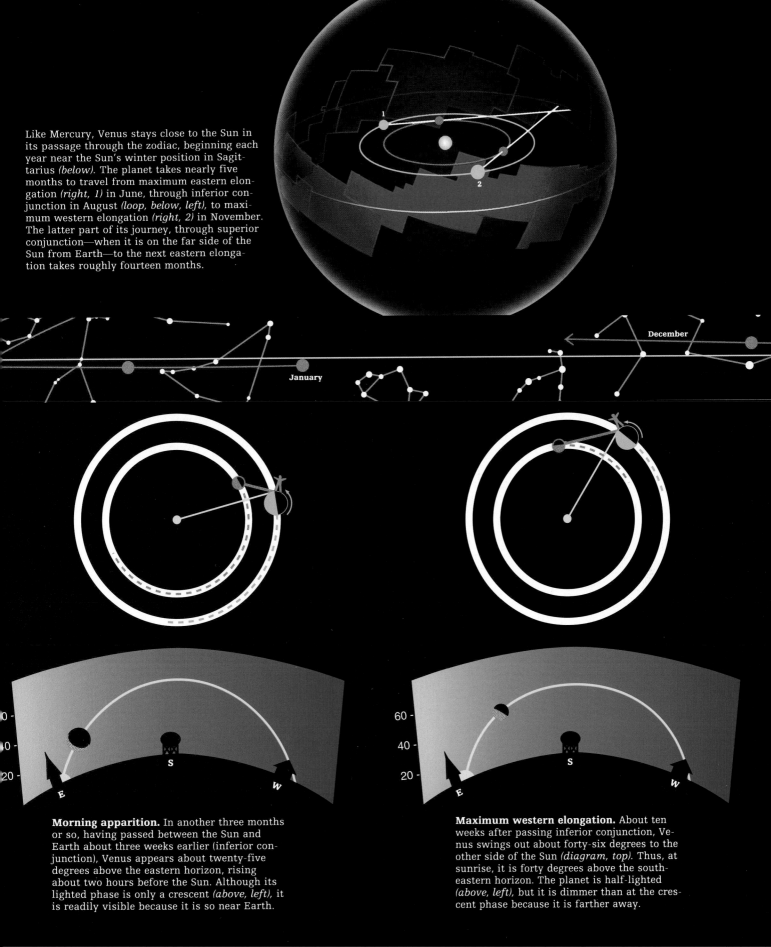

Like Mercury, Venus stays close to the Sun in its passage through the zodiac, beginning each year near the Sun's winter position in Sagittarius *(below)*. The planet takes nearly five months to travel from maximum eastern elongation *(right, 1)* in June, through inferior conjunction in August *(loop, below, left)*, to maximum western elongation *(right, 2)* in November. The latter part of its journey, through superior conjunction—when it is on the far side of the Sun from Earth—to the next eastern elongation takes roughly fourteen months.

December

January

Morning apparition. In another three months or so, having passed between the Sun and Earth about three weeks earlier (inferior conjunction), Venus appears about twenty-five degrees above the eastern horizon, rising about two hours before the Sun. Although its lighted phase is only a crescent *(above, left)*, it is readily visible because it is so near Earth.

Maximum western elongation. About ten weeks after passing inferior conjunction, Venus swings out about forty-six degrees to the other side of the Sun *(diagram, top)*. Thus, at sunrise, it is forty degrees above the southeastern horizon. The planet is half-lighted *(above, left)*, but it is dimmer than at the crescent phase because it is farther away.

MARS AT OPPOSITION

Orbiting beyond Earth, Mars is not limited to horizon-hugging appearances in the morning or evening sky. Depending on where it is in its roughly two-year orbital journey, it can be seen throughout the night, and it rises well up in the sky—more than seventy degrees above the horizon for an observer at forty degrees north latitude. Since the planet's distance from Earth ranges from about 48 million to more than 200 million miles, its apparent size and brightness undergo marked changes. Viewing is best at opposition, when Mars is lined up opposite the Sun in Earth's sky and the distance between the two planets is minimized.

Oppositions occur about every twenty-five and a half months—the longest such period of any of the outer planets—but because the orbit of Mars is eccentric, its nearness to Earth during opposition varies. The best oppositions occur when Mars is near perihelion, closest to the Sun and thus to Earth, allowing viewing bonanzas every fifteen to seventeen years.

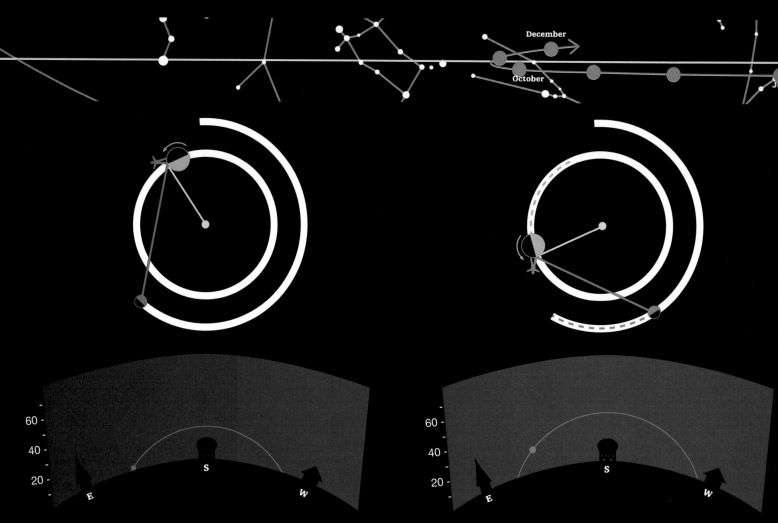

Midwinter. As Earth comes around from behind the Sun a few months after conjunction *(diagram, top)*, the angular distance between Mars and the Sun is about forty-five degrees. A Northern Hemisphere observer finds the planet rising at 5:00 a.m. in the southeast *(above)*, where it is observable for only about

Early spring. At 5:00 a.m. in early spring, with a widened angular distance from the Sun, Mars is farther above the horizon. Because Earth is catching up to Mars and the distance between them has narrowed, Mars appears somewhat brighter and bigger than it did three months earlier.

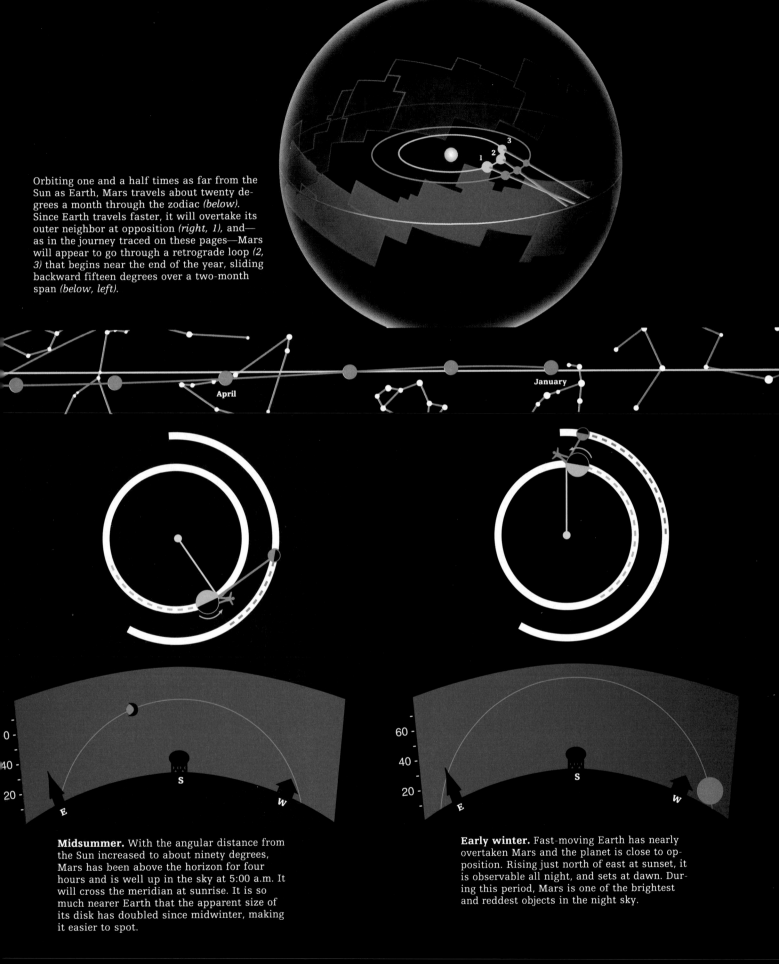

Orbiting one and a half times as far from the Sun as Earth, Mars travels about twenty degrees a month through the zodiac *(below)*. Since Earth travels faster, it will overtake its outer neighbor at opposition *(right, 1)*, and—as in the journey traced on these pages—Mars will appear to go through a retrograde loop *(2, 3)* that begins near the end of the year, sliding backward fifteen degrees over a two-month span *(below, left)*.

April

January

Midsummer. With the angular distance from the Sun increased to about ninety degrees, Mars has been above the horizon for four hours and is well up in the sky at 5:00 a.m. It will cross the meridian at sunrise. It is so much nearer Earth that the apparent size of its disk has doubled since midwinter, making it easier to spot.

Early winter. Fast-moving Earth has nearly overtaken Mars and the planet is close to opposition. Rising just north of east at sunset, it is observable all night, and sets at dawn. During this period, Mars is one of the brightest and reddest objects in the night sky.

THE SLOW-MOVING OUTER PLANETS

Traveling slowly in their far-flung orbits, Jupiter, Saturn, Uranus, and Neptune are overtaken by Earth almost once a year. During their respective periods of opposition, Jupiter is second only to Venus in brightness, but distant Uranus is barely visible to the naked eye, and Neptune requires binoculars or a telescope.

For ten months of the year, the outer planets can be seen during the night, each with its own schedule for rising and setting. However, all conform to the same annual viewing cycle: On a given date that begins the cycle, the planet will rise at dawn, only to be quickly overpowered by the Sun. Emerging earlier each night, it will rise at dusk about six months later and be visible all night long. After about ten months, it will rise earlier in the day and set shortly after dusk. Thus, for the next two months, the planet will be above the horizon only during the daylight hours. Then the cycle will begin anew.

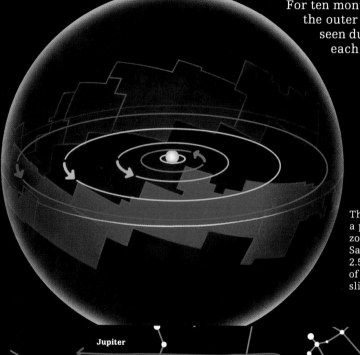

The outer planets travel their distant orbits at a ponderous pace. Jupiter's path through the zodiac averages one constellation per year. Saturn moves through one constellation every 2.5 years. Uranus completes only one percent of its orbit in a year, and Neptune covers slightly more than one-half percent.

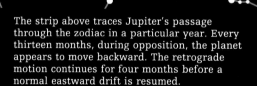

The strip above traces Jupiter's passage through the zodiac in a particular year. Every thirteen months, during opposition, the planet appears to move backward. The retrograde motion continues for four months before a normal eastward drift is resumed.

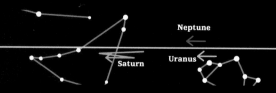

Here, Saturn, Uranus, and Neptune are grouped fairly close together in the direction of Sagittarius, but Saturn, fastest of the three, is pulling away. Because they move so slowly against the background stars and Earth keeps overtaking them, these planets spend two-thirds of the year in a retrograde loop.

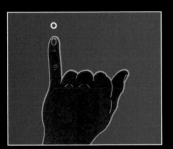

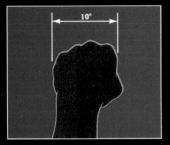

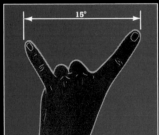

Celestial objects can be located by their altitude and azimuth, as shown at top. An observer can make rough measurements by holding a hand at arm's length as indicated above. The tip of the little finger is about one degree across—twice the angular size of the full moon.

Key characteristics of selected short-period comets that visit the inner Solar System are listed at right. Their orbital periods range from 3.28 years for Encke to almost 80 years for Halley's comet. Other items include the date of perihelion, or closest approach to the Sun; the perihelion distance (in astronomical units—the average distance from Sun to Earth, or about 93 million miles); the aphelion distance, or farthest point from the Sun; the semimajor axis, representing the average distance from the Sun; and the orbital inclination to the ecliptic. (An inclination of more than ninety degrees indicates retrograde motion, opposite to the planets' orbital direction.)

Comet Name	Orbital Period (Years)	Perihelion Date	Perihelion Distance (AU)	Aphelion Distance (AU)	Semimajor Axis of Orbit (AU)	Inclination (Degrees)
Halley	75.99	Feb. 9, 1986	.587	35.29	17.94	162.2
Parker-Hartley	8.89	Aug. 15, 1987	3.025	5.55	4.29	5.2
Shoemaker-Holt 1	9.55	May 21, 1988	3.053	5.95	4.50	4.4
Helin-Roman-Crockett	8.12	Sept. 10, 1988	3.470	4.61	4.04	4.2
Tempel 2	5.29	Sept. 16, 1988	1.383	4.69	3.04	12.4
d'Arrest	6.39	Feb. 4, 1989	1.292	5.59	3.44	19.4
Churyumov-Gerasimenko	6.59	June 18, 1989	1.300	5.73	3.52	7.1
Gunn	6.84	Sept. 24, 1989	2.472	4.74	3.60	10.4
Lovas 1	9.09	Oct. 10, 1989	1.680	7.03	4.35	12.2
Gehrels 2	7.94	Nov. 3, 1989	2.348	5.61	3.98	6.7
Clark	5.51	Nov. 28, 1989	1.556	4.68	3.12	9.5
Kopff	6.46	Jan. 20, 1990	1.585	5.35	3.47	4.7
Sanguin	12.50	Apr. 2, 1990	1.814	8.96	5.39	18.7
Russell 3	7.50	May 17, 1990	2.517	5.15	3.83	14.1
Peters-Hartley	8.13	June 21, 1990	1.626	6.46	4.04	29.8
Tritton	6.34	July 8, 1990	1.436	5.41	3.42	7.1
Encke	3.28	Oct. 28, 1990	0.331	4.09	2.21	11.9
Johnson	6.97	Nov. 18, 1990	2.313	4.98	3.65	13.7
Kearns-Kwee	8.96	Nov. 22, 1990	2.215	6.42	4.32	9.0
Wild 2	6.37	Dec. 16, 1990	1.578	5.30	3.44	3.2
Swift-Gehrels	9.21	Feb. 22, 1991	1.355	7.43	4.39	9.3
Wolf-Harrington	6.51	Apr. 4, 1991	1.608	5.37	3.49	18.5
Van Biesbroeck	12.43	Apr. 24, 1991	2.401	8.33	5.37	6.6
Hartley 1	5.92	Apr. 28, 1991	1.795	4.75	3.27	25.6
Harrington-Abell	7.59	July 6, 1991	1.774	5.95	3.86	10.2
Machholz	5.24	July 22, 1991	0.126	5.91	3.02	60.1
Arend-Rigaux	6.82	Oct. 2, 1991	1.438	5.75	3.60	17.9
Faye	7.34	Nov. 16, 1991	1.593	5.96	3.78	9.1
Giacobini-Zinner	6.61	Apr. 13, 1992	1.034	6.01	3.52	31.8
Smirnova-Chernykh	8.57	Aug. 5, 1992	3.572	4.81	4.19	6.6

Shower Name	Constellations	Date of Peak Activity	No. Visible Per Hour	Associated Comet
Quadrantids	Boötes, Draco, Hercules	January 4	40	—
Lyrids	Lyra, Hercules	April 21	15	Thatcher
Eta Aquarids	Aquarius	May 4	20	Halley
Delta Aquarids	Aquarius	July 28	20	—
Perseids	Perseus	August 12	50	Swift-Tuttle
Orionids	Orion	October 21	25	Halley
Southern Taurids	Taurus	November 3	15	Encke
Leonids	Leo	November 16	15	Temple-Tuttle
Geminids	Gemini	December 13	50	—
Ursids	Ursa Minor	December 22	15	Tuttle

Meteor showers—intense displays of space debris thought to be associated with particular comets—occur at fixed times during the year. The chart at left shows the details of selected meteor showers. The names given to the spectacular events, which occur over a few hours or even several days, allude to constellations in the meteors' apparent direction of origin. The Perseids, for example, seem to emanate from Perseus, the Lyrids from the constellation Lyra.

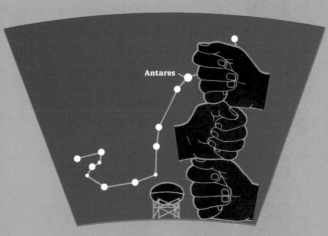

Antares

A fist held at arm's length is about ten degrees in angular size, offering a rough way of measuring altitude. For example, to find Antares, a bright star in the constellation Scorpius, line up a fist with the horizon, place your other fist on top of it, and continue in this fashion as needed. As shown in the illustration at left, Antares is two and a half fists high, indicating an altitude of twenty-five degrees.

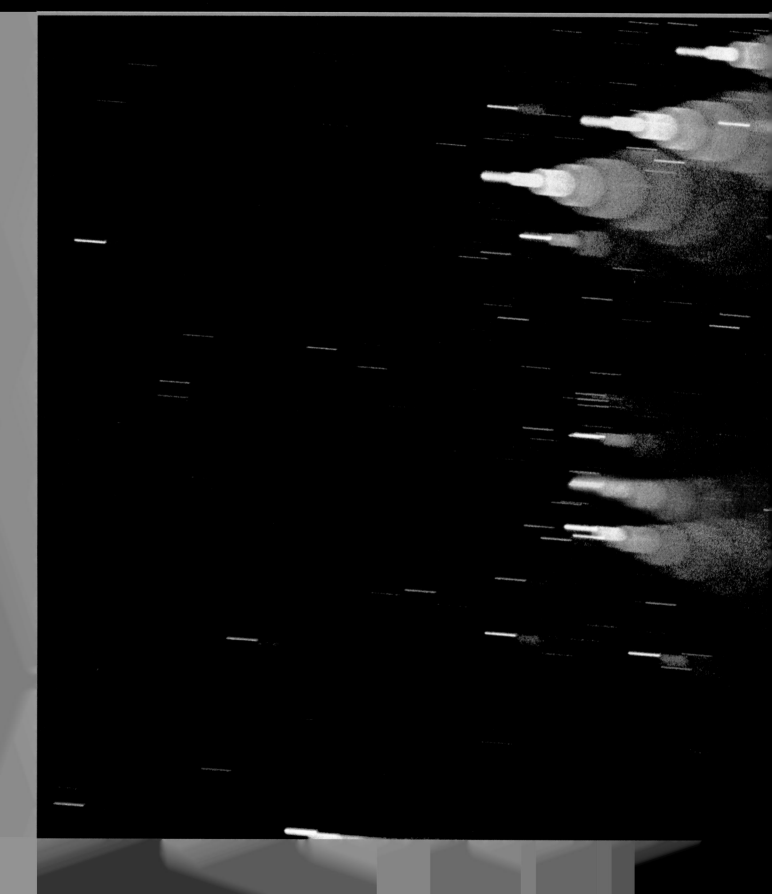

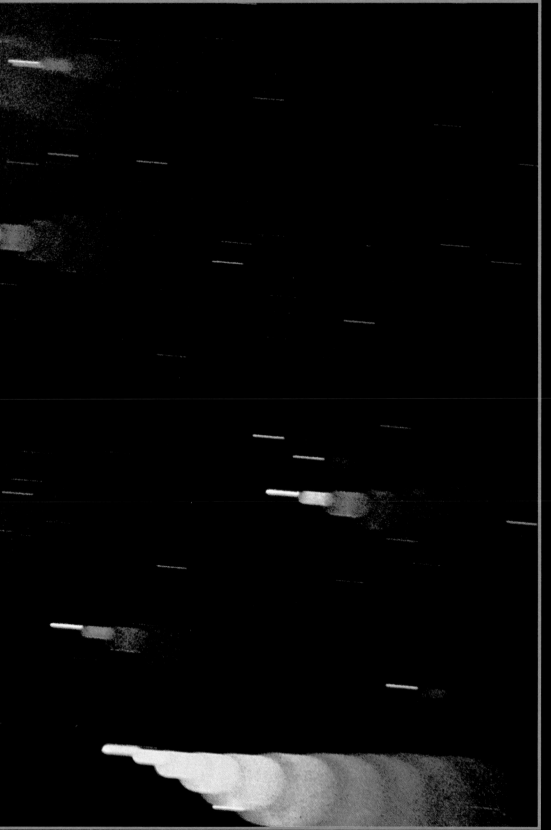

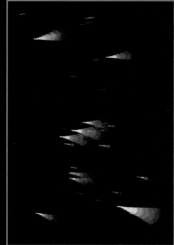

The stars of the constellation Orion sketch multicolored trails in the night sky in a photograph *(above)* made by varying the focus during a long exposure. Betelgeuse glows red-orange in the upper left. In the closeup at left, the three blue stars that make up Orion's belt align diagonally above the pink glow of the Orion nebula *(center)*, while Rigel, seventh-brightest star in the heavens, shines at lower right. Stars' colors are generally determined by their temperature: The hottest stars are blue, and the coolest ones are red.

Sclear, dark night, a sharp-eyed observer far from city lights might detect as many as 2,000 stars without the aid of a telescope (6,000 if he or she watches until dawn). But their true numbers are beyond comprehension. The Milky Way galaxy alone contains more than 200 billion of these celestial bodies—and it is only one galaxy among hundreds of billions in the universe.

Although some stars, like the Sun, travel alone, most orbit the galactic center in gravitational associations numbering from two to many thousand members *(pages 86-87)*. These spheres of shining gas are a diverse lot, ranging in size and temperature from hot white dwarfs, scarcely larger than Earth and blazing with surface temperatures between 4,000 and 100,000 degrees Kelvin, to red supergiants, glowing at a relatively cool 3,000 degrees and voluminous enough to fill the Solar System out to the orbit of Saturn.

tronomical technique for wringing information from mere glowing pinpoints is spectroscopy—the analysis of starlight. The first hint of light's secrets came in 1666, when Isaac Newton passed a beam of sunlight through a glass prism and discovered the rainbow of colors that lies hidden within white light. Borrowing from the Latin word for "apparition," he named the red-through-violet array a spectrum.

The true father of astronomical spectroscopy, however, was probably the German optician Joseph von Fraunhofer, who, in 1814, set up a telescope and a prism to examine sunlight entering a room through a narrow slit in the window shutter. Fraunhofer found that the Sun's spectrum was crossed by a large number of dark, vertical lines of varying width and sharpness.

Theorizing that the lines formed some sort of code generated by the Sun itself, he turned his new device, later named the spectroscope, on Venus, Mars, and the Moon. Because the three bodies reflect the Sun's light and are not themselves luminous, the patterns of lines in all three spectra were the same as those for the Sun. When he examined the stars, however, he found that no two stellar spectra were alike; each was marked by a different arrangement of lines.

Although Fraunhofer continued his experiments and made some prescient conjectures as to the nature of the lines, he died without solving the mystery. Thirty-three years later, in 1859, Gustav Kirchhoff and Robert Bunsen picked up the trail when they burned various elements in their laboratory and passed the light from these flames through a spectroscope. Each element's spectrum had a characteristic pattern of sharply defined lines that were bright and colored rather than dark.

It soon became clear that these bright emission lines, so called because they are produced when substances are heated to incandescence, could be matched with the dark lines that appeared in stellar spectra. Kirchhoff concluded that as light from a hot star passes through a surrounding atmosphere of cooler gases, the gases absorb their characteristic wavelengths from the light, leaving dark gaps in the overall spectrum and producing, in effect, a combined signature of all the elements in the star's makeup.

Scientists quickly parlayed these findings into a deeper understanding of stellar composition and structure, learning, for example, that the Sun and stars contain elements that are common on Earth, such as calcium, iron, and sodium. They also found an element in the Sun's spectrum that had not yet been discovered on Earth—and named it helium (from *helios,* the Greek word for "sun"). Later experiments showed that spectral lines could reveal other characteristics as well, such as a star's age and density, the speed at which it rotates around its axis, and the strength of its magnetic field.

Armed with these tools, astronomers began to plumb the once-inaccessible secrets of the stars, from the processes that fuel their fires to the sometimes violent way they die in explosive cataclysms known as supernovae. Building on the information gleaned from the inhabitants of the Milky Way, scientists have begun to reach ever deeper into the cosmos, examining the structure of neighboring galaxies and studying objects so far away that their light has been traveling almost since the beginning of time.

ILLUSION AND REALITY

One of the most difficult challenges for early astronomers was distinguishing reality from illusion in the night sky. The constellations, for example, are the product of human imagination: The arrangements of stars on the two-dimensional celestial dome led ancient observers to name them for a variety of shapes *(below)*.

The realization that the stars were vastly distant brought efforts to determine just how far away they were. Astronomers once thought that because light intensity diminishes with distance, a dim object is probably farther away than a brighter one. But that notion proved an unreliable gauge. Because of their mass, age, or temperature, some stars are intrinsically more luminous and hence may shine more brightly than others that are closer to Earth. Eventually, by correlating painstaking measurements of apparent stellar movement, brightness, and spectra, scientists arrived at more reliable methods for gauging distance and, in turn, the size of the Milky Way.

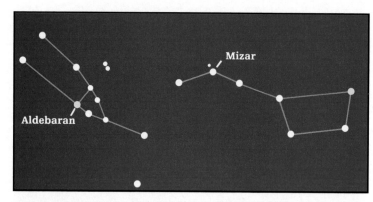

Star Name	Bayer's 1603	Flamsteed's 1629	Henry Draper	Harvard Revised	Bonn Survey
Aldebaran	α Tau	87 Tau	—	HR 1457	BD⁺16° 629
Mizar	ζ UMa	—	HD 116656	HR 5054	BD⁺55° 1598

Constellations. Many ancient cultures named collections of stars that form patterns largely because of their seeming proximity to one another as viewed from Earth. For example, Taurus *(far left)* suggested a bull, and the Big Dipper *(left)* resembled, among other things, a ladle. (The Big Dipper is also part of the constellation Ursa Major, or Great Bear.) The stars themselves go by many names. The chart lists some of the names for Aldebaran (from the Arabic word for "the follower"), the brightest star in Taurus, and Mizar (from the Arabic for "the groin"), the second star from the end of the handle of the Big Dipper. Some schemes simply use numbers or a prefix—such as alpha, beta, or gamma—before the constellation name to signify the star's order of brightness in the grouping. Thus, Dubhe, the brightest star in Ursa Major, is called Alpha Ursae Majoris.

The question of brightness. Astronomers rate stellar brightness according to a scale based on one dating to the second century BC, which designated the brightest stars as "first magnitude" and the faintest stars visible to the naked eye as "sixth magnitude." The modern scale *(right)* extends in both directions, including very faint twenty-seventh-magnitude objects that are visible only with sophisticated telescopes as well as extremely bright objects, like the Sun, whose magnitudes are measured in negative numbers.

These measurements all refer to an object's apparent magnitude *(right, middle)*, which is a combination of the star's actual light output and its distance from Earth. To compare objects of different intrinsic luminosities, astronomers need to compensate for the effects of distance and come up with a measure of how bright an object would appear if it were viewed at a standard distance from Earth. By convention, this new measure is called absolute magnitude *(far right)*. When very dim and faraway objects are brought in to the standard distance, their absolute magnitudes will be much brighter than their apparent magnitudes; the reverse occurs for bright objects that are nearby.

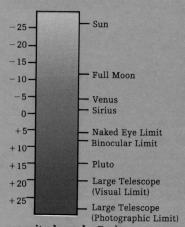

−25	Sun
−20	
−15	
−10	Full Moon
−5	Venus
0	Sirius
+5	Naked Eye Limit
+10	Binocular Limit
+15	Pluto
+20	Large Telescope (Visual Limit)
+25	Large Telescope (Photographic Limit)

The magnitude scale. Each magnitude is quantified to be exactly 2.512 times as dim as the one before. Thus, Sirius, which has a magnitude of −1.4, is about 100 billion times brighter than the dimmest known celestial object, a star with a magnitude of 27, which can only be electronically imaged by a powerful telescope.

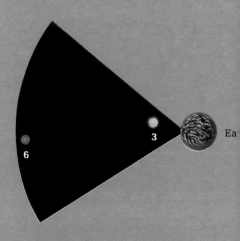

Apparent magnitude. As observed from Earth, a sixth-magnitude star *(dark yellow)* is perceived to be considerably dimmer than a nearby third-magnitude star. However, the difference between them may be the effect of the stars' actual luminosities, their distances from Earth—or both.

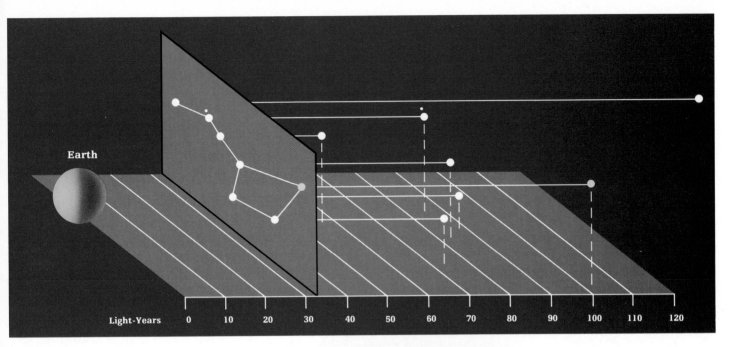

A stellar illusion. As shown in the distance plot above, the apparent relationship among stars in a constellation is an optical effect caused by the eye's inability to gauge real celestial distances from sources of light. For example, Alkaid—the end star in the Big Dipper's handle—is actually twice as far from Earth as any other star in the constellation; its greater intrinsic luminosity makes it appear on a plane with the Big Dipper's other stars. In reality, of course, the stars are all at different distances, and the dipper is merely an imaginative construct.

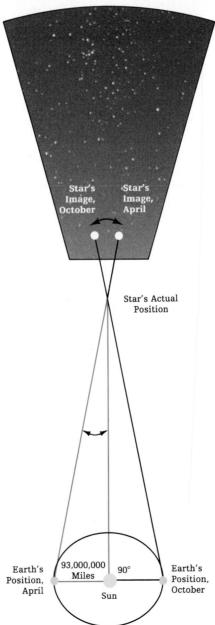

Star's Image, October / Star's Image, April

Star's Actual Position

Earth's Position, April

93,000,000 Miles

90°

Earth's Position, October

Sun

A celestial yardstick. The oldest method for determining stellar distances is trigonometric parallax *(left)*. From the Greek for "change," parallax is the apparent shift in a nearby star's position against the backdrop of more distant stars as Earth travels halfway around its orbit. The star is photographed twice—in April and October in the example at left—and its apparent movement across the background is measured on the photographs as an angle *(top arrow)*, greatly exaggerated here for clarity. Half of this angle *(bottom arrow)* yields one angle of a right triangle *(red)* whose vertices are the Sun, Earth, and the star. Given the Earth-Sun distance, simple trigonometry allows the calculation of the Earth-star distance. The technique is accurate for stars within about 200 light-years. Beyond that, parallaxes become too small to measure accurately.

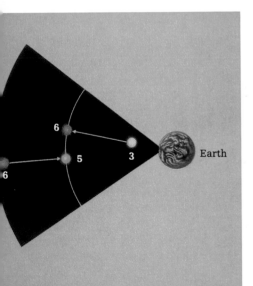

Earth

Absolute magnitude. When mathematically brought in to a standard distance of 10 parsecs (32.6 light-years), the sixth-magnitude star turns out to be a 2.5-times-brighter fifth-magnitude object *(bright yellow)*, marking it as intrinsically more luminous than the other star, which drops to an absolute magnitude of 6.

83

Decoding Stellar Spectra

Because stars radiate energy over a wide range of electromagnetic wavelengths *(below)*, a stellar spectrum is a kind of illustrated record of the energy transactions that have taken place when light from the star's energetic, hot interior passes through the cooler and less energetic outer atmosphere. Certain wavelengths are absorbed by various gases, producing absorption lines at characteristic positions along the spectrum *(bottom)*. By studying the position, width, number, and strength, or darkness, of the lines, astronomers can tell not only what chemical elements the star is made of but, among other things, its temperature *(opposite, bottom)*, roughly how old it is, and some of its movement in space.

The Hertzsprung-Russell (H-R) diagram *(opposite)* classifies stars by their luminosity, expressed in absolute magnitude, and spectral class, which includes color and temperature. The hottest, most energetic stars emit most of their radiation as short-wavelength blue light; the coolest emit long-wavelength red light. The most massive stars also tend to be the shortest-lived, exhausting their nuclear fuel within several million years and suddenly exploding as supernovae. Less massive stars can live for tens of billions of years or more.

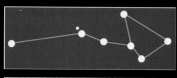

Tracking a star. Because stars are so far away from Earth, their movement as they orbit the center of the Milky Way can be detected only through painstaking observation. Stellar motion has two components, one along Earth's line of sight (radial velocity), the other perpendicular to it (proper motion). Tracking a star over several decades yields the proper motion. The star's Doppler shift *(below, right)* indicates its radial velocity. By combining these two components algebraically, astronomers can compute the star's true trajectory if its distance from Earth is known.

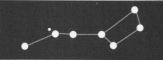

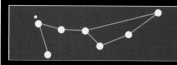

The Big Dipper through time. Over hundreds of thousands of years, stellar motions can significantly alter the way constellations look from Earth. In the three diagrams above, for example, astronomers have extrapolated the appearance of the Big Dipper 100,000 years ago *(top)* and 100,000 years in the future *(bottom)* from the present-day motions of its component stars *(middle)*. The greatest shifts are in Alkaid, at the end of the handle, and Dubhe, at the lip of the ladle; the other stars move through space together and exhibit little relative change.

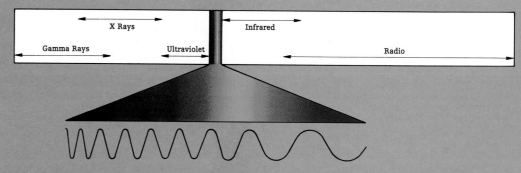

The spectrum. Electromagnetic radiation ranges from high-energy, short-wavelength gamma rays *(above, left)* to low-energy, long-wavelength radio *(above, right)*. The visible-light portion spans wavelengths between 4,000 angstroms *(violet)* and 8,000 angstroms *(red)*. The actions of electrons in the atoms of various elements making up the star can produce absorption lines in different parts of the visible spectrum, depending on the element.

Doppler effect. The observed frequency of a light-wave is affected by the line-of-sight relative motion of source and observer. At right, two sources emit light of a certain wavelength. An observer perceives waves from the approaching source as arriving at shorter intervals, shifting the observed frequency toward the blue end of the spectrum. With the receding source, the observed frequency is shifted toward red.

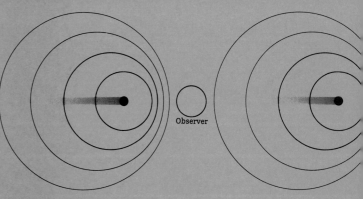

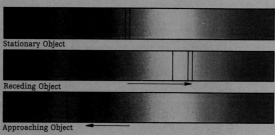

Redshift. An object at rest *(left)* produces absorption lines for a given element at particular positions on the spectrum. As all wavelengths from an object receding from an observer stretch *(middle)*, absorption lines shift redward from their usual position; those from an approaching object move toward blue. (Shifts are exaggerated for clarity.)

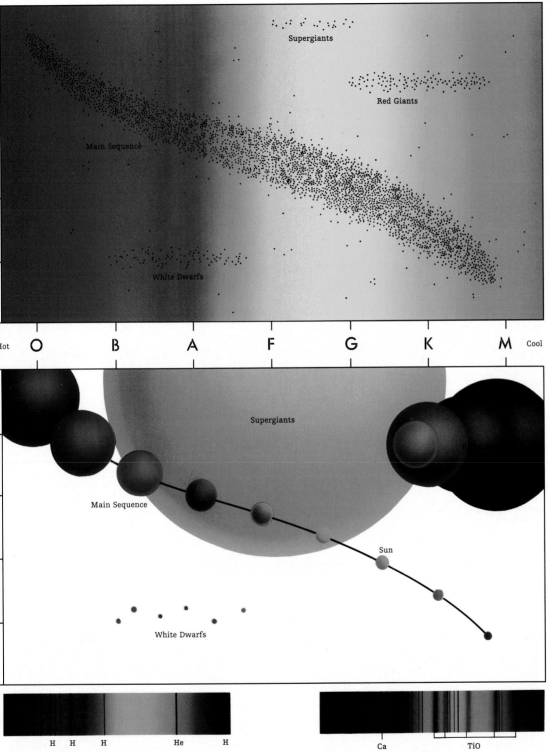

Supergiants

Red Giants

Main Sequence

White Dwarfs

Hot **O** **B** **A** **F** **G** **K** **M** Cool

Supergiants

Main Sequence

Sun

White Dwarfs

H H H He H

Ca TiO

Hertzsprung-Russell diagram.
Devised in the early 1900s, the diagram plots a star's absolute magnitude against its spectral class—labeled in order of decreasing surface temperature with the letters O, B, A, F, G, K, and M (and memorized through the mnemonic "Oh, Be A Fine Girl—Kiss Me"). Fainter stars appear near the bottom on the vertical axis, brighter ones near the top; and temperature decreases from left to right. The broad diagonal band, called the main sequence, associates lower surface temperature with lower luminosity and includes more than 90 percent of all stars. Brilliant but cool giants fall in the upper right quadrant, hot but dim white dwarfs in the lower left sector.

A matter of size. For stars on the main sequence, both temperature and luminosity are correlated with size. The most massive stars are the class O and B stars—very hot and very bright; small M stars are cold and dim. Off the main sequence, however, surface area, or size, rather than temperature, is the stronger influence on luminosity. Red giants and supergiants are only about half as hot as the Sun, but they can be a hundred to a million times more luminous, and planet-size white dwarfs, although generally hotter than the Sun, are much dimmer.

A hot star. The elements that leave their signatures in stellar spectra vary according to a star's surface temperature. The spectrum of a very hot, first-magnitude, main sequence B star *(above)* consists primarily of strong hydrogen (H) and helium (He) absorption lines.

A cool star. Cooler stars such as the red giants, which are off the main sequence, show absorption lines of heavier elements such as titanium oxide (TiO) and neutral calcium (Ca) *(above)*.

85

A Celestial Assortment

Any sweep of the glittering night sky will reveal stars at all stages of evolution, starting and ending with the glowing clouds of gas and dust called nebulae *(opposite)* that are both the formative matter of new stars and the massive shrouds cast off by the aged, thereby replenishing the galaxy's supply of starmaking material. Although most stars appear to shine steadily, some exhibit more changeable natures, from the sudden, blazing appearance of novae *(left)* to the regular pulses of Cepheid variables *(right).* Scientists take advantage of pairs of stars to ascertain stellar mass *(bottom)*; with solitary stars, only indirect estimates based on luminosity are possible.

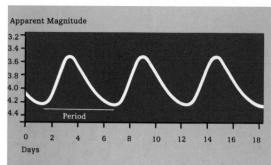

Cepheid variables. The oscillating brightness profile of Delta Cephei, which changes by a factor of two every 5.4 days, is characteristic of a class of stars known as Cepheid variables. Cepheids undergo periodic fluctuations in size that affect their light output.

Novae. One of the most spectacular types of variable stars occurs when a white dwarf star in a binary system begins to rob a main sequence companion of gaseous matter. The accreting gas fuels a flareup that can temporarily increase the robber star's luminosity by a factor of millions. Nova Cygni 1975, for example—shown at the height of its brilliance in the top photo—rapidly exhausted its new fuel and returned to its normal invisibility; an arrow marks its position in the lower photo, taken three months later. Astronomers believe Nova Cygni will not flare again for at least 10,000 years.

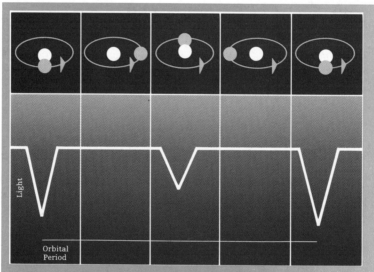

Eclipsing binaries. Light fluctuations also result from the mutual eclipses of pairs of stars whose orbits are viewed nearly edge-on from Earth. The light curve at left (schematized for clarity) approximates that of Beta Lyrae, a system that includes a large B-type star and a smaller A- or F-type partner. When the smaller, dimmer star passes in front of the larger one, reducing the major source of the system's light, the total light output of the system drops sharply. Just over six days later, when the larger star does the eclipsing, the dip in light output is less than half as severe.

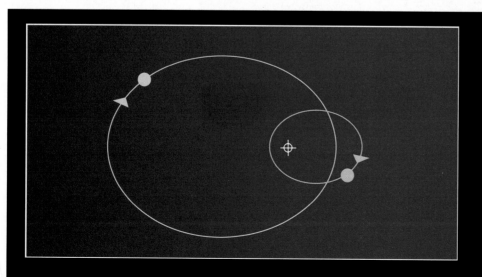

Judging stellar mass. When two or more stars orbit a common center of mass, as in the binary system represented at left, astronomers can use the stars' motions to find their masses. Scientists first determine each star's orbital period and the long diameter of its orbit from observations made over a number of years, and apply Kepler's laws of orbital motion to find the total mass of the system. The relative masses of the two stars may then be derived from the ratio of their orbital diameters: The more massive star, orbiting nearer to the system's center of gravity, has a smaller orbit. Finally, given total mass and relative mass, astronomers can calculate the individual mass of each star.

The Orion nebula. Located below the three stars in Orion's belt and just visible to the naked eye is a stellar nursery, a vast cloud of gas and dust where the densest clumps contract to give birth to new stars. High-energy ultraviolet radiation from the hot stellar fledglings is absorbed by hydrogen atoms in the cloud and reradiated as the nebula's signature reddish light.

The Pleiades. Named for the daughters of Atlas in Greek mythology, these hot, young stars in Taurus are enveloped by the blue glow of their own light, reflected by dust particles in what may be the remnants of the cloud from which they formed.

A globular cluster. Orbiting the Milky Way along paths that trace a vast, bubblelike halo are dense groups of ancient stars called globular clusters. M13 (above) is a collection of roughly a hundred thousand stars in the constellation Hercules.

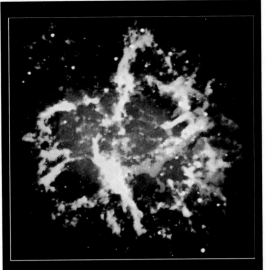

The Crab nebula. These filaments of glowing gas and dust in Taurus are the remains of a massive star that went supernova in AD 1054.

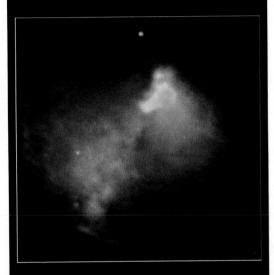

The Dumbbell nebula. This so-called planetary nebula in the constellation Vulpecula is a shell of gas sloughed off by a dying white dwarf star in the center.

The Trifid nebula. Divided by lanes of dust and gas, this nebula in Sagittarius is a stellar nursery where clouds of hydrogen and helium glow pink from the radiation of newborn stars.

LOW-WATTAGE NEIGHBORS

Gazing on the spangled dome of the night sky, an observer on Earth might think the Sun resides fairly near to a number of stellar luminaries. First among them would be Sirius A, whose apparent magnitude of −1.46 *(pages 82-83)* makes it the brightest star in the heavens. As it happens, both Sirius A and Alpha Centauri—fourth in brightness— would be considered near neighbors of the Sun, lying 8.6 and 4.4 light-years away, respectively. But Canopus, the second brightest star, is nearly 100 light-years distant, a sign of its great intrinsic luminosity.

Indeed, as the charts opposite reveal, of the twenty brightest stars in Earth's sky, only three fall within a dozen light-years of the Sun. The rest are distant powerhouses of electromagnetic radiation: Deneb, for instance, is nearly 1,500 light-years away.

By contrast, of the Sun's twenty nearest neighbors, most are intrinsically faint. Despite their proximity, only nine are visible to the naked eye. Also, as shown in the diagram below, several stars are actually multiple systems—a trait shared with about half the stars in the galaxy.

The solar neighborhood. (1) Proxima Centauri, Alpha Centauri A, Alpha Centauri B. **(2)** Barnard's Star. **(3)** Wolf 359. **(4)** Lalande 21185. **(5)** Luyten 726-8 A, UV Ceti (L726-8 B). **(6)** Sirius A, Sirius B. **(7)** Ross 154. **(8)** Ross 248. **(9)** Epsilon Eridani. **(10)** Ross 128. **(11)** Luyten 789-6. **(12)** Groombridge 34 A, Groombridge 34 B. **(13)** Epsilon Indi. **(14)** 61 Cygni A, 61 Cygni B. **(15)** Struve 2398 A, Struve 2398 B. **(16)** Tau Ceti. **(17)** Procyon A, Procyon B. **(18)** Lacaille 9352. **(19)** G 51-15. **(20)** Luyten 725-32.

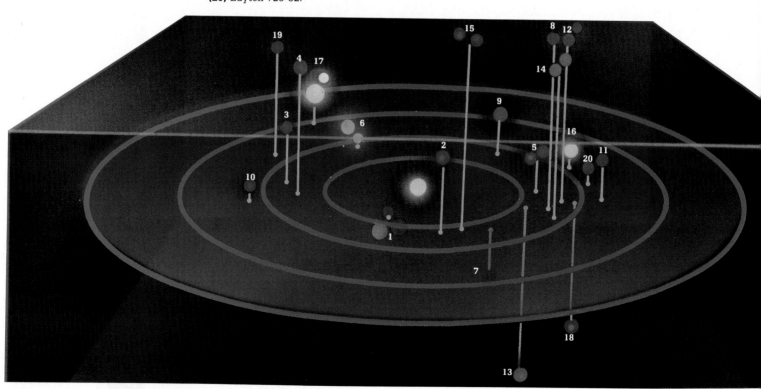

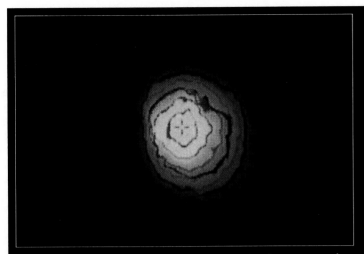

In this computer-enhanced image, an orange halo of gas surrounds Betelgeuse, the second brightest star in the constellation Orion. This red supergiant may go supernova within some millions of years.

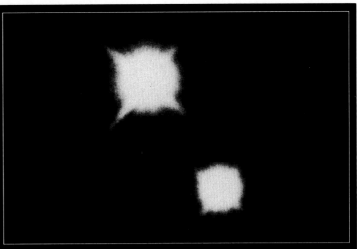

Alpha Centauri A and Alpha Centauri B, with apparent magnitudes of −0.01 and 1.33, respectively, belong to a three-star system that is the Sun's nearest neighbor. Proxima Centauri is not visible here.

THE TWENTY NEAREST STARS

Star Name	Right Ascension Hours	Minutes	Declination Degrees	Minutes	Distance (Light-Years)	Apparent Magnitude	Absolute Magnitude
Proxima Centauri	14	26	−62	28	4.3	+11.05	+15.5
Alpha Centauri A	14	36	−60	38	4.38	−0.01	+4.4
Alpha Centauri B	14	36	−60	38	4.38	+1.33	+5.7
Barnard's Star	17	55	+4	33	5.9	+9.54	+13.3
Wolf 359	10	54	+7	19	7.6	+13.53	+16.7
Lalande 21185	11	01	+36	18	8.1	+7.50	+10.5
Sirius A	6	43	−16	39	8.6	−1.46	+1.4
Sirius B	6	43	−16	39	8.6	+8.68	+11.6
Luyten 726-8 A	1	36	−18	13	8.9	+12.45	+15.3
UV Ceti (L726-8 B)	1	36	−18	13	8.9	+12.95	+15.3
Ross 154	18	47	−23	53	9.4	+10.6	+13.3
Ross 248	23	39	+43	55	10.3	+12.29	+14.8
Epsilon Eridani	3	31	−9	38	10.8	+3.73	+6.1
Ross 128	11	45	+1	06	10.8	+11.10	+13.5
Luyten 789-6	22	36	−15	36	10.8	+12.18	+14.6
61 Cygni A	21	05	+38	30	11.1	+5.22	+7.6
61 Cygni B	21	05	+38	30	11.1	+6.03	+8.4
Epsilon Indi	22	00	−57	00	11.2	+4.68	+7.0
Procyon A	7	37	+5	21	11.2	+0.37	+2.7
Procyon B	7	37	+5	21	11.2	+10.70	+13.0
Tau Ceti	1	41	−16	12	11.4	+3.50	+13.7
Struve 2398 A	18	42	+59	33	11.5	+8.90	+10.9
Struve 2398 B	18	42	+59	33	11.5	+9.68	+11.9
Groombridge 34 A	0	15	+43	44	11.6	+8.07	+10.3
Groombridge 34 B	0	15	+43	44	11.6	+11.10	+13.3
Lacaille 9352	23	03	−36	08	11.7	+7.36	+9.6
G 51-15	8	27	+26	57	11.9	+14.8	+17.0
Luyten 725-32	10	01	−17	16	12.4	+11.5	+13.6

THE TWENTY BRIGHTEST STARS

Star Name	Hours	Minutes	Degrees	Minutes	Distance (Light-Years)	Apparent Magnitude	Absolute Magnitude
Sirius A	6	43	−16	39	8.6	−1.46	+1.4
Canopus	6	23	−52	40	98	−0.72	−3.1
Arcturus	14	13	+19	27	36	−0.06	−0.3
Alpha Centauri A	14	36	−60	38	4.4	−0.01	+4.4
Vega	18	35	+38	44	26.5	+0.04	+0.5
Capella	5	13	+45	57	45	+0.05	−0.7
Rigel	5	12	−8	15	900	+0.14	−6.8
Procyon A	7	37	+5	21	11.2	+0.37	+2.6
Betelgeuse	5	53	+7	24	520	+0.41	−5.5
Achernar	1	36	−57	29	118	+0.51	−1.0
Beta Centauri	14	00	−60	08	490	+0.63	−4.1
Altair	19	48	+8	44	16.5	+0.77	+2.2
Aldebaran	4	33	+16	25	68	+0.86	−0.2
Spica	13	23	−10	54	220	+0.91	−3.6
Antares	16	26	−26	19	520	+0.92	−4.5
Pollux	7	42	+28	09	35	+1.16	+0.8
Fomalhaut	22	55	−29	53	22.6	+1.19	+2.0
Deneb	20	40	+45	06	1,500	+1.26	−6.9
Beta Crucis	12	45	−59	24	490	+1.28	−4.6
Alpha Crucis	12	24	−62	49	120	+1.39	−4.0

THE MILKY WAY: THE SUN'S HOME

The pale river of stars that crosses the heavens is actually an edge-on view of the disklike galaxy that is home to the Sun and more than 200 billion other stars. The notion that the Milky Way ("galaxy" is from the Greek word for "milk") is just one of hundreds of billions of similar stellar collections was confirmed only in the early part of this century *(pages 104-105)*. Since then, increasingly powerful astronomical tools have let scientists ferret out many of the galaxy's secrets. For example, in the 1950s, astronomers armed with radio telescopes finally proved what most had long believed: that the Milky Way, like many of the galaxies in the known universe, is a spiral. More recently, similar instruments have penetrated the clouds of interstellar gas and dust that block the view of optical instruments to reveal unexpected features at the galactic core *(opposite, bottom)*.

One conundrum still awaiting definitive solution is the question of why spiral galaxies exist at all. Differential rotation—the tendency of stars, dust, and gas near the galaxy's center to orbit more rapidly than those farther out—can create a spiral structure, much as cream stirred into a cup of coffee will swirl. But the same rotation should also cause the pattern to smear out relatively quickly. One theory posits the existence of density waves, spiral-shaped disturbances that move through the galactic disk *(opposite, top)*. The gravitational attraction in regions of increased density causes diffuse clouds of hydrogen gas to compress, triggering star formation that outlines the spiral pattern.

In a false-color radio image looking toward the Milky Way's center, the galactic plane forms a thick band roughly matching the more familiar stellar swath but spiked with structures not visible to the naked eye. Projecting above the plane *(left)*, a dark streamer called the North Polar Spur *(1)* may be radio-emitting gas left over from a local supernova that occurred about one million years ago. At far right, the swirling Gum nebula *(2)* is the remnant of the Vela supernova, heated to radio-brightness by the shock wave of the explosion. The only feature not part of the Milky Way itself is Centaurus A *(3)*, a powerful radio source associated with the galaxy NGC 5128, which is about 15 million light-years away.

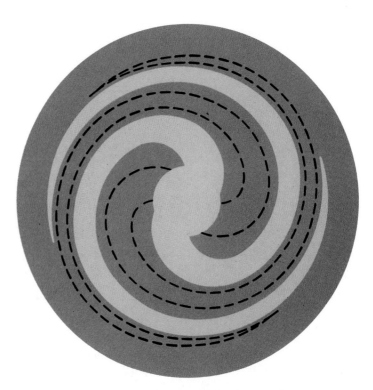

According to one theory, as orbiting stars and gas follow a circular path *(pink)* around the galactic center, they intersect a slower-moving wave of density *(light blue)*. At those junctures *(box)*, stars slow down before moving through, but diffuse clouds of gas accumulate, compress, and give birth to new stars—thus lighting up the spiral arm.

After millions of years, the density wave has rotated to a new position, where a burst of star formation defines new spiral arms; the old arms *(dashed line)* vanish as their stars grow dim or disperse. Useful as density-wave theory is in explaining some forms of spiral galaxies, it does not address the question of how a density wave begins in the first place.

Surprise at the center. In the mid-1970s, analysis of radio emissions given off by hydrogen gas showed that the Milky Way was not the uniform, flat disk defined by the galaxy's spiral arms *(left, blue)* but instead held a second disk *(yellow)* that is tilted some twenty degrees to the galactic plane. Spanning about 8,000 light-years and rotating at eighty-one miles per second (three times faster than the stars and gases in the outer disk region), the inner disk lies well within the galaxy's nuclear bulge *(lavender)* and seems to harbor even further surprises *(right)*. Globular clusters, huge groupings containing anywhere from hundreds of thousands to a few million ancient red stars, follow highly eccentric and inclined orbits, creating a kind of halo around the galaxy.

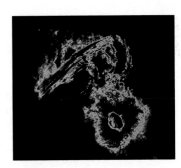

Sagittarius A. A radio image of the heart of the Milky Way, which lies in the direction of the constellation Sagittarius, reveals filaments some 130 light-years long but only 3 light-years wide. The filaments are perpendicular to the galactic plane and may be shaped by electrons spiraling around a powerful magnetic field. Scientists speculate that the huge amounts of energy being generated at the galaxy's center signal the presence of a voracious black hole.

THE STARRY FIRMAMENT

In the desert or the mountains, or out in the country far from city lights, the sight is simply breathtaking—a ragged, luminous ribbon, interrupted here and there by dark patches, that sweeps across the sky from horizon to horizon. Even where viewing conditions are relatively poor, the faintest glimmer of the Milky Way's wispy band makes an awesome impression. It is, after all, direct visible evidence of the galaxy's structure.

The spectacle is a phenomenon of perspective, the result of the Solar System's position within the disk of the galaxy, about two-thirds of the way out from the center *(above)*. Thus, earthbound observers looking along the plane of the disk see its billions of stars, as well as interstellar clouds of dust and gas, concentrated into the narrow strip of the Milky Way. The stars scattered throughout the rest of the night sky constitute those relatively thin portions of the disk above and below the Solar System.

As shown on the celestial sphere at right, because the plane of Earth's orbit around the Sun is tilted about sixty-three degrees to that of the galactic disk, the Milky Way deviates from the ecliptic *(yellow line)* by the same angle and stretches across a completely different region of the heavens. But like the ecliptic, it varies in position with the seasons, and its features change as Earth makes its annual passage. During summer, autumn, and winter, it is high in the sky and clearly visible. In July, the Milky Way is at its brightest, because Earth's nightside faces toward the center of the galaxy, located in the direction of the constellation Sagittarius *(opposite, lower left)*. In December, looking away from the galactic center toward Orion *(opposite, far right)*, the view is not nearly as brilliant. And during the spring, when Earth's nightside faces out of the plane of the galaxy, the Milky Way is low on the horizon and almost impossible to make out.

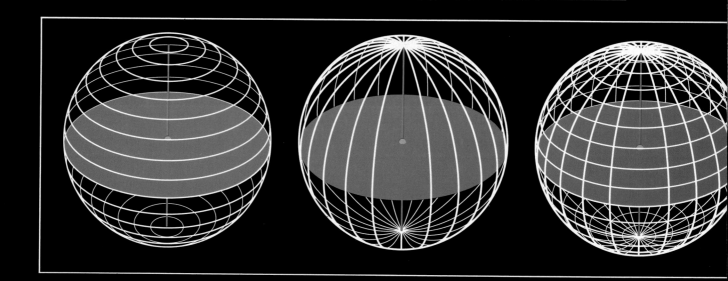

elestial coordinates. Stars occupy rel-
tively fixed positions on the celestial
phere that are defined by the grid sys-
em shown at left. (In contrast, altitude
nd azimuth *[pages 68-69]* change with
arth's rotation.) Declination *(far left)* is
neasured in degrees above and below
ne celestial equator *(purple),* from plus
inety degrees at the north celestial
ole to minus ninety degrees at the
outh. Right ascension *(middle)* corre-
ponds to longitude and is divided into
wenty-four hours, going counterclock-
vise (eastward) from zero hour at the
ernal equinox. With the combined grid
near left), astronomers can mark the
ocation of any star.

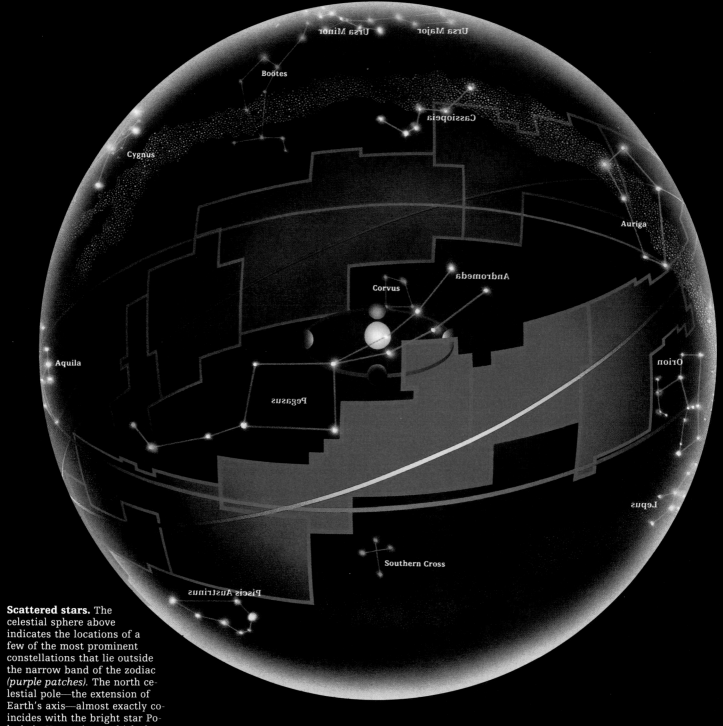

Scattered stars. The celestial sphere above indicates the locations of a few of the most prominent constellations that lie outside the narrow band of the zodiac *(purple patches).* The north celestial pole—the extension of Earth's axis—almost exactly coincides with the bright star Polaris in Ursa Minor, which thus barely moves during the course of the night. No equivalent marker star exists for the south celestial pole.

PATTERNS AND PERSPECTIVES

In addition to the twelve constellations that make up the zodiac, dozens of other star patterns populate the night sky. In the second century AD, the Greek astronomer Ptolemy published a list of forty-eight groupings; today, astronomers recognize a total of eighty-eight, many of which are too far south to have been seen by the ancients.

Like the Moon and planets, stars appear to move westward during the night as Earth rotates beneath them. Unlike the members of the Solar System, however, stars do not hew to the ecliptic. Some are so close to the celestial poles that they never rise or set, circling counterclockwise in the north and clockwise in the south. A constellation's position—and whether it is visible at all—depends on the hour, the date, and an observer's latitude. Only at the equator can all eighty-eight be seen during the year. The drawings at right depict the view at midnight in early October from four different latitudes; the blue planes represent the plane of the horizon for each location.

From the North Pole. Polaris sits directly overhead. Orion is on the horizon, with the celestial equator *(purple)* running through its belt. As Earth rotates eastward *(purple arrow)*, Orion will move westward *(red arrow)*. The Southern Cross lies well below the horizon and cannot be seen.

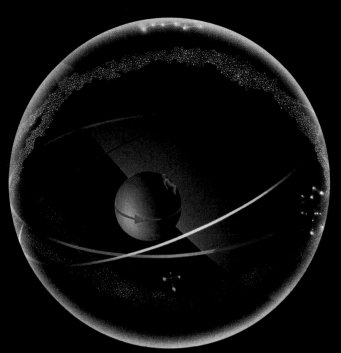

From forty degrees north. Polaris is forty degrees above the northern horizon. (Its altitude always matches the observer's latitude.) Orion is fairly high toward the south and will cross the horizon—inclined fifty degrees to the celestial equator—at an angle when it sets. The Southern Cross remains hidden.

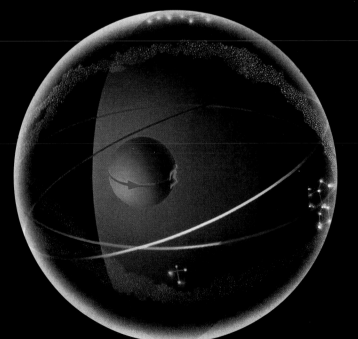

From the equator. At zero degrees latitude, Polaris is zero degrees high—that is, right on the northern horizon. Orion and the celestial equator are straight overhead, and Orion will set due west. The Southern Cross is visible low in the southern sky.

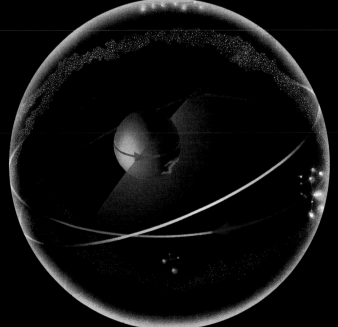

From forty degrees south. Polaris lies out of sight below the northern horizon. Orion is visible to the north, the Southern Cross to the south. At this time of year—early spring in the Southern Hemisphere—the sky over the South Pole is still light at midnight.

THE BACKYARD SKY

Because a large percentage of the world's population lives at midnorthern latitudes—in North America, Europe, the Soviet Union, China, and Japan—star guides tend to focus on celestial sights visible from forty degrees north. The drawings on this page represent the midwinter sky at this latitude looking toward the south *(below)* and toward the north *(bottom)*; each view is shown at two different times, three hours apart, to illustrate how the Milky Way and the constellations move during the night.

To the south, the zodiac constellations arc high in the sky, following the ecliptic as they rise in the east and set in the west. To the north, not all the constellations rise and set; some appear to draw a counterclockwise circle around the celestial pole *(page 101)*.

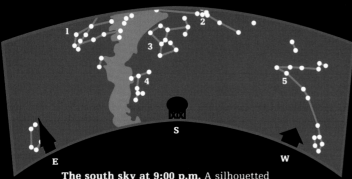

The south sky at 9:00 p.m. A silhouetted church represents the eastern horizon, a house the western horizon, and a water tower due south. Gemini *(1)* rides high in the eastern sky; high in the south are Taurus *(2)*, Orion *(3)*, and Canis Major *(4)*, with its bright star Sirius. In the west, Pisces *(5)* will soon set. The Milky Way runs vertically just east of south.

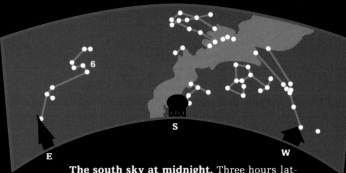

The south sky at midnight. Three hours later, Earth's eastward rotation at the rate of fifteen degrees per hour has effectively shifted all the stars westward *(right)* forty-five degrees of arc. Thus, Pisces has disappeared below the western horizon and Leo *(6)* is well risen in the east.

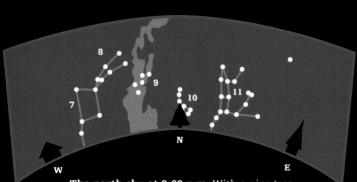

The north sky at 9:00 p.m. With a pine tree marking due north, the house (west) is now to the left, the church (east) is to the right. Pegasus *(7)* and Andromeda *(8)* are beginning to set to the west of the Milky Way. Cassiopeia *(9)* lies west of Ursa Minor *(10)* and Ursa Major *(11)* (east).

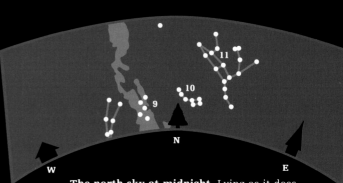

The north sky at midnight. Lying as it does near the celestial pole, Ursa Minor *(10)* has rotated only slightly around the North Star, Polaris, while Cassiopeia *(9)* and Ursa Major *(11)* have traced longer arcs of their wider circles. Pegasus has disappeared altogether in the west *(left)*.

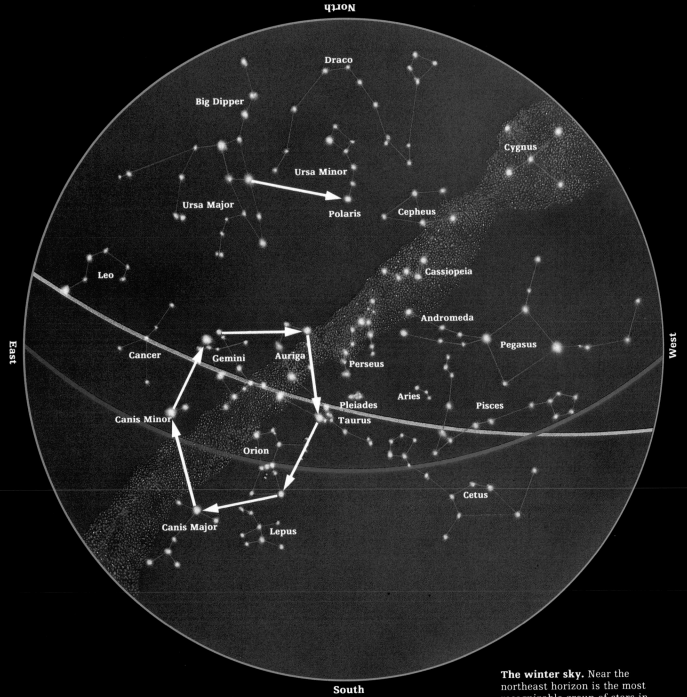

Draco

Big Dipper

Ursa Minor

Ursa Major

Polaris

Cepheus

Cygnus

Leo

Cassiopeia

Andromeda

Pegasus

East

Cancer

Gemini

Auriga

Perseus

West

Pleiades

Aries

Pisces

Taurus

Canis Minor

Orion

Cetus

Canis Major

Lepus

South

CHANGES THROUGH THE SEASONS

The star map above and those on the following pages show the full dome of the sky for each of the four seasons as it appears from forty degrees north latitude. The maps are based on stellar positions at 9:00 p.m. on four specific dates—the first of January, April, July, and October—shifting as the stars rise about four minutes earlier each day as Earth circles the Sun.

At more northerly latitudes, each chart's south horizon will be higher, hiding the most southerly stars but revealing additional ones to the north. The opposite holds true for latitudes farther south.

To use these star charts, hold them overhead, with the labels for north, south, east, and west aligned with those directions. For example, when facing north, turn the book upside down so that north is at the bottom, south at the top.

The winter sky. Near the northeast horizon is the most recognizable group of stars in the heavens—the Big Dipper, part of Ursa Major. The two outermost stars of its bowl point to Polaris (arrow). Arching overhead is the Milky Way, which passes between Orion and Gemini toward the south. As indicated by arrows, bright stars in Orion, Canis Major, Canis Minor, Gemini, Auriga, and Taurus form a rough circle around the band of the Milky Way. Sirius in Canis Major is the brightest star visible from Earth.

97

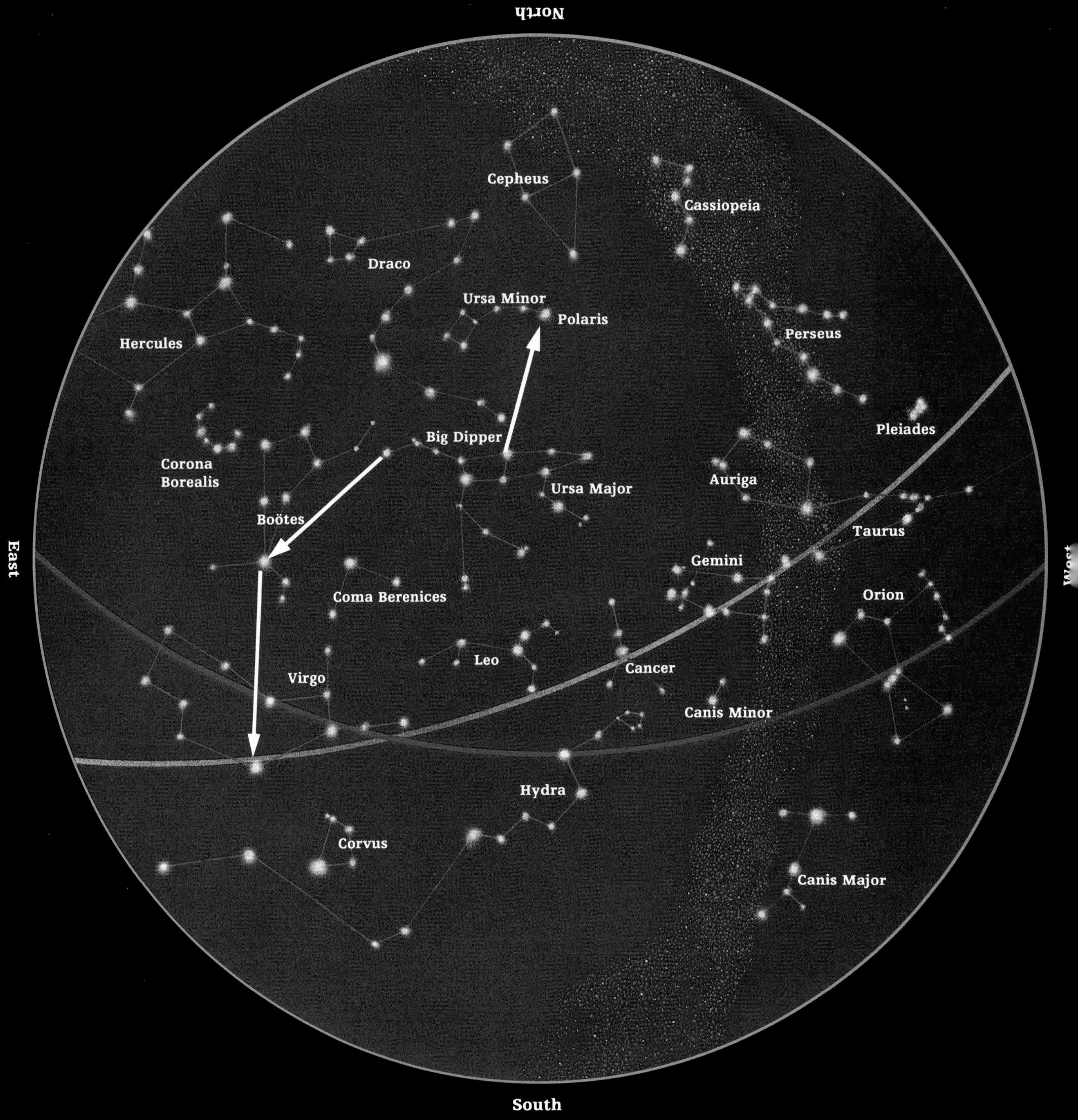

Cepheus

Cassiopeia

Draco

Ursa Minor

Polaris

Perseus

Hercules

Pleiades

Big Dipper

Corona
Borealis

Ursa Major

Auriga

Taurus

Boötes

Gemini

Orion

Coma Berenices

Cancer

Virgo

Leo

Canis Minor

Hydra

Corvus

Canis Major

East

West

South

The spring sky. The Big Dipper has moved
almost directly overhead, slightly to the north;
its bowl stars Dubhe and Merak always serve
to point the way to Polaris. Extending the
curve of the Big Dipper's handle leads first to
spring's brightest star, orange Arcturus in
Boötes, then onward to Spica in Virgo. The
prominent constellation high in the southern
half of the sky is Leo, with the bright star
Regulus marking its heart. The Milky Way
now hangs low in the western sky and is
much less noticeable. Orion and other winter
constellations are just visible near the western
horizon, setting shortly after dark.

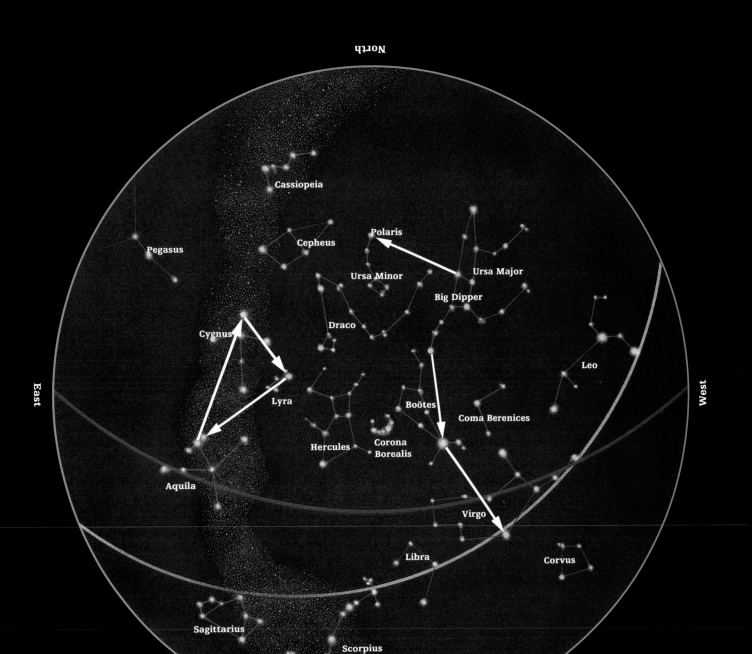

North

Cassiopeia

Pegasus

Cepheus

Polaris

Ursa Minor

Ursa Major

Big Dipper

Draco

Cygnus

Leo

Lyra

Boötes

Coma Berenices

East

West

Hercules

Corona
Borealis

Aquila

Virgo

Libra

Corvus

Sagittarius

Scorpius

South

The summer sky. Once again, the Milky Way is clearly apparent and now at its brightest, stretching across the eastern half of the sky. Lodged within it are Cassiopeia to the north and Cygnus—also known as the Northern Cross—almost overhead. Among the summer constellations, the three brightest stars are Vega in Lyra, Altair in Aquila, and Deneb in Cygnus, which together form the Summer Triangle *(arrows)*. Near the southern horizon are Scorpius, with red Antares, and teapot-shaped Sagittarius, which lie in the direction of the galaxy's central bulge. The Big Dipper has moved west of Polaris in the northern sky.

North

Ursa Major

Big Dipper

Auriga

Polaris   Ursa Minor

Corona Borealis

Cassiopeia

Draco

Perseus   Cepheus

Taurus

Pleiades

Hercules

Cygnus

Andromeda

Lyra

Aries

Pisces   Pegasus

East

West

Cetus

Aquila

Aquarius

Sculptor   Capricornus

Piscis Austrinus   Sagittarius

South

The autumn sky. Having shifted around Polaris, the Big Dipper is at its lowest, down
near the northern horizon. Cassiopeia is high
in the sky on the opposite side of Polaris, with
Andromeda and the Great Square of Pegasus
just to the south. A line drawn south through
the two western stars of the square points to
the brightest star of the autumn constellations, Fomalhaut. The Milky Way runs overhead from northeast to southwest. Descending
toward the west is the Summer Triangle, and
just beginning to rise in the east are the
bright winter stars of Taurus and Auriga.

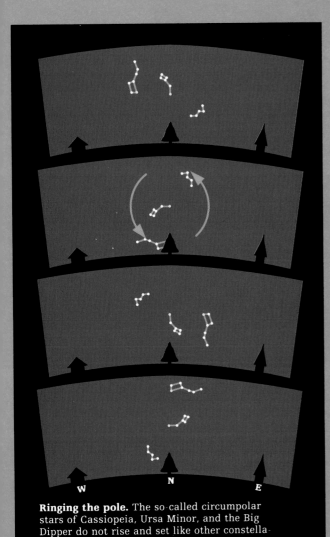

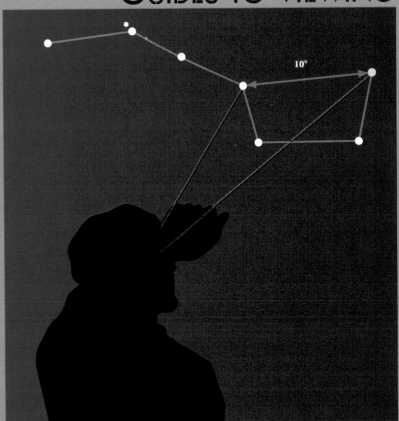

Ringing the pole. The so-called circumpolar stars of Cassiopeia, Ursa Minor, and the Big Dipper do not rise and set like other constellations. Instead, they circle Polaris in a counterclockwise direction, completing one round every twenty-three hours and fifty-six minutes.

Gauging distances. One of the trickier aspects of stargazing is relating the distances between objects on a chart to their actual separation in the sky. A good way to judge is by comparing one's fist held at arm's length to the size of the Big Dipper's bowl, which is equal to about ten degrees. For most people, fist and bowl will be about the same width. Thus, when one star is thirty degrees—or three bowl widths—from another on a chart, it will be about three fists away in the sky.

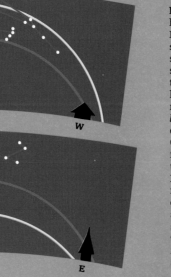

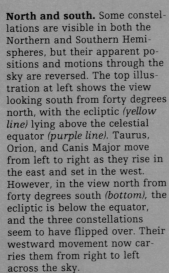

North and south. Some constellations are visible in both the Northern and Southern Hemispheres, but their apparent positions and motions through the sky are reversed. The top illustration at left shows the view looking south from forty degrees north, with the ecliptic *(yellow line)* lying above the celestial equator *(purple line)*. Taurus, Orion, and Canis Major move from left to right as they rise in the east and set in the west. However, in the view north from forty degrees south *(bottom)*, the ecliptic is below the equator, and the three constellations seem to have flipped over. Their westward movement now carries them from right to left across the sky.

Seen edge-on *(far left)*, the equatorial disk of galaxy NGC 891, in the constellation Andromeda, appears only as a thin, cloudy band cutting across the galaxy's glowing central bulge of stars. But NGC 7479 *(below)*, in Pegasus, presents its full face to Earth, revealing much greater detail. This false-color image highlights the curving spiral arms *(purple)* extending from a central barlike structure *(orange)*.

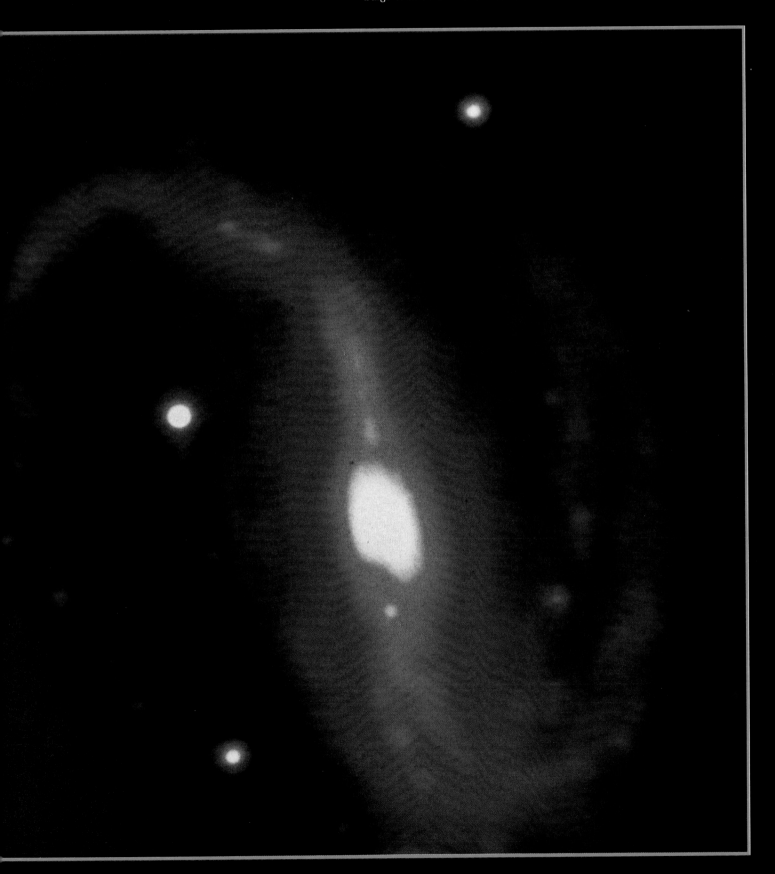

**F**or hundreds of years, astronomers were puzzled by a strange phenomenon in the night sky: faint, fuzzy patches of light known as nebulae, from the Latin word for "mist" or "clouds." In 1784, the French astronomer Charles Messier published a list of 103 of these objects, noting their celestial coordinates so that he could distinguish them from comets, which looked much the same but did not have fixed positions. Messier, however, made no attempt to explain what his catalog entries might be.

One intriguing possibility was proposed by the great German philosopher Immanuel Kant, who was fascinated by astronomy and had read widely on the subject. Contrary to the standard view that the Milky Way was the only galaxy, or large collection of stars, in the cosmos, Kant suggested that it was but one of many such systems, all of which were separated from one another by enormous distances. According to this theory, these so-called island universes were so remote that their stars did not appear as individual points of light, blurring instead into the hazy clouds that Messier had observed. Kant would prove to be right, of course, but clinching evidence would not emerge for nearly 150 years.

In the meantime, sky watchers using more powerful telescopes than Messier's did manage to distinguish stars within certain nebulae. And in the 1840s, Irish astronomer William Parsons noticed that object M51 (its designation in Messier's catalog) had a distinct spiral structure, a pattern that would later earn it the name Whirlpool *(page 124-125)*. He soon found other spiral-shaped nebulae, lending credence to the hypothesis that these were separate stellar systems, each rotating around a central hub. But try as he might, he was unable to make out individual stars within the spirals, and the issue remained unsettled.

The problem was that there was no way of knowing how far away any of these nebulae were and whether they actually lay beyond the bounds of the Milky Way. At the time, the only way to gauge the remoteness of a celestial object was by measuring its parallax, or the degree to which it shifted against the motionless background of very distant stars as Earth moved from one side of the Sun to the other. This method was good out to only about 200 light-years; beyond that, parallax shift was undetectable and distance estimates unreliable.

Then, in the early years of the twentieth century, American astronomer Henrietta Leavitt discovered that a certain kind of pulsating star known as a Cepheid variable (after the first to be detected, Delta Cephei) could serve as an astronomical yardstick because of a unique relationship between its rate of variation and its absolute magnitude: The longer a Cepheid took to reach maximum brightness, the brighter it was. By comparing its pulsation rate with that of a Cepheid whose absolute magnitude had been calculated by other means, one could gauge any Cepheid's true luminosity. Then, knowing how bright a star really was as well as its apparent brightness from Earth, one could determine its distance according to the inverse-square law, which states that an object's luminosity diminishes in proportion to the square of its distance.

Armed with this knowledge, Edwin Hubble, an astronomer at the Mount Wilson Observatory in California, set out to find Cepheids in one of the best-known spirals, the great Andromeda nebula. Eventually, in 1923, he found one. Applying Leavitt's period-luminosity law, he calculated that Andromeda was about 800,000 light-years away, far beyond even the most generous estimates of the Milky Way's dimensions. Although Hubble's figure was well short of the actual distance, now known to be more than two million light-years, there could be no doubt about the implications: Andromeda and, presumably, many other of the nebulae were full-fledged galaxies.

A few years later, Hubble came up with an even more astounding finding. Not only was the cosmos teeming with galaxies, but redshift measurements *(pages 84-85)* indicated that they were all rushing away from one another at rates proportional to their distance. The universe was growing larger by the second, as if flung outward by some gigantic explosion. Astronomers would have to reevaluate all they knew about the size, the composition, and the very history of the cosmos. And the galaxies, it seemed, would be the new focus of their attention.

THE MILKY WAY AND ITS NEIGHBORS

The Local Group. (1) Milky Way. **(2)** Draco. **(3)** Ursa Minor. **(4)** Small Magellanic Cloud. **(5)** Large Magellanic Cloud. **(6)** Carina. **(7)** Sextans C. **(8)** Ursa Major. **(9)** Pegasus. **(10)** Sculptor. **(11)** Fornax. **(12)** Leo I. **(13)** Leo II. **(14)** Maffei I. **(15)** NGC 185. **(16)** NGC 147. **(17)** NGC 205. **(18)** M32. **(19)** Andromeda I. **(20)** Andromeda III. **(21)** Andromeda (M31). **(22)** M33. **(23)** LGS 3. **(24)** IC 1613. **(25)** NGC 6822. **(26)** Sextans A. **(27)** Leo A. **(28)** IC 10. **(29)** DDO 210. **(30)** Wolf-Lundmark-Melotte. **(31)** IC 5152.

Although vast distances separate them, galaxies seldom qualify as loners. Most reside in groups known as clusters, defined by astronomers as at least a few dozen galaxies within a radius of a few million light-years. The Milky Way itself is part of such a gathering, called the Local Group, which includes some thirty systems of varying sizes, bound together by their gravitational pull on one another.

The map below charts the members of the Local Group from the perspective of the Milky Way *(1)*. Concentric circles mark intervals of 650,000 light-years, and vertical lines indicate positions above or below the

Milky Way's plane. The cluster's gravitational center lies about midway between the two largest galaxies, the Milky Way and Andromeda *(21)*, each of which is orbited by a small group of satellite systems.

Three of the Local Group's galaxies can be seen with the naked eye: Andromeda from the Northern Hemisphere, and the Small and Large Magellanic Clouds *(4 and 5)* from the Southern Hemisphere. The others are visible only with the use of telescopes. Their names refer to the astronomical catalog in which they were first listed, or to the constellation where they are found, or to their discoverers.

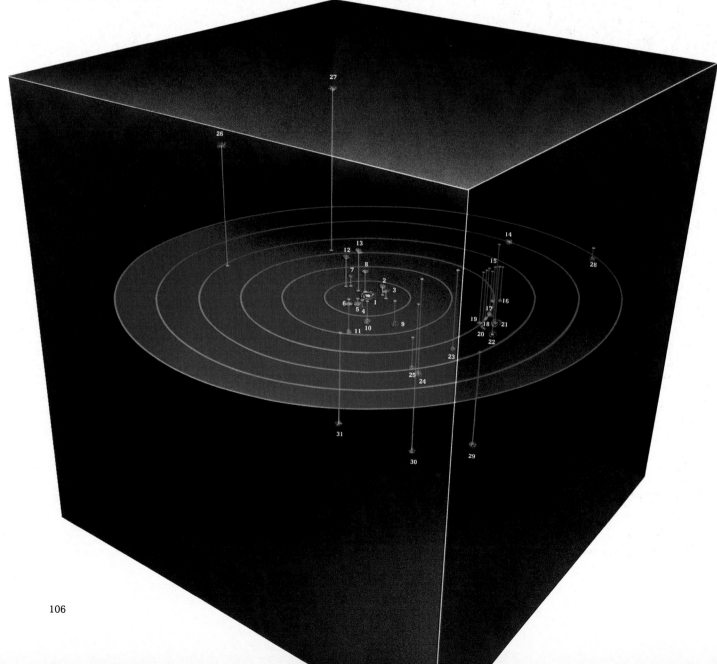

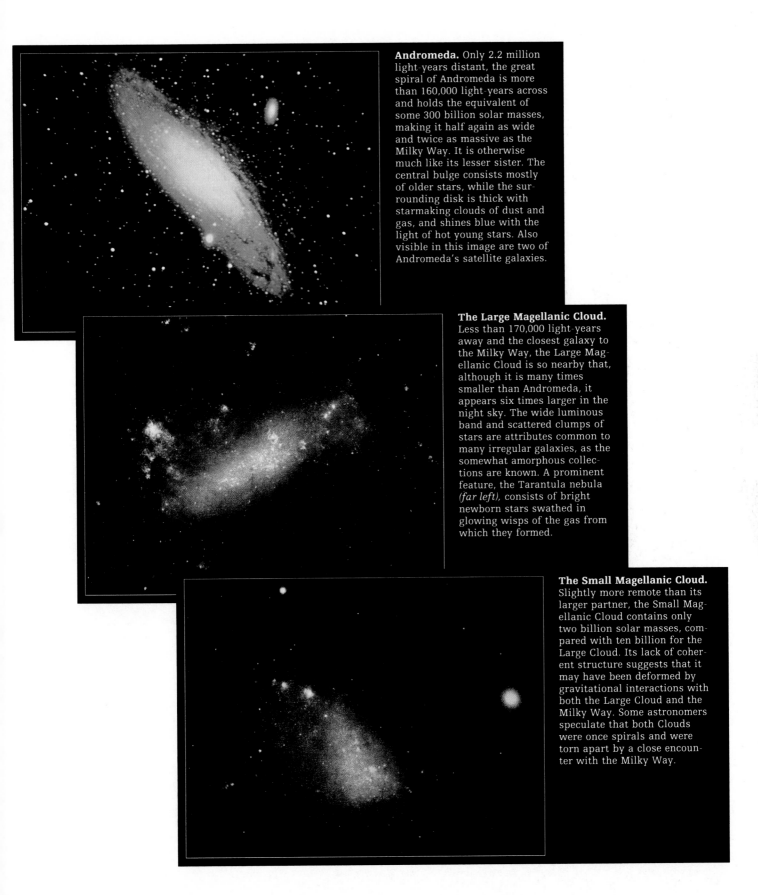

Andromeda. Only 2.2 million light-years distant, the great spiral of Andromeda is more than 160,000 light-years across and holds the equivalent of some 300 billion solar masses, making it half again as wide and twice as massive as the Milky Way. It is otherwise much like its lesser sister. The central bulge consists mostly of older stars, while the surrounding disk is thick with starmaking clouds of dust and gas, and shines blue with the light of hot young stars. Also visible in this image are two of Andromeda's satellite galaxies.

The Large Magellanic Cloud. Less than 170,000 light-years away and the closest galaxy to the Milky Way, the Large Magellanic Cloud is so nearby that, although it is many times smaller than Andromeda, it appears six times larger in the night sky. The wide luminous band and scattered clumps of stars are attributes common to many irregular galaxies, as the somewhat amorphous collections are known. A prominent feature, the Tarantula nebula *(far left),* consists of bright newborn stars swathed in glowing wisps of the gas from which they formed.

The Small Magellanic Cloud. Slightly more remote than its larger partner, the Small Magellanic Cloud contains only two billion solar masses, compared with ten billion for the Large Cloud. Its lack of coherent structure suggests that it may have been deformed by gravitational interactions with both the Large Cloud and the Milky Way. Some astronomers speculate that both Clouds were once spirals and were torn apart by a close encounter with the Milky Way.

107

From Cluster to Supercluster

During the 1950s, as astronomers collected distance measurements to more and more galaxies, a startling image began to emerge of the Local Group's place in the cosmic order. The Milky Way's home cluster, it turned out, is part of a much larger association whose basic units are not mere galaxies but entire clusters. Known as the Local Supercluster, this vast assembly spans more than 100 million light-years and consists of several scores of clusters, as well as a smattering of galaxies in between.

As shown in the diagram below, which features only the largest members of the system, the Local Supercluster centers on its most massive element, the Virgo cluster *(1)*, a so-called rich cluster harboring thousands of galaxies. The Local Group *(29)* lies near the periphery, about 60 million light-years from Virgo. (Concentric circles indicate distances of 25 million light-years.) Most of the other clusters reside in or very close to the plane that passes through both Virgo and the Local Group, represented by the disk in the illustration; the regions of space above and below the general vicinity of this plane are almost completely empty.

The Local Supercluster is far from the only one of its kind in the heavens, and astronomers have identified about fifty other superclusters containing an average of a dozen rich clusters apiece. In these terms, the Local Supercluster is a lightweight, Virgo being its only rich cluster and many of the others just as poor in galaxies as the relatively sparse Local Group.

The Local Supercluster.
(1) Virgo. **(2)** Sombrero. **(3)** NGC 5061. **(4)** NGC 4699. **(5)** NGC 5087. **(6)** NGC 4697. **(7)** NGC 4995. **(8)** Virgo W. **(9)** NGC 3813. **(10)** NGC 3613. **(11)** NGC 4123. **(12)** NGC 3998. **(13)** NGC 4151. **(14)** NGC 4036. **(15)** Ursa Major. **(16)** NGC 3079. **(17)** NGC 2768. **(18)** NGC 2841. **(19)** M96. **(20)** NGC 2541. **(21)** Coma I. **(22)** M51. **(23)** NGC 4258. **(24)** M94. **(25)** NGC 5643. **(26)** M81. **(27)** Centaurus. **(28)** IC 342. **(29)** Local Group. **(30)** Sculptor.

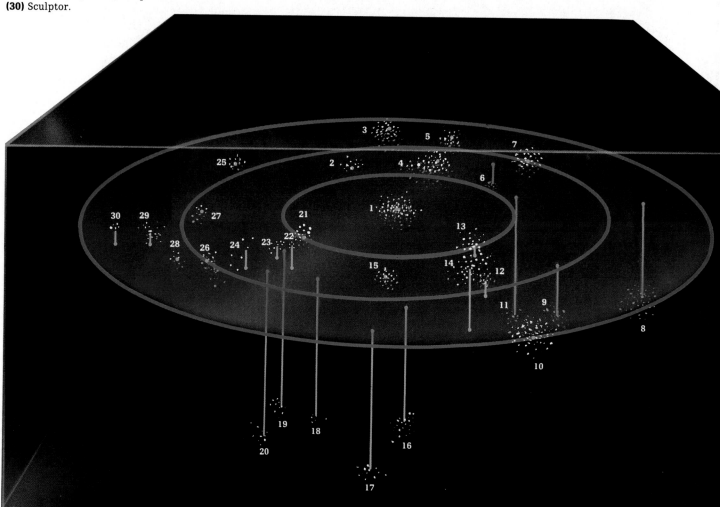

The Virgo cluster. This photograph of a tiny portion of the teeming Virgo cluster includes two of its largest, brightest members, the elliptical galaxies M84 and M86 *(right and center)*, as well as a handful of smaller spirals. The field of view here covers about one square degree of the sky; the full cluster extends over 120 square degrees and has a diameter of approximately 20 million light-years.

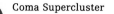

Networks of Superclusters

No matter what direction they look in the sky, astronomers find vast filamentary strands of superclusters stretching for hundreds of millions of light-years across the universe. In some cases, tenuous chains of galaxies or clusters seem to link these superclusters to each other, forming networks of awesome proportions.

Equally astounding are colossal volumes of space, some measuring more than 300 million light-years across, that are practically devoid of galaxies. Although most surveys, such as the one that produced the map below, can cover only limited portions of the sky, these large-scale structural patterns inevitably appear. Theorists have yet to fully explain how these profoundly puzzling entities could have formed.

Perseus Supercluster

A three-dimensional survey.
Three cones of space that have been intensively studied from Earth *(center)* reveal the extended structures of three superclusters, whose main clusters are pictured in the accompanying photographs *(opposite)*. The dots on the map represent individual galaxies, which were charted out to distances of more than 500 million light-years. The supercluster chains seem to bound huge regions of emptiness.

110

Hercules Supercluster

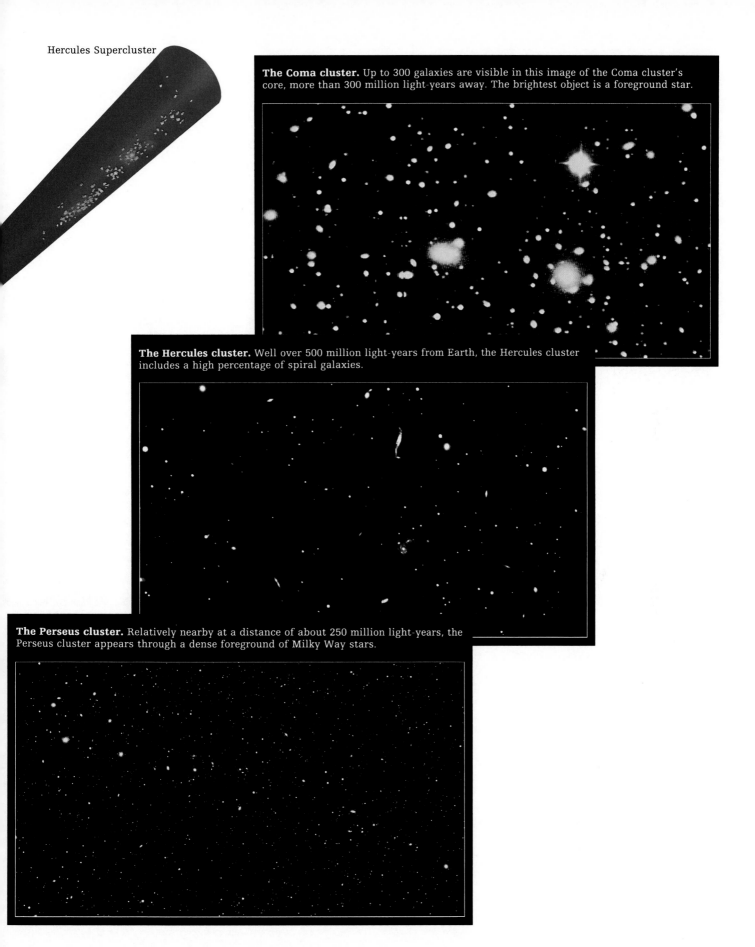

The Coma cluster. Up to 300 galaxies are visible in this image of the Coma cluster's core, more than 300 million light-years away. The brightest object is a foreground star.

The Hercules cluster. Well over 500 million light-years from Earth, the Hercules cluster includes a high percentage of spiral galaxies.

The Perseus cluster. Relatively nearby at a distance of about 250 million light-years, the Perseus cluster appears through a dense foreground of Milky Way stars.

Type E0. The giant galaxy M87 in Virgo represents one extreme in the elliptical class: Its outline barely deviates from a perfect circle, marred only by a jet of gas apparently ejected from the nucleus.

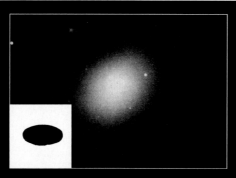

Type E3. One of the Virgo cluster's largest members, M86 is more oval in shape than M87. The steady increase in brightness from the outer edge toward the core suggests a uniform internal structure.

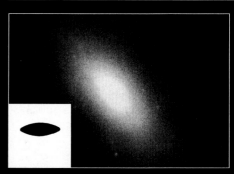

Type E6. One grade shy of the most elongated type of elliptical, NGC 3377—part of a large group of galaxies in Leo—consists of a small core surrounded by a diffuse, almost disklike region.

Type Sa. Spiral galaxy NGC 2811 exhibits the relatively large central bulge and tightly wound spiral arms of its type. Sa galaxies are composed mostly of old stars and create new ones only fitfully.

Type Sb. Well-defined, more open arms that wrap around a smaller nucleus place NGC 4622 in the second category of ordinary spirals. The disk is composed primarily of young and newborn stars.

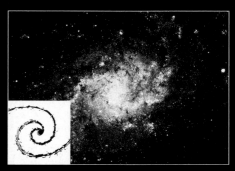

Type Sc. Known as the Pinwheel galaxy, M33 has very widely splayed, indistinct arms that emanate from a small nucleus. It is one of the nearest galaxies to Earth, only 2.4 million light-years distant.

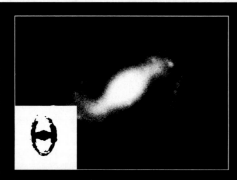

Type SBa. The barred spiral NGC 175 has a clearly delineated bar extending beyond a well-defined central bulge and ending in two distinct spiral arms.

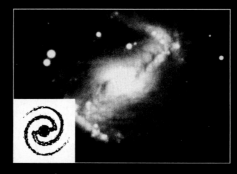

Type SBb. A somewhat degraded version of the barred spiral, NGC 5383 has a less pronounced central region that tapers off into more diffuse arms.

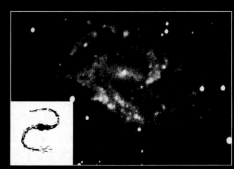

Type SBc. Spidery and indistinct, NGC 2525 exhibits only the faintest suggestion of a narrow bar running through its tiny core and connecting its sinuous arms.

Galaxy Type	Mass (Solar Masses)	Diameter (10^3 Light-Years)	Absolute Magnitude	Age of Star Population	Spectral Type	Interstellar Matter
Spiral	10^9 to 10^{12}	20 to 300 or more	-15 to -22.5	Old and Young	A to K	Gas and Dust
Elliptical	10^6 to 10^{13}	2 to 500 (approx.)	-9 to -23	Old	G to K	Little Gas and Dust
Irregular	10^8 to 10^{11}	5 to 30	-13 to -20	Old and Young	A to F	Much Gas, Some with Dust and Some without Dust

TYPECASTING THE GALAXIES

Galaxies are a diverse breed, but most fall into a few clear categories based on their shape. The examples on these two pages illustrate the major classes and subclasses according to a scheme published by Edwin Hubble in 1936.

The broadest distinction is between regular and irregular galaxies: those with a well-defined structure and those that look like random splashes of stars. The regular galaxies subdivide into the bloblike ellipticals and the more intricate spirals, which are either ordinary (with an almost spherical nucleus) or barred (with an elongated central region). A scale of values—a, b, c, and d for spirals and 0 to 7 for ellipticals—indicates variations in such factors as an elliptical's roundness.

Hubble correctly hypothesized a third class of regulars—lenticular, or lens-shaped, galaxies—that share features of the first two groups. Altogether, his categories still encompass most known galaxies.

Lenticular galaxy. Combining the rounded, armless shape of an elliptical with the bulge-and-disk structure of a spiral, NGC 5102 is a prime example of a lenticular galaxy. Once considered an evolutionary stage between the two larger groups, lenticulars are now thought to be separate in origin.

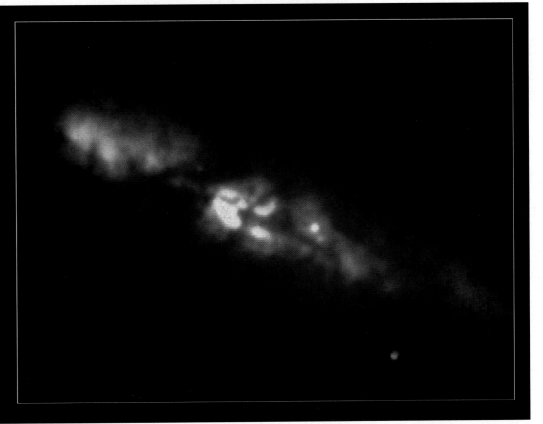

Irregular galaxy. Because it has no clear symmetric structure or rotational pattern, M82 qualifies as one of the small group of irregular galaxies—about five percent of all star systems. It belongs to a certain class of irregulars with highly chaotic distributions of stars, dust, and gas. The evidence seems to indicate that M82 has been disturbed and deformed by a strong gravitational interaction with its large spiral neighbor M81.

Samples from the Menagerie

Hubble's venerable classification system, while encompassing a vast majority of galaxies, leaves out several identifiable types. Some, such as the dwarf galaxy at bottom, have stretched the limits of existing categories. Others offer valuable insights into the origin and evolution of all galaxies.

Perhaps the most compelling of these objects, the protogalaxies *(below),* are also among the most far removed and hardest to detect. Close to the very edge of the observable universe, these vast, dense clouds of hydrogen show signs of having collapsed just enough to commence star formation.

Because they are so distant and their light has taken since nearly the beginning of the universe to reach Earth, they provide a first-hand look at the era when galaxies were starting to come to life.

As for what has happened to galaxies since then, certain examples of so-called peculiar galaxies *(opposite)* help fill in the picture. Sophisticated computer manipulation of data on such galaxies has led to the conclusion that many of the most bizarre galactic structures result from gravitational interactions between pairs of systems that pass near each other or actually collide.

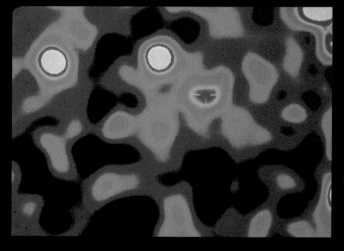

A galaxy aborning? This computerized infrared image reveals the location of a potential protogalaxy *(cross hairs)* more than 15 billion light-years from Earth. False colors from dark blue to light blue, green, yellow, red, and white indicate increasingly strong infrared signals. The intensity of the radiation at the source in question suggests that it may be a huge contracting cloud of hydrogen just beginning to shine with newborn stars. The two white spots are foreground stars that are only slightly brighter although very much closer.

Miniature ellipticals. A member of the Local Group, the dwarf galaxy Fornax harbors about 20 million stars—a tiny percentage of the scores of billions in larger systems. Classified as ellipticals because of their shape, dwarfs bear a striking resemblance to objects not considered galaxies at all: globular clusters, spherical bundles of stars that orbit at the outer limits of many galaxies, including the Milky Way. Dwarfs qualify as full-fledged galaxies in part because they seem to have formed at about the same time as other galaxies; globular clusters developed later on.

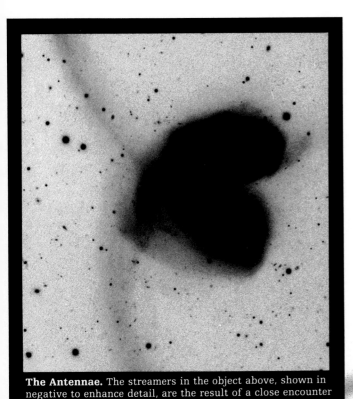

A tale of interaction. The three illustrations at left are based on a computer simulation of a close encounter between two equal-size galaxies. To reduce the variables, the galaxies are represented as simple disks rather than complex spirals. At top, the galaxies start to approach each other; rotating in opposite directions, they begin to orbit their common center of mass *(arrows)*. After 300 million years *(middle)*, the galaxies have pulled bridges of stars from their partner's near edge and left stellar streamers trailing behind. About 400 million years later *(bottom)*, both disks are significantly diminished, and some stars in the tails have gained enough velocity to escape their galaxies altogether.

The Antennae. The streamers in the object above, shown in negative to enhance detail, are the result of a close encounter between two galaxies (simulated at right) that began hundreds of millions of years ago.

When galaxies meet. In this five-step portrayal of a simulation, two disklike galaxies rotating in opposite directions head toward each other from an initial separation of about two galactic diameters *(top)*. Some 600 million years later, they meet. Each galaxy's stars are so widely dispersed that stellar collisions are extremely rare, but both gravitational fields are profoundly affected. By step three, the galaxies have rebounded to less than one diameter apart, and their disks have become severely distorted: Most of their mass has collected in buttonlike shapes toward the middle, while the disks fan out in the opposite direction. In the last two steps, the galaxies collide and then separate again—but not nearly as far—and their stars begin to mix. The process will continue until the two systems have completely merged.

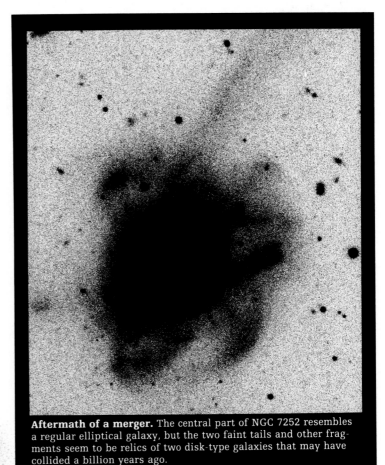

Aftermath of a merger. The central part of NGC 7252 resembles a regular elliptical galaxy, but the two faint tails and other fragments seem to be relics of two disk-type galaxies that may have collided a billion years ago.

MYSTERIOUS COSMIC POWERHOUSES

Despite clear dissimilarities, several types of galaxies are classified together because of one shared characteristic: They are all churning out huge amounts of energy from their cores. Some of these so-called active galaxies have very bright, compact nuclei that may fluctuate wildly in luminosity; others are strong sources of radio waves or other forms of electromagnetic radiation that testify to some sort of violent activity.

Precisely what causes that activity is still unknown, but in most cases the leading culprit is a supermassive black hole, a hypothetical object of unimaginable density that squeezes many millions of solar masses into a dimensionless point. So gravitationally powerful that not even light can escape it, a black hole at the heart of a galaxy would continually suck in interstellar material, heating it and subjecting it to extreme pressure, thereby causing it to radiate intensely before being swallowed forever.

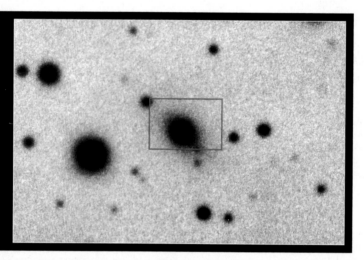

A galaxy's flickering heart. The original example of a class of objects that now bear its name, BL Lacertae *(box)* was mistakenly identified as a variable star when it was first discovered in 1929. The spectral characteristics of its fuzzy periphery, however, closely resemble those of elliptical galaxies, leading to the conclusion that it is indeed an elliptical, dominated by a very luminous nucleus. Scientists are not sure what causes the periodic fluctuations in its brightness.

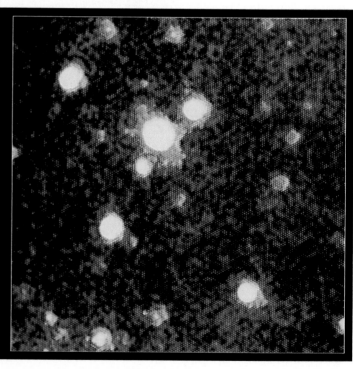

A beacon from deep space. The brightest object near the center of this false-color image is a quasar, the first to be found at the heart of a galaxy cluster. Quasars, or quasistellar radio sources, are so named because their light seems to come from a single point and because the initial ones to be detected radiate intensely at radio wavelengths. Quasars are tremendously remote; the one shown here is measured at seven billion light-years. Given that distance, they are the most intrinsically luminous objects in the universe, hundreds of times brighter than whole galaxies. Astronomers believe they may in fact be the nuclei of young galaxies, and that their exceptional energies result from supermassive black holes.

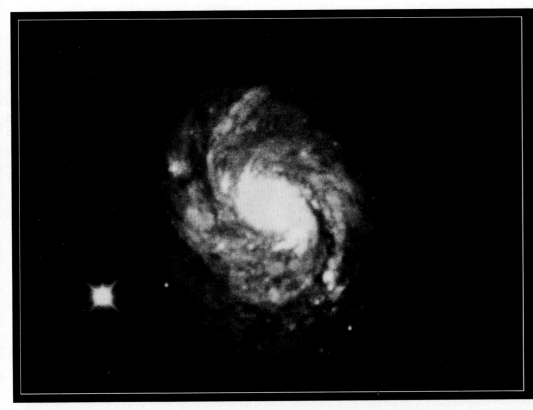

Brilliance at the core. This spiral system with a blazing, almost star-like nucleus belongs to a class of galaxies known as Seyferts, after their discoverer, American astronomer Carl Seyfert, who spotted the first one in 1943. Spectral analysis indicates that the central regions of Seyferts contain extremely hot, turbulent gas whipping around at thousands of miles per second—a sign of some kind of gravitational behemoth at their cores. Like the BL Lacertae objects, they vary in luminosity, typically over the course of a few months.

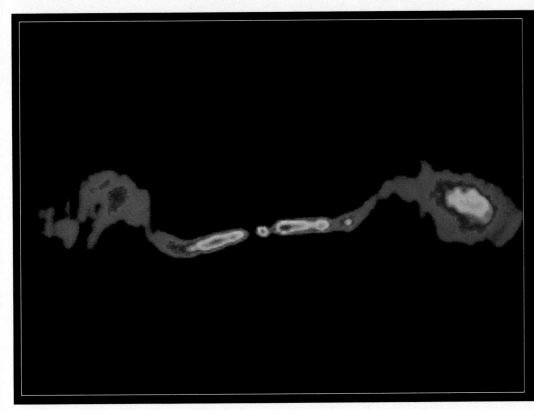

Radio jets and lobes. This false-color image of radio emissions from the elliptical galaxy 3C449 reveals a surprising feature invisible in optical photographs: twin clouds of plasma—superheated gas whose atoms have been stripped of electrons—connected by thin streamers to the galactic nucleus. The intensity of the signals from the thin regions *(yellow and red)* indicates that they are jets of gas ejected from the nucleus at near light-speed. Theorists speculate that the jets emanate from the two ends of a black hole's spin axis, where a certain amount of infalling material is channeled by powerful magnetic fields and shot back out into space. Disrupted by intergalactic dust and gas, the jets spread out to form lobes.

STRUCTURE AT THE LARGEST SCALE

To one particular class of astronomers, whose focus is the universe as a whole, the architecture of individual galaxies is essentially irrelevant. Even clusters and superclusters hold but a passing interest. For cosmologists, as these scientists are known, the structures of central significance are the largest ones of all—those that emerge only in the most wide-ranging, far-reaching surveys, showing great masses of galaxies in clumps and chains bordering regions equally impressive for their emptiness. By uncovering such patterns, students of nature's grandest design hope to learn more about the forces that created the universe and caused it to evolve as it has.

But the task has never been an easy one. When the first large-scale assemblies such as the Local Group and the Local Superclus-

ter *(pages 106-109)* were being detected, charting the crucial third dimension of distance was a painstaking process that required hours or days of telescope time for each galaxy, simply to collect enough light to gauge the object's redshift and thus its recessional velocity, the key indicator of how far away it might be. Many catalogers have opted for faster two-dimensional maps, such as the one below, claiming that patterns are nonetheless visible.

More recently, the use of extremely sensitive electronic light detectors has greatly speeded up distance measurements and made possible increasingly extensive three-dimensional surveys. By taking depth into account, maps such as the one shown at right give a truer, if no less perplexing, picture of cosmic structure.

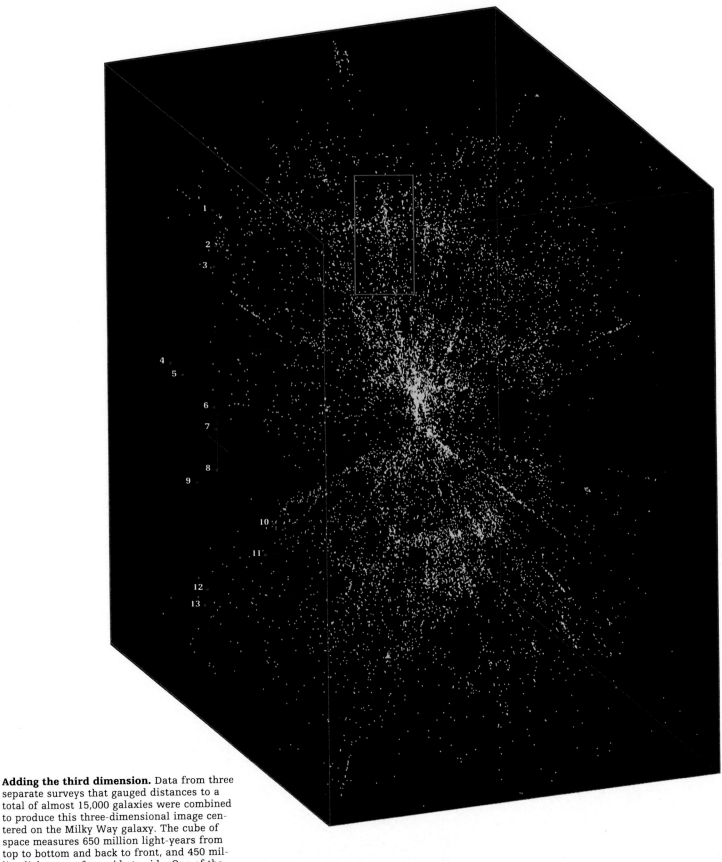

Adding the third dimension. Data from three separate surveys that gauged distances to a total of almost 15,000 galaxies were combined to produce this three-dimensional image centered on the Milky Way galaxy. The cube of space measures 650 million light-years from top to bottom and back to front, and 450 million light-years from side to side. One of the largest of the structures, toward the top of the cube *(red box)*, includes the Coma cluster *(2)*. Blank areas that lie to the left and right of center could not be completely surveyed because dust in the galactic plane obscures the view from Earth.

(1) Great Wall. **(2)** Coma cluster. **(3)** Center for Astrophysics void. **(4)** Great Attractor. **(5)** Centaurus cluster. **(6)** Virgo cluster. **(7)** Coma-Sculptor cloud. **(8)** Fornax cluster. **(9)** Pavo-Indus-Telescopium cloud. **(10)** Perseus cluster. **(11)** Pisces cluster. **(12)** A wall in the southern sky. **(13)** A void in the southern sky.

A wedge of space. The illustration above represents a single slice from Margaret Geller and John Huchra's galaxy survey in a celestial sphere centered on the Milky Way. Each wedge, its apex at an observatory in Arizona, is almost 120 degrees wide and 6 degrees thick, and it extends to 450 million light-years from Earth. This particular slice shows a vaguely human-shaped structure that includes the Coma cluster seen on page 119.

SURVEYING BY THE SLICE

Among the most intriguing galactic surveys is one being conducted by astronomers Margaret Geller and John Huchra of the Harvard-Smithsonian Center for Astrophysics. Focusing only on that half of the celestial sphere visible from their observing post in southern Arizona, the two began in 1985 by plotting the distances and locations of galaxies within a single fan-shaped wedge of space *(opposite)*. By adding selected slices over time, they have created a stunning portrait of galaxy distribution.

Because the data exist in a computer, they can be manipulated and presented graphically to show the view from all sorts of angles *(below)*, revealing how patterns in adjacent slices fit together. By this means, in 1989 Geller and Huchra discovered the largest coherent structure ever seen—a gigantic sheet of galaxies that they dubbed the Great Wall *(bottom)*. Their survey did not even encompass all of it. The find only added to the mystery of cosmic architecture. Gravity, which might account for the creation of smaller patterns, could not have fashioned anything so mammoth.

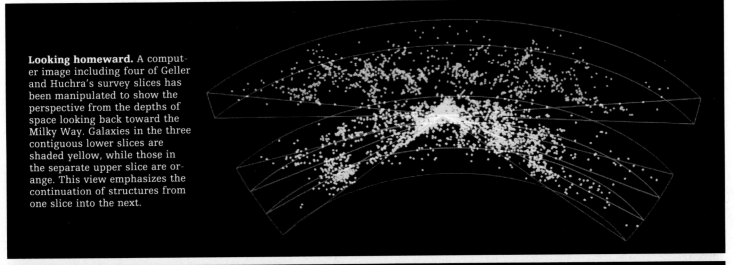

Looking homeward. A computer image including four of Geller and Huchra's survey slices has been manipulated to show the perspective from the depths of space looking back toward the Milky Way. Galaxies in the three contiguous lower slices are shaded yellow, while those in the separate upper slice are orange. This view emphasizes the continuation of structures from one slice into the next.

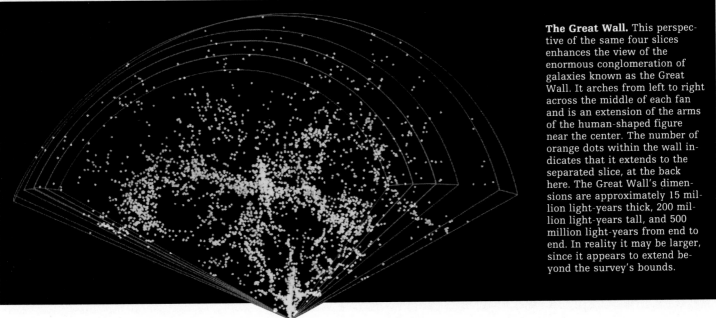

The Great Wall. This perspective of the same four slices enhances the view of the enormous conglomeration of galaxies known as the Great Wall. It arches from left to right across the middle of each fan and is an extension of the arms of the human-shaped figure near the center. The number of orange dots within the wall indicates that it extends to the separated slice, at the back here. The Great Wall's dimensions are approximately 15 million light-years thick, 200 million light-years tall, and 500 million light-years from end to end. In reality it may be larger, since it appears to extend beyond the survey's bounds.

LESSONS FROM THE BIG BANG

Creation's smooth glow. Leftover radiation from the Big Bang fills all of space in this map of microwave emissions detected by the Cosmic Background Explorer (COBE) satellite early in 1990. Cooled to a uniform 2.7 degrees above absolute zero by billions of years of travel through the cosmos, the radiation is remarkably even, as indicated by the broad purple region that covers most of the image; the pink and blue areas at upper right and lower left are distortions in the recorded signals caused by the Milky Way's motion against the pervasive background. But COBE did not reveal slight irregularities in the initial flood of energy that would explain why matter has clumped into the enormous structures visible today.

Edwin Hubble's discovery that space is expanding, carrying galaxies away from one another at a rate proportional to their distance, did far more than provide a convenient yardstick for measuring the remoteness of celestial objects. To begin with, it implied that all matter and energy had once been contained in an infinitely dense singularity but had somehow exploded into existence some 15 to 20 billion years ago in a cataclysmic event now known as the Big Bang. In 1965, radio astronomers Arno Penzias and Robert Wilson offered confirmation of the theory when they detected cool radiation pervading all of space—apparently the leftover glow from the Big Bang.

Precisely what the Big Bang was like, how it influenced the subsequent evolution of the universe, and what it portends for the future are among the most difficult questions facing today's cosmologists. Recognizing that the deeper one looks in space,

the farther back one is looking in time, some investigators hope eventually to be able to chart stages of cosmic evolution back to when the glow of the Big Bang first began to permeate space. Other studies focus only on the background radiation itself, trying to detect irregularities that could have led to the clumpiness of the present universe.

As for the fate of the cosmos, the crucial determinant is how much matter the universe contains and how fast it is expanding, a factor known as the critical density. If the universe holds more than the equivalent of about three hydrogen atoms per cubic meter, it has enough mass—and, thus, enough gravity—to overcome the expansion; the cosmos will ultimately collapse in on itself. Below the critical density, expansion will continue forever. Some estimates suggest that eternal expansion lies in store, but other theorists believe enough undetected matter exists to balance the scales.

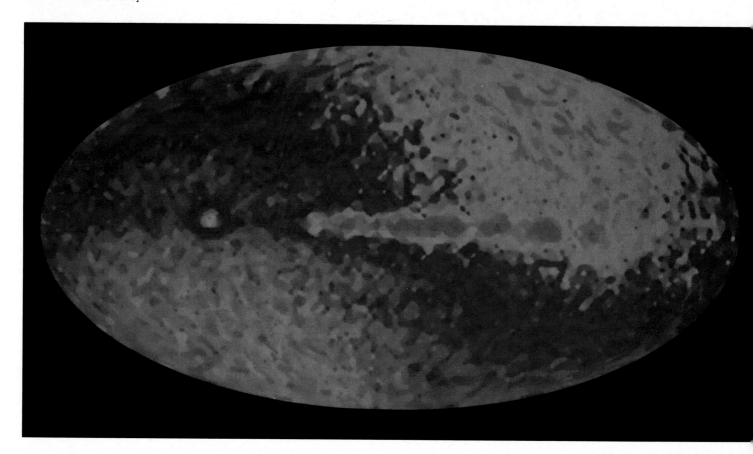

Perspective on the past. Because light has a finite speed, the farther away a celestial object is, the longer its light has taken to reach Earth. As the schematic drawing at right illustrates, cosmic history thus unfolds in reverse as astronomers look ever deeper into space. The stars of the Milky Way *(bottom)* and nearby galaxies, whose light has been traveling for a few million years at most by the time it reaches Earth, represent the universe as it is today. Earlier stages in galactic evolution include quasars, presumably the brightly burning hearts of young galaxies, and the even more remote protogalaxies, fragments of vast clouds of primordial gases. Prior to protogalaxy formation, matter existed primarily as individual atoms of hydrogen and helium. The earliest detectable radiation is the cosmic microwave background, the afterglow of the Big Bang itself, whose light had previously been blocked by a dense fog of ionized hydrogen and helium—scattered atomic nuclei and unbound electrons that were too highly energized to come together and form stable atoms.

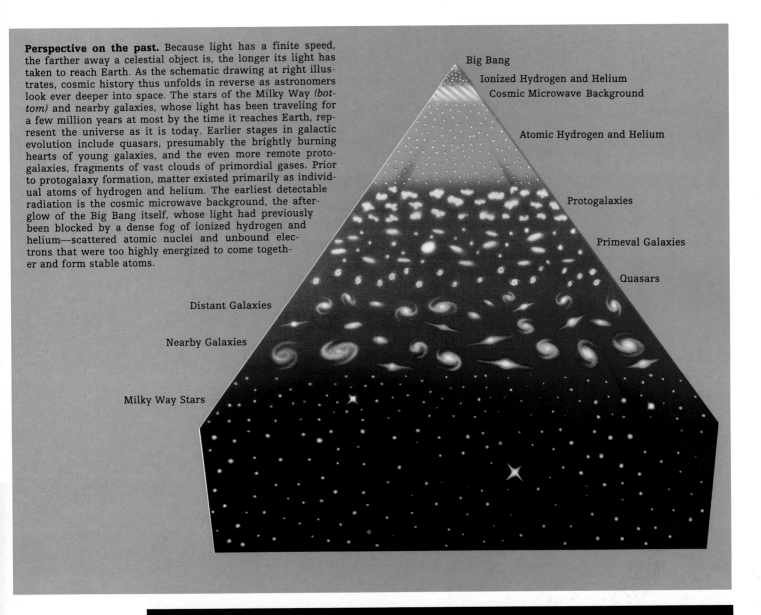

Big Bang

Ionized Hydrogen and Helium

Cosmic Microwave Background

Atomic Hydrogen and Helium

Protogalaxies

Primeval Galaxies

Quasars

Distant Galaxies

Nearby Galaxies

Milky Way Stars

The universe's three fates. One of the most significant questions in all of cosmology is, What will become of the universe? Theorists acknowledge three possibilities, depicted in the diagram at right. Each red line represents the history of the universe, with time plotted horizontally and the size of the universe vertically. Each fate depends on the relationship between the universe's actual mass density and its critical density—the amount of matter necessary to generate enough gravitational pull to precisely balance the outward force of expansion. If the actual density is lower than the critical density, gravity will be too weak and the expansion will go on forever *(top line)*. If the two are equal, expansion will continue but at a slower and slower rate, approaching zero velocity *(middle line)*. And if the universe is denser than the critical value, it will eventually stop growing as gravity overwhelms expansion, and then collapse back in on itself *(bottom line)*. Scientists do not yet know the universe's true density and cannot tell enough from its rate of expansion at present *(yellow bar)* to determine which of the three paths the actual cosmos is following.

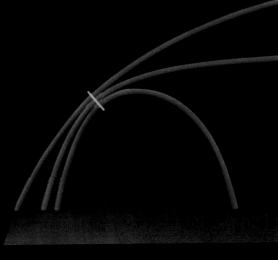

A GALAXY HUNTER'S GUIDE

The vast majority of the billions of galaxies in the universe are so far away and so faint that they are invisible to all but the most powerful telescopes. But a few thousand galactic objects are near enough or bright enough to be spotted with relatively inexpensive equipment.

The trick to observing these systems is knowing precisely where to look. As in the case of planets and stars, the familiar patterns of the constellations offer the readiest guideposts. Once an object has been located, seeing it clearly can still be somewhat difficult; galaxies will appear as indistinct, cloudy patches of light. Experienced sky watchers use a technique called averted vision to get the best view: By not staring directly at an object, but looking slightly to one side, they use the more sensitive light receptor cells of their peripheral vision, which makes the object appear brighter.

The illustrations on these pages indicate where to find a few of the most prominent galaxies and quasars. Only the brightest stars in each constellation are shown here; on clear nights, many more will be visible.

Target constellations. The Sun-centered celestial sphere at right shows Earth's position for each of the four seasons in relation to those constellations where galaxies and quasars can be found. Because of its location near the north celestial pole, Ursa Major—home to three prominent galaxies—is visible from the Northern Hemisphere throughout the year. But Andromeda and Virgo, which lie much closer to the ecliptic plane *(yellow band),* appear only during certain seasons, Andromeda in autumn and winter, and Virgo in spring and summer.

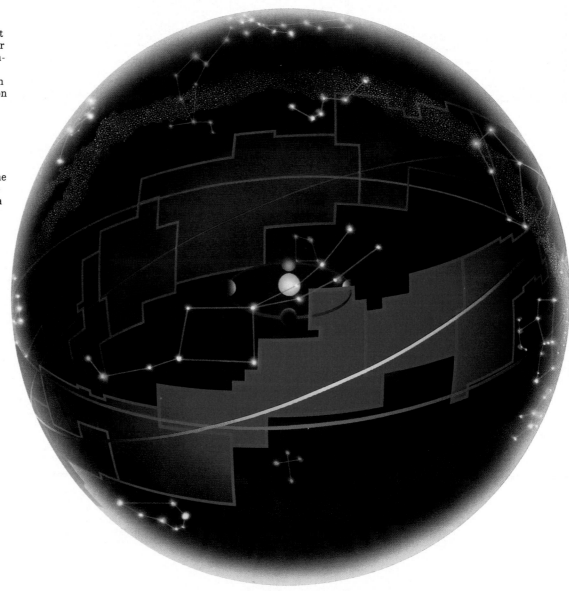

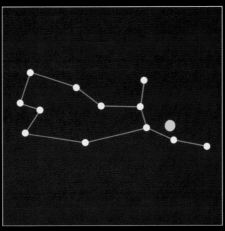

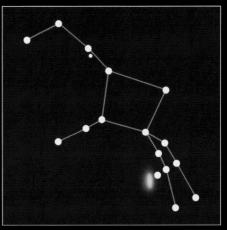

The Big Dipper's three neighbors. Directly below the star at the end of the Big Dipper's handle is M51, a spiral galaxy also known as the Whirlpool. Best viewed in spring and early summer, when the Big Dipper is high overhead in the Northern Hemisphere, the Whirlpool is extremely faint and may be hard to spot under less-than-perfect conditions. The dot above and to the right of the Dipper's bowl represents two galaxies, M81 and M82, both visible within the same field of view of most small telescopes. The best way to find them is to follow an imaginary line running from the lower left to the upper right of the bowl.

A quasar in Virgo. Best seen in the Northern Hemisphere looking toward the south during spring and early summer, the constellation Virgo is home to the first quasar ever detected, designated 3C273 *(unconnected dot)*. Analyzing its spectrum in 1963, Dutch astronomer Maarten Schmidt discovered that its light was redshifted by 16 percent, equivalent to a distance of almost three billion light-years, which made it the most distant object in the heavens at the time. The brightest quasar in the sky, 3C273 looks very much like a dim blue star through a telescope.

Finding Andromeda. Shown above as it appears to observers in the Northern Hemisphere looking north in the autumn or winter, the constellation Andromeda extends from the lower right star of the square of Pegasus. The galaxy Andromeda lies north of the constellation's two middle stars and is most easily located by focusing on a fourth-magnitude star just to its right. Even when stargazing conditions are not particularly good, the galaxy's bright nucleus is readily apparent through binoculars or a small telescope; on clear, dark nights, the wispy oval of its surrounding disk also stands out.

The southern sky. The map at left outlines the major constellations of the Southern Hemisphere within a radius of forty degrees from the south celestial pole and indicates the locations of the Milky Way's two closest neighbors, the Large and Small Magellanic Clouds. Because they extend over relatively large areas, they are actually best seen with binoculars or a low-power telescope, which have wide fields of view. The Large Cloud covers eleven degrees of the sky and stretches from the constellation Dorado into Mensa. The Small Cloud is about twenty-two degrees to the west in Tucana and measures four degrees across. The galaxies are visible year-round for observers in southern Australia and South Africa and are best seen in winter, when they are highest above the horizon.

125

A TELESCOPE PRIMER

The first telescopic eye on the cosmos, a tiny spyglass crafted by the great Italian scientist Galileo Galilei in 1609, consisted of a convex lens and a concave eyepiece at opposite ends of a tube. Today, sky watchers can choose from a range of viewing instruments that are all vastly more capable than Galileo's pioneering device.

Direct descendants of his design are called refractor telescopes. As explained below, they work by bending light with glass lenses of various shapes. The early refractors produced fuzzy images with rainbow halos, a problem known as chromatic aberration, caused by unequal bending of different light wavelengths. In the mid-eighteenth century, telescope makers discovered that lenses made of different types of glass and formed of both convex and concave parts would cancel out the differential bending and eliminate the halos. Meanwhile, Isaac Newton had taken a completely new tack: In 1668, he produced the first workable reflecting telescope, which used a curved mirror to focus light, and thus dodged chromatic difficulties. In the 1930s, these two lines of development came together in the so-called catadioptric telescope, a hybrid that uses both mirrors and lenses.

All three types have their pros and cons. The refractor is rugged and good for observing planetary detail, but comparatively bulky and expensive. The reflector is cheaper and better for deep-sky viewing but may need more maintenance. The catadioptric occupies the middle ground in price and has a size advantage: It is significantly more compact than the others.

A refracting telescope. Refraction is the bending of light as it enters a medium of different density—in the case of a telescope *(below, left)*, passing from air to higher-density glass and back to air. The light passes through a so-called objective lens at the large front end of the scope, which brings it to a focus near the opposite end, forming an image that is magnified by the eyepiece. (The result of this path is an inverted image.) The objective lens and the eyepiece are each typically a combination of convex and concave lenses, which bend light in opposite ways *(bottom)*, thereby canceling out chromatic aberration.

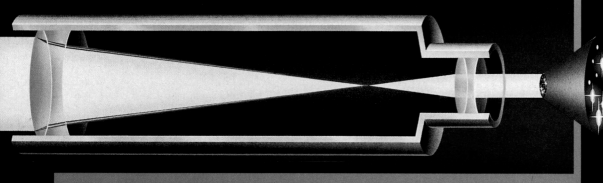

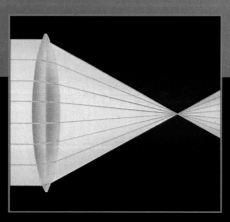

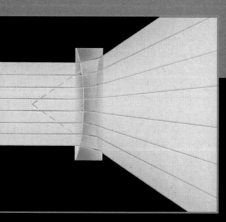

The art of light-bending. The angle of the encounter between the lens and incoming light rays (depicted here as arriving perpendicular to the lens) determines the degree of bending. In a lens that is convex on both its front and back sides *(far left)*, light bends more at the thinner edges than at the center, bringing incoming light rays to a common focus. A concave lens—thinner in the center than at the edges—causes incoming parallel rays to diverge. The observer sees the light as originating from a so-called virtual focus *(dotted lines)*.

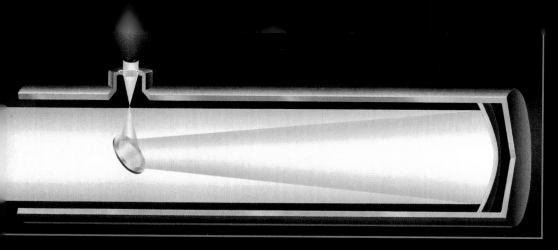

A reflecting telescope. A New-tonian reflecting scope, the type devised by Isaac Newton, col-lects and focuses light with a parabolic concave mirror. This primary mirror reflects the light back up the tube to a small flat mirror *(far left)*, which deflects the converging rays sideways before they come to a focus. An eyepiece set in the side of the tube magnifies the image.

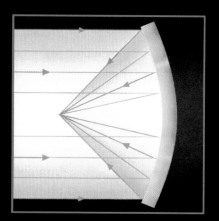

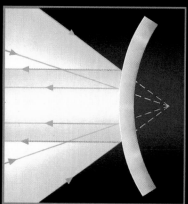

Modes of reflection. The con-cave primary mirror brings in-coming parallel rays to a com-mon focus *(far left)*. Some reflecting telescopes—known as the Cassegrain type, after their inventor—use a convex second-ary mirror *(left)* to intercept light from the primary and di-rect it back through a hole in the primary mirror's center and on to an eyepiece. This folding of the light-path reduces the size of the telescope.

A catadioptric telescope. Especially popular among amateur astronomers, the catadioptric design typically uses a primary mirror with a spherical concave surface, which is much eas-ier to make than the parabolic concave mirror used in Newtonian telescopes. But because such a mirror is prey to a focusing problem called spherical aberration, a thin correcting lens is positioned over the front edge of the telescope tube to eliminate the distortion. Just behind this lens is a small, convex secondary mirror that redirects the light from the prima-ry mirror back to the eyepiece. The design pic-tured here, called a Schmidt-Cassegrain, is less than half the length of an equivalent Newtonian reflector.

The most important factor in a telescope's performance is its aperture—the size of its objective lens or primary mirror. The larger the aperture, the more light is collected and therefore the greater the scope's ability to snare faint objects. A scope with a two-inch aperture, for example, can pick out stars as faint as about magnitude 11 (invisible to the naked eye), whereas a four-inch telescope can see stars to about magnitude 12.5, or four times fainter *(pages 82-83)*. Also, the larger the aperture, the greater the resolution of the image, meaning that more details can be distinguished.

Another performance key is focal length—the distance from the objective lens or primary mirror to the point where the image comes to focus. Focal length is often expressed indirectly by dividing the focal length by the aperture, yielding the so-called f-number, often stamped on a telescope. The longer the focal length (or higher the f-number for any given aperture), the larger the image.

Finally, magnification, or power, is the ratio of the scope's focal length to that of the eyepiece. The higher the power, the smaller the field of view *(opposite)*. Power can be changed for different viewing purposes by changing the eyepiece.

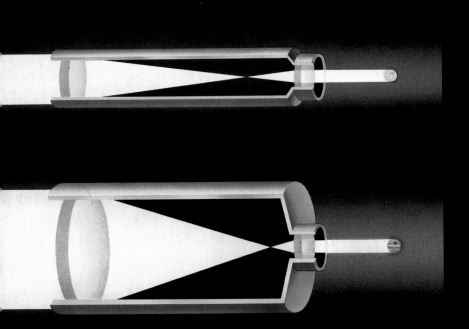

Aperture and focal length. In the diagrams at left and below, the interplay of aperture and focal length is illustrated with three refractor telescopes; the principles hold true for reflectors as well. The top telescope has a relatively small aperture and short focal length, producing an image of Jupiter that is neither very sharp nor bright. The middle telescope has the same focal length but an aperture with twice the diameter; as a result, it yields an image that is much sharper and four times as bright. The bottom telescope has the same aperture as the middle scope but twice the focal length. Because it collects the same amount of light but spreads it over four times the image area, the image has only a quarter the surface brightness—but higher magnification is easier. The two larger-aperture scopes both have virtues. The one with the shorter focal length is less awkward to use and would be especially good for viewing large but dim deep-sky objects, such as galaxies or nebulae. The bottom telescope would be well-suited for viewing the planets, which are small and need high magnification.

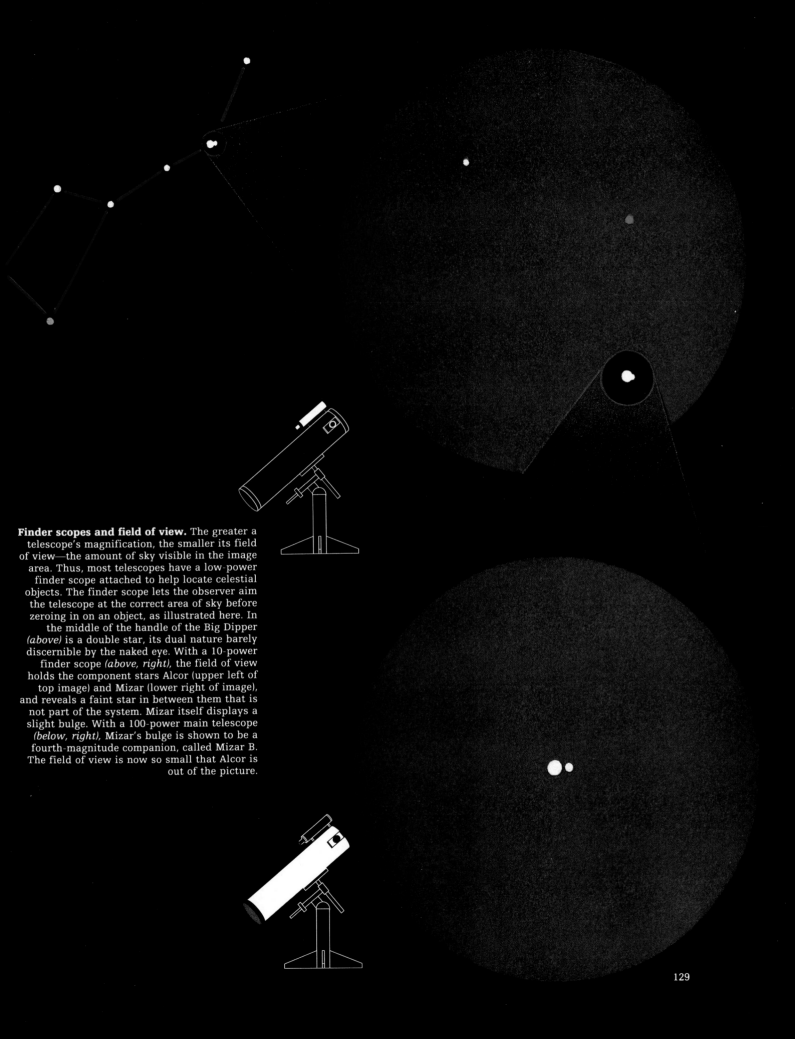

Finder scopes and field of view. The greater a telescope's magnification, the smaller its field of view—the amount of sky visible in the image area. Thus, most telescopes have a low-power finder scope attached to help locate celestial objects. The finder scope lets the observer aim the telescope at the correct area of sky before zeroing in on an object, as illustrated here. In the middle of the handle of the Big Dipper *(above)* is a double star, its dual nature barely discernible by the naked eye. With a 10-power finder scope *(above, right)*, the field of view holds the component stars Alcor (upper left of top image) and Mizar (lower right of image), and reveals a faint star in between them that is not part of the system. Mizar itself displays a slight bulge. With a 100-power main telescope *(below, right)*, Mizar's bulge is shown to be a fourth-magnitude companion, called Mizar B. The field of view is now so small that Alcor is out of the picture.

A Choice of Mounts

Telescopes need sturdy mounts for two reasons: to stabilize the instrument so that the image doesn't jiggle, and to allow the telescope to follow the apparent movement of celestial objects as Earth turns. The so-called altazimuth mount is adjustable on two axes, one for the vertical movement of an object as it rises and sets (its altitude), the other for the object's horizontal movement (its azimuth). To follow an object's path in the course of an evening, the telescope is manually adjusted on both axes.

A simpler, but more expensive, approach is taken by the equatorial mount. One of its two axes is aligned with the north celestial pole, parallel to Earth's own axis of rotation. Rotating the telescope around this axis shifts the telescope east and west. The second, or declination, axis is set at the desired object's declination, determined by the object's position above or below the celestial equator *(pages 92-93)*. Once the object is in view, the declination axis is fixed in position, and the telescope has only to be rotated steadily around its polar axis to keep the object in sight. Most equatorial mounts come with an electric drive that automates the rotation around the polar axis.

An altazimuth mount. Two perpendicular axes of rotation allow the telescope to be moved vertically *(purple arrow)* and horizontally *(green arrow)*. To keep a star or other celestial object in view as Earth turns, adjustments must be made once or twice a minute.

An equatorial mount. In this type of mount, the telescope's vertical, or polar, axis is pointed at the north celestial pole, near Polaris, aligning the telescope with Earth's axis of rotation. Swinging the telescope around this axis *(blue arrow)* moves it toward celestial east or west. Movement around the other axis shifts the telescope toward celestial north or south. Because sky objects trace an arc from east to west during the night, the telescope will follow them unerringly by steadily turning on its polar axis. No motion is required on the other axis because an object's north-south position (its declination) does not change.

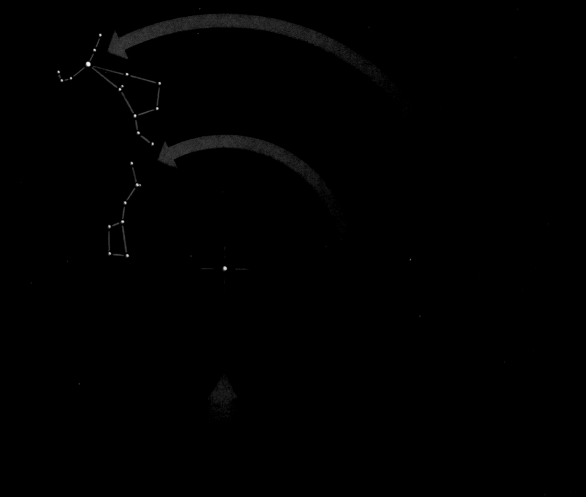

Tracking the stars. An observer looking north during July in the Northern Hemisphere could see the constellations Boötes and the Big Dipper circle from east to west in the course of the evening. To track their arcing path, a telescope must be able to compensate for the combination of vertical and horizontal movement.

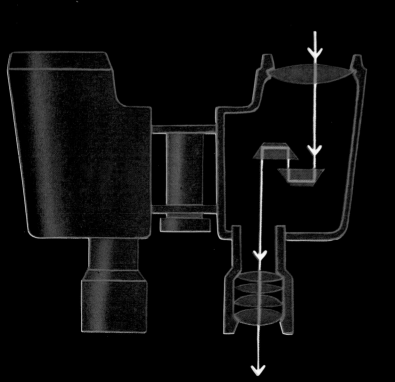

A role for binoculars. A good pair of binoculars is much less expensive than a good telescope, and because they are easy to use with star maps and reference books, they are ideal for introducing an observer to serious stargazing. In essence, binoculars consist of two refractor telescopes that have been joined together and given the added feature of internal prisms that fold the light-path both to save size and to turn the image right side up. Magnification and aperture size are usually inscribed on the instrument. For example, 8x30 binoculars have a magnification of 8 power and an aperture of 30 millimeters. Large-aperture binoculars are best for celestial viewing, but high magnification is less of an asset both because it narrows the field of view and because it exaggerates motion, requiring a tripod for stability.

Venus and the Moon. In the sky above Tulsa, Oklahoma, the waxing crescent Moon glides past the bright disk of Venus just before setting. The event was recorded in a series of four-second exposures taken every ten minutes for about three and a half hours.

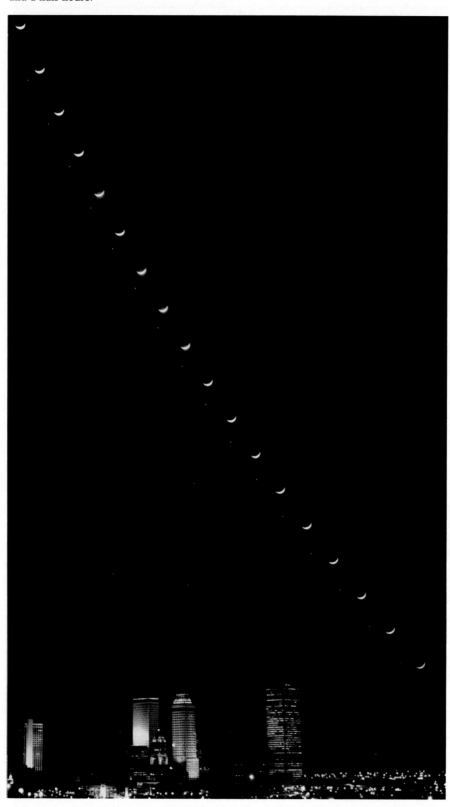

SKY WATCHERS' GALLERY

The beauty of the Solar System and many of the celestial objects beyond its bounds is visible to the naked eye or through a small telescope. Armed with a star map, an elementary knowledge of celestial motion, and patience, an amateur can easily observe all the planets except Pluto as they traverse the zodiac, and witness the rising and setting of the stellar groupings whose fixed patterns have served as navigation guides for many generations of earthly travelers.

With the addition of a standard 35-millimeter camera, some fast film, and a few other pieces of simple equipment, a backyard astronomer can also record the celestial pageant on film, a practice known as astrophotography. The images shown here, for example, represent a range of possibilities, from relatively close-to-home alignments of planets and moons to the distant glory that is the heart of the Milky Way.

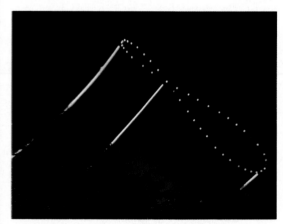

Analemma. The Sun's path, photographed from Watertown, Massachusetts, at the same time on forty-five mornings over the course of a year, reveals the tilt of Earth's axis by tracing a figure-eight shape known as the analemma. (If the axis were perpendicular to the plane of the ecliptic and Earth traveled in a circular orbit, all of the solar images would coincide.) The highest and lowest points mark the solstices, but because Earth's orbit around the Sun is elliptical rather than circular, the ascending and descending paths cross not at the equinoxes but in April and August. (The three streaks were made in June, August, and December by leaving the shutter open from sunrise to 8:30 a.m.)

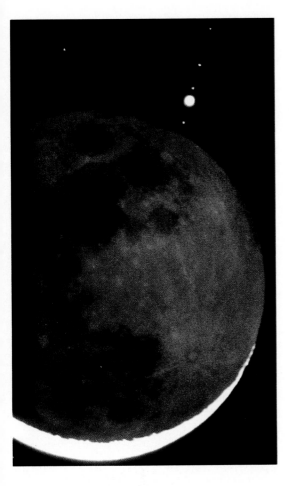

Jupiter and the Galileans. Photographed from Auberry, California, through a fourteen-inch Schmidt-Cassegrain telescope, Jupiter and its four largest satellites are emerging from behind a waning crescent Moon. In the lead is Callisto, followed by Ganymede, Io, Jupiter itself, and finally Europa.

Milky Way. The bright hub of the galaxy, best viewed from the Southern Hemisphere, where it passes overhead, is the centerpiece of this full-sky view of the Milky Way taken with a fisheye lens from the Australian Outback. To the right of a meteor streak above the galactic heart is a reddish region of ionized hydrogen. The ruddy North America nebula glows at top, while Jupiter shines in a patch of light at lower left.

Mars among the stars. In this image, shot during a recent late autumn from Los Angeles, the Red Planet *(far left)* passes near the Pleiades, a star cluster situated between the constellations Aries and Taurus in the zodiac. The photographer used a four-inch refracting telescope and exposed the film for thirty minutes.

BIBLIOGRAPHY

Books

Abell, George O., David Morrison, and Sidney C. Wolff. *Exploration of the Universe* (5th ed.). Philadelphia, Pa.: Saunders College Publishing, 1987.

Audouze, Jean, and Guy Israël (eds.). *The Cambridge Atlas of Astronomy*. Cambridge, England: Cambridge University Press, 1985.

Baker, Robert H. *Astronomy* (8th ed.). Princeton, N.J.: D. Van Nostrand, 1964.

Baugher, Joseph F. *The Space-Age Solar System*. New York: John Wiley & Sons, 1988.

Beatty, J. Kelly, and Andrew Chaikin (eds.). *The New Solar System* (3d ed.). Cambridge, England: Cambridge University Press, 1990.

Berry, Richard. *Discover the Stars*. New York: Harmony Books, 1987.

Briggs, Geoffrey, and Fredric Taylor. *The Cambridge Photographic Atlas of the Planets*. Cambridge, England: Cambridge University Press, 1986.

Brown, Bruce, and Lane Morgan. *The Miracle Planet*. New York: Gallery Books, 1990.

Burgess, Eric. *Uranus and Neptune: The Distant Giants*. New York: Columbia University Press, 1988.

Burnham, Robert, Jr. *Burnham's Celestial Handbook: An Observer's Guide to the Universe beyond the Solar System*. New York: Dover Publications, 1978.

Chapman, Robert D., and John C. Brandt. *The Comet Book: A Guide for the Return of Halley's Comet*. Boston, Mass.: Jones and Bartlett Publishers, 1984.

Chartrand, Mark R. *Skyguide: A Field Guide to the Heavens*. New York: Golden Press, 1990.

Consolmagno, Guy, and Dan M. Davis. *Turn Left at Orion: A Hundred Night Sky Objects to See in a Small Telescope—and How to Find Them*. Cambridge, England: Cambridge University Press, 1989.

Cosmic Mysteries (Voyage Through the Universe series). Alexandria, Va.: Time-Life Books, 1990.

Couper, Heather, and Nigel Henbest. *New Worlds: In Search of the Planets*. Reading, Mass.: Addison-Wesley, 1985.

Cunningham, Clifford J. *Introduction to Asteroids: The Next Frontier*. Richmond, Va.: Willmann-Bell, 1988.

Dickinson, Terence. *Night Watch: An Equinox Guide to Viewing the Universe*. Camden East, Ontario: Camden House, 1983.

Dodd, Robert T. *Thunderstones and Shooting Stars: The Meaning of Meteorites*. Cambridge, Mass.: Harvard University Press, 1986.

Ferris, Timothy. *Galaxies*. New York: Stewart, Tabori, & Chang Publishers, 1982.

Frazier, Kendrick. *Solar System* (Planet Earth series). Alexandria, Va.: Time-Life Books, 1985.

Frontiers of Time (Voyage Through the Universe series). Alexandria, Va.: Time-Life Books, 1990.

Galaxies (Voyage Through the Universe series). Alexandria, Va.: Time-Life Books, 1988.

Gibson, Edward G. *The Quiet Sun*. Washington, D.C.: National Aeronautics and Space Administration, 1973.

Greeley, Ronald. *Planetary Landscapes*. Boston, Mass.: Allen & Unwin, 1987.

Hamblin, W. Kenneth, and Eric H. Christiansen. *Exploring the Planets*. New York: Macmillan, 1990.

Harrington, Philip S. *Touring the Universe through Binoculars: A Complete Astronomer's Guidebook*. New York: John Wiley & Sons, 1990.

Hartmann, William K.:
Astronomy: The Cosmic Journey. Belmont, Calif.: Wadsworth, 1982.
Moons and Planets (2d ed.). Belmont, Calif.: Wadsworth, 1983.

Hawking, Stephen W. *A Brief History of Time: From the Big Bang to Black Holes*. New York: Bantam Books, 1988.

Hoffman, Mark S. (ed.). *The World Almanac and Book of Facts, 1990*. New York: Pharos Books, 1990.

Hunt, Garry, and Patrick Moore. *Atlas of Uranus*. Cambridge, England: Cambridge University Press, 1989.

Hunten, D. M., et al. (eds.). *Venus*. Tucson: The University of Arizona Press, 1983.

Jones, Barrie William. *The Solar System*. Oxford, England: Pergamon Press, 1984.

Karttunen, H., et al. (eds.). *Fundamental Astronomy*. Berlin: Springer-Verlag, 1987.

Kaufmann, William J., III:
Discovering the Universe. New York: W. H. Freeman, 1987.
Galaxies and Quasars. San Francisco: W. H. Freeman, 1979.
Universe. New York: W. H. Freeman, 1985.

Knight, David C. *The Moons of Our Solar System*. New York: William Morrow, 1980.

Littmann, Mark. *Planets Beyond: Discovering the Outer Solar System*. New York: John Wiley & Sons, 1990.

MacRobert, Alan. *Backyard Astronomy*. Cambridge, Mass.: Sky Publishing, 1990.

Maloney, Terry. *Telescopes: How to Choose and Use Them*. New York: Sterling, 1968.

Miczaika, G. R., and William M. Sinton. *Tools of the Astronomer*. Cambridge, Mass.: Harvard University Press, 1961.

Miles, Frank, and Nicholas Booth (eds.). *Race to Mars: The Mars Flight Atlas*. New York: Harper & Row Publishers, 1988.

Miller, Russell. *Continents in Collision* (Planet Earth series). Alexandria, Va.: Time-Life Books, 1983.

Mitton, Simon (ed.). *The Cambridge Encyclopaedia of Astronomy*. London: Jonathan Cape, 1977.

Moore, Patrick:
The Atlas of the Universe. London: Mitchell Beazley, 1970.
Exploring the Night Sky with Binoculars. Cambridge, England: Cambridge University Press, 1986.

Moore, Patrick (ed.). *The International Encyclopedia of Astronomy*. New York: Orion Books, 1987.

Moore, Patrick, et al. *The Atlas of the Solar System*. New York: Crescent Books, 1990.

Morrison, David. *Voyages to Saturn.* Washington, D.C.: National Aeronautics and Space Administration, 1982.

Morrison, David, and Tobias Owen. *The Planetary System.* Reading, Mass.: Addison-Wesley, 1987.

Muirden, James. *Astronomy Handbook.* New York: Arco Publishing, 1982.

Murray, Bruce (ed.). *Readings from Scientific American: The Planets.* New York: W. H. Freeman, 1983.

Osterbrock, Donald E. (ed.). *Stars and Galaxies: Citizens of the Universe.* New York: W. H. Freeman, 1990.

Ottewell, Guy.:
Astronomical Calendar 1990. Greenville, S.C.: Furman University Astronomical Workshop, 1989.
Astronomical Calendar 1991. Greenville, S.C.: Furman University Astronomical Workshop, 1990.
The Astronomical Companion. Greenville, S.C.: Furman University Astronomical Workshop, 1979.
To Know the Stars: A Simple Guide to the Night Sky. Greenville, S.C.: Furman University Astronomical Workshop, 1984.

Raymo, Chet. *365 Starry Nights: An Introduction to Astronomy for Every Night of the Year.* New York: Prentice Hall Press, 1982.

Reiber, Duke B. (ed.). *The NASA Mars Conference* (Vol. 71, Science and Technology series). Washington, D.C.: National Aeronautics and Space Administration, 1988.

Rey, H. A. *The Stars: A New Way to See Them.* Boston, Mass.: Houghton Mifflin, 1976.

Richter, Nikolaus B. *The Nature of Comets* (rev. ed.). Translated by Arthur Beer. London: Methuen & Co. Ltd., 1963.

Ridpath, Ian (ed.). *Norton's 2000.0: Star Atlas and Reference Handbook.* New York: John Wiley and Sons, 1989.

Ronan, Colin A. *The Practical Astronomer.* New York: Bonanza Books, 1981.

Rükl, Antonín. *The Amateur Astronomer.* Translated by Olga Kuthanová. London: Octopus Books, 1979.

Ryan, Peter. *Solar System.* New York: Viking Press, 1978.

Sagan, Carl, and Ann Druyan. *Comet.* New York: Random House, 1985.

Sandage, Allan. *The Hubble Atlas of Galaxies.* Washington, D.C.: Carnegie Institution of Washington, 1961.

Smith, Peter J. (ed.). *The Earth.* New York: Macmillan, 1986.

Smoluchowski, Roman. *The Solar System: The Sun, Planets, and Life.* New York: Scientific American Books, 1983.

Snow, Theodore P. *Essentials of the Dynamic Universe: An Introduction to Astronomy* (2d ed.). St. Paul, Minn.: West Publishing, 1987.

Tully, R. Brent, and J. Richard Fisher. *Nearby Galaxies Atlas.* Cambridge, England: Cambridge University Press, 1987.

The Visible Universe (Voyage Through the Universe series). Alexandria, Va.: Time-Life Books, 1990.

Whitney's Star Finder. New York: Alfred A. Knopf, 1989.

Zeilik, Michael, and Elske v. P. Smith. *Introductory Astronomy and Astrophysics* (2d ed.). Philadelphia, Pa.: Saunders College Publishing, 1987.

Zirin, Harold. *Astrophysics of the Sun.* Cambridge, England: Cambridge University Press, 1988.

Periodicals

Baum, Judy M. "Voyager 2 Answering Scientists' Major Questions about Neptune." *Chemical & Engineering News*, September 11, 1989.

Beatty, J. Kelly. "Discovering Pluto's Atmosphere." *Sky & Telescope*, December 1988.

Berry, Richard:
"Neptune Revealed." *Astronomy*, December 1989.
"Triumph at Neptune." *Astronomy*, November 1989.

Cook, William J.:
"The Secrets of Venus." *U.S. News & World Report*, May 13, 1991.
"Voyager's Last Picture Show." *U.S. News & World Report*, September 11, 1989.

Dyer, Alan. "Tracking the Great White." *Astronomy*, March 1991.

Elliot, J. L., et al. "Pluto's Atmosphere." *Icarus*, 1989, Vol. 77, pp. 148-170.

Geller, Margaret J. "Mapping the Universe: Slices and Bubbles." *Mercury*, May-June 1990.

Geller, M. J., and J. P. Huchra. "Mapping the Universe." *Science*, November 17, 1989.

Gore, Rick. "Neptune: Voyager's Last Picture Show." *National Geographic*, August 1990.

Gregory, Stephen A., and Laird A. Thompson. "Superclusters and Voids in the Distribution of Galaxies." *Scientific American*, March 1982.

Horgan, John. "Universal Truths." *Scientific American*, October 1990.

"Hubble Space Telescope: A New View of the Universe." *Observer*, Winter 1991.

"Images." *Sky & Telescope*, March 1991.

Kasting, James F., Owen B. Toon, and James B. Pollack. "How Climate Evolved on the Terrestrial Planets." *Scientific American*, February 1988.

Kerr, Richard A.:
"Geysers or Dust Devils on Triton?" *Science*, October 19, 1990.
"Triton Steals Voyager's Last Show." *Science*, September 1, 1989.

Kinman, T. D. "The Surface Brightness of the Nebulosity in BL Lacertae." *The Astrophysical Journal*, April 15, 1975.

Larson, Richard B. "Galaxy Building." *Publications of the Astronomical Society of the Pacific*, July 1990.

McKinnon, William B. "Around Venus in 37 Days." *Nature*, December 1990.

Maddox, S. J., et al. "The APM Galaxy Survey—I." *Monthly Notices of the Royal Astronomical Society*, April 15, 1990.

Miner, Ellis D. "Voyager 2's Encounter with the Gas Giants." *Physics Today*, July 1990.

"Neptune and Triton: Worlds Apart." *Sky & Telescope*,

February 1990.

"New Distance to the LMC." *Sky & Telescope,* April 1991.

Ostro, Steven J., et al. "Radar Images of Asteroid 1989 PB." *Science,* June 22, 1990.

Preston, Richard. "Beacons in Time: Maarten Schmidt and the Discovery of Quasars." *Mercury,* January-February, 1988.

Smith, Bruce A. "Voyager's Discoveries Mount on Final Rush to Neptune." *Aviation Week & Space Technology,* August 28, 1989.

"A Stellar Volcano." *Observer,* Winter 1991.

"A Storm on Saturn." *Observer,* Winter 1991.

Waldrop, M. Mitchell. "Astronomers Go Up against the Great Wall." *Science,* November 17, 1989.

Wilford, John Noble. "Peering to Edge of Time, Scientists Are Astonished." *New York Times,* November 20, 1989.

Williams, Debra. "Venus Unclouded." *Space,* January-February, 1991.

Other Sources

"Magellan Achieves Primary Mission Objective Early." Press release. Washington, D.C.: National Aeronautics and Space Administration, April 4, 1991.

"Magellan Completes Mapping of Venus Highland Region." Press release. Washington, D.C.: National Aeronautics and Space Administration, February 22, 1991.

"Magellan Mapping of Venus Provides Significant New Knowledge." Press release. Washington, D.C.: National Aeronautics and Space Administration, January 25, 1991.

"Magellan: The Unveiling of Venus." NASA publication no. 300-345. Pasadena, Calif.: Jet Propulsion Laboratory, March 1989.

"Names of Notable Women to be Proposed for Venus Features." Press release. Washington, D.C.: National Aeronautics and Space Administration, March 8, 1991.

National Aeronautics and Space Administration: Photograph caption, *Magellan.* Photo number P-36547/MGN-6. Washington, D.C.: NASA, August 24, 1990. Photograph caption, *Magellan.* Photo number P-36711/MGN 17. Washington, D.C.: NASA, September 24, 1990. Photograph caption, *Magellan.* Photo number P-37125/MGN 18. Washington, D.C.: NASA, November 16, 1990. Photograph caption, *Magellan.* Photo number P-37138/MGN 20. Washington, D.C.: NASA, November 16, 1990. Photograph caption, *Magellan.* Photo number P-37264. Washington, D.C.: December 5, 1990.

Young, Carolynn (ed.). "The Magellan Venus Explorer's Guide." NASA publication no. 90-24. Pasadena, Calif.: Jet Propulsion Laboratory, August 1, 1990.

INDEX

Numerals in italics indicate an illustration of the subject mentioned.

A

Absolute magnitude, 83, *charts* 89; of galaxies, *chart* 112
Absorption lines, 80-81, *84, 85*
Achernar (star), *chart* 89
Active galaxies, *116-117*
Adams, John Couch, 52
Air currents: Earth, *31*
Aldebaran (star), *chart* 89; location, *66*; names for, *chart* 82
Alkaid (star): location, *83*; shifts over time, *84*
Alpha Centauri A and B (stars), *map 88, 89, chart* 89
Alpha Crucis (star), *chart* 89
Alpha Regio, Venus: domed hills, *29*
Altair (star), *chart* 89, *map* 99
Altazimuth mount for telescope, *130*
Altitude and azimuth, 68, 77, 130
Amalthea (moon of Jupiter), *41*
Amor asteroids: orbit, *61*
Analemma, *132*
Andromeda (constellation): as galactic guidepost, *124, 125*; galaxies in, *102, 125*; viewing, *96, map* 100
Andromeda (galaxy), *107*; Hubble's study of, 105; location of, *106, 125*
Antarctic Circumpolar Current, *31*
Antares (star), *chart* 89; location, *67, 77, map* 99
Antennae (galaxies), *115*
Aperture of telescopes, *128*
Aphelion vs. perihelion: asteroids, *61*; comets, *14, chart* 77; Mars, *36*; Mercury, *22, 23*; Pluto, *56*
Aphrodite Terra, Venus, *28*
Apollo asteroids: orbit, *61*
Apparent magnitude, *82, charts* 89
Aquarius (constellation), *63, 67*; viewing, *69*
Aquila (constellation): star in (Altair), *map* 99
Arcturus (star), *chart* 89, *map* 98
Arend-Rigaux (comet), *chart* 77
Argyre Basin, Mars: dust storm, *36*
Ariel (moon of Uranus), *49*
Aries (constellation), *66*
Asteroids, *60-61*; belt, *16, 40*, 60, *61*; double, *60*; Earth approachers, *61*; orbits, *61*; types, *60*
Astrophotography, amateur, *132-133*
Aten asteroids: orbit, *61*
Atmospheres, *chart* 17; Earth, *30*; Jupiter, *42*; Mercury, *22*; Neptune, *54, 55*; Pluto, *56*; Saturn, *46*; Sun, *18, 19*; Titan, *44, 45*; Uranus, *50, 51*; Venus, *26, 27*
Auriga (constellation): bright stars in, locating, *map* 97, *map* 100
Aurorae: Earth, *30*; Jupiter, *43*
Australia: meteorite craters, *63*
Autumn: equinox, *13, 69*; star map, *100*
Azimuth and altitude, 68, 77, 130

B

Background radiation, cosmic, *122*
Barnard's Star, *map* 88, *chart* 89
Barred spiral galaxies, *103, 112*
Beta Centauri (star), *chart* 89
Beta Crucis (star), *chart* 89
Beta Lyrae (star system): light curve, *86*
Betelgeuse (star), *89, chart* 89
Big Bang: leftover radiation from, *122*
Big Dipper (constellation), *82, maps 97-100*; circumpolar movement of, *101*; distances of stars in, *83*; galaxies in, *125*; gauging distances with, *101*; telescope observation of, *129, 131*; through time, *84*
Binary asteroid, *60*
Binary stars, *86*
Binoculars for celestial viewing, *131*
Black holes in galaxies, 116, 117
Blink comparator: Tombaugh's use of, 56
BL Lacertae (galaxy), *116*
Boötes (constellation), *map* 98; tracking, *131*
B star: spectrum, *85*
Bunsen, Robert, 81

C

C, S, and M asteroids, *60*
Callisto (moon of Jupiter), *41, 133*
Caloris Basin, Mercury, *24*
Cancer (constellation), *66*
Canis Major (constellation): viewing, *96, map* 97, *101*
Canis Minor (constellation), *map* 97
Canopus (star), *chart* 89
Capella (star), *chart* 89
Capricornus (constellation), *67*; viewing, *69*
Carbonaceous (C) asteroids, *60*
Carbon dioxide: Venus, 27
Cassegrain reflecting telescope, *127*
Cassiopeia (constellation): viewing, *96, maps* 99-100, *101*
Castor and Pollux (stars), *66*
Catadioptric telescopes, 126, *127*

Celestial mechanics. *See* Orbits
Celestial sphere, *10-11, 12-13*; constellations beyond zodiac, *94*; coordinates on, *92*; galactic guideposts, *124*; latitude and, *95*; Milky Way on, *93*; star maps, *97-100*; visible half of, *68*; zodiac on, *13, 64-65*
Centaurus A (radio source), *90*
Cepheid variables (stars), 105; brightness profile of, *86*
Ceres (asteroid), *60*
Channels: Mars, *38*; Venus, *28*
Charon (moon of Pluto), 56
Christy, James, 56
Chromatic aberration, *126*
Chromosphere, *18, 19*
Churyumov-Gerasimenko (comet), *chart* 77
Circumpolar stars, *101*
Cirrus clouds: Neptune, *54*
Clark (comet), *chart* 77
Clouds: Jupiter, *42*; Neptune, *54*; Venus, *26, 27*
Clovis meteorite, *62*
Clusters and superclusters of galaxies, *2-3, 106, 108, 109, 110-111*
Coma, comet's, *59*
Coma cluster of galaxies, *111*
Comets, *58-59, chart* 77; and meteor showers, *63, chart* 77; orbits, *14, 58, 59, chart* 77; source of, *58*; tails, *59*
Computer simulation of galactic interactions, *115*
Conjunction vs. opposition, 14
Constellations: alterations over time, *84*; circumpolar stars, *101*; extra-zodiacal, *94*; as galactic guideposts, *124-125*; as imaginative constructs, *82, 83*; latitude and, *95*; maps of, *97-100*; meteor showers in, *63, chart* 77; movement during night, *96*; Orion, *63, 78-79, 95, 96, maps 97-98, 101*; seasonal changes, *10-11, 69*; tracking with telescope, *131*. *See also* Zodiac
Continental drift, 32, *33*
Convection currents: Earth, *31*; Jupiter, *42*
Convection zone of Sun, *18, 19*
Copernicus, Nicolaus, 12
Cores: Earth, *33*; Jupiter, *43*; Mars, *39*; Mercury, *25*; Pluto, *57*; Saturn, *47*; Sun, *18*; Uranus, *51*
Coriolis effect: Earth, *31*; Jupiter, *42*
Corona, *18, 19*

Coronal holes, *18*, 19
Coronal mass ejection, *21*
Coronal plasma and solar wind, 20, *21*
Cosmic Background Explorer (COBE) satellite: emissions detected by, *122*
Cosmic background radiation, *122*
Crab nebula, *87*
Craters: Callisto, *41;* Earth, *63;* Mars's moons, *37;* Mercury, *24, 25;* Moon, *35;* Uranus's moons, *49;* Venus, *28*
Critical density of universe, 122, 123
Crusts: Earth, *33;* Mars, *39;* Mercury, *25;* Pluto, *57*
Currents: Earth, *31;* Jupiter, *42;* Venus, *27*
Cygnus (constellation), *map* 99

D
Dark side of Moon, *35*
D'Arrest (comet), *chart* 77
Days, solar vs. sidereal, *15;* Mercury, 15, 22, 23
Declination, *92*, 130
Deimos (moon of Mars), *37*
Delta Aquarids (meteor shower), 63, *chart* 77; location, *63*
Delta Cephei (star): brightness profile of, *86*
Delta ring of Uranus, *50*
Deneb (star), *chart* 89, *map* 99
Density waves, 90, *91*
Deuteron, *18*
Doppler effect, *84*
Dorado (constellation): and Large Magellanic Cloud, *125*
Dubhe (star): shifts over time, *84*
Dumbbell nebula, *87*
Dust storms: Mars, *36*
Dust tail vs. plasma tail of comet, *59*
Dwarf galaxies, *114*

E
Earth, *30-33;* atmosphere, *30;* aurorae, *30;* data, *chart* 17, 30; heat exchange, 30, *31;* interior, *33;* interplanetary magnetic field at, *21;* magnetosphere, *30;* Mars's similarities to, 36; meteorite craters, *63;* meteorites, *62;* and Moon, 34, *35;* ocean currents, *31;* orbit, 12; rotational axis, 12, *13, 35;* tectonic plates, *32, 33;* vegetation zones, *32;* winds, *31. See also* Earth-based observations
Earth-approaching asteroids: orbits, *61*
Earth-based observations: astrophotography, *132-133;* estimating angles, *77;* estimating distances, *101;* meteor showers, 63, *chart* 77; par-

allax measurement, *83*, 104; planets, visibility of, *14, 22, 26, 70-76;* retrograde motion of Jupiter, *15, 76;* rotation, effect of, *65, 68;* from Southern Hemisphere, *95, 101, 125;* telescopes, use of, *126-131. See also* Celestial sphere; Constellations
Eclipses, 34
Eclipsing binary stars, *86*
Ecliptic, *13;* Northern vs. Southern Hemisphere, *101;* orbital inclinations to, *16, chart* 17, *22, 34, 56, 64, chart* 77; seasonal shifts in, 68, *69;* and zodiac, *13, 64-65, 66-67. See also* Celestial sphere
Eisila Regio, Venus: volcano, *29*
Elliptical galaxies, *112, chart* 112, 113; BL Lacertae, *116;* dwarf, *114;* radio (3C449), *117;* in Virgo cluster, *109, 112*
Elysium Mons (volcano), Mars, *38*
Emission lines, 81
Encke (comet), *chart* 77; path of, *59*
Epsilon Eridani (star), *map* 88, *chart* 89
Epsilon Indi (star), *map* 88, *chart* 89
Epsilon ring of Uranus, *50*
Equatorial mount for telescope, *130*
Equinoxes, *13*, 69
Eros (asteroid): orbit, *61*
Eta Aquarids (meteor shower), *chart* 77
Europa (moon of Jupiter), *41, 133*
Evening apparition: Mercury, *70;* Venus, *72*
Expansion of universe, 105

F
Fall: equinox, *13*, 69; star map, *100*
Faye (comet), *chart* 77
Fibrils: Sun, *19*
Finder scopes, use of, *129*
Flora (asteroid), *60*
Flux tubes: Sun, *20*
Focal length of telescopes, *128*
Fomalhaut (star), *chart* 89, *map* 100
Fornax (galaxy), *map* 106, *114*
Fraunhofer, Joseph von, 80-81
Freyja mountain range, Venus, *29*
Fusion reactions in Sun, *18*

G
G 51-15 (star), *map* 88, *chart* 89
Galaxies, 102-125; active, *116-117;* dwarf, *114;* evolution of, *123;* groups of, *2-3, 106, 108, 109, 110-111, 118-121;* interactions of, 107, 113, 115; irregular, *107, chart* 112, *113;* nascent (protogalaxies), *114;* as nebulae, 104, 105; observing, *124-125;* peculiar, *115;* spiral structure, theory of, 90, *91;* types, classification of, *112, chart* 112,

113. See also Milky Way galaxy
Galilean moons of Jupiter, *41, 133;* orbits, *40*
Galileo Galilei, 44, 126
Galileo Regio, Ganymede, *41*
Gamma ray photons in Sun, *18*
Ganymede (moon of Jupiter), *41, 133*
Gehrels 2 (comet), *chart* 77
Geller, Margaret: galactic survey by, *120-121*
Gemini (constellation), *63, 66;* viewing, *69, 96, map* 97
Geminids (meteor shower), 63, *chart* 77; location, *63*
Geocentric vs. heliocentric views, 12
Geographos (asteroid): orbit, *61*
Giacobini-Zinner (comet), *chart* 77
Globular clusters, *87, 91;* vs. dwarf galaxies, *114*
Golubkina crater, Venus, *28*
Gondwana (ancient landmass), *33*
Gravitational interactions: tidal, *35*
Great Dark Spot: Neptune, *54, 55*
Great Red Spot: Jupiter, *42*
Great Wall of galaxies, *121*
Great White Spot: Saturn, *46*
Greeks and Trojans (asteroids), *61*
Greenhouse effect: Venus, *27*
Groombridge 34 A and B (stars), *map* 88, *chart* 89
Gum nebula, *90*
Gunn (comet), *chart* 77
Gyres (circular ocean currents), *31*

H
Halley, Edmond, 58
Halley's comet, *58, chart* 77; path of, *59*
Harrington-Abell (comet), *chart* 77
Hartley 1 (comet), *chart* 77
Heat exchange: Earth, 30, *31*
Helin-Roman-Crockett (comet), *chart* 77
Heliocentric vs. geocentric views, 12
Helium: Sun's production of, *18*
Hellas Basin, Mars, *38*
Helmet streamers, *21*
Hercules (constellation): globular cluster in, *87*
Hercules cluster of galaxies, *111*
Herschel, William, 48
Hertzsprung-Russell (H-R) diagram, 84, *85*
Hoba meteorite, *62*
Hubble, Edwin, 105; classification scheme for galaxies, *112-113*
Hubble Space Telescope: images by, *46*
Huchra, John: galactic survey by, *120-121*
Hyades (stars), 66
Hydrogen: Jupiter, 43; Saturn, 47; Sun's conversion of, to helium, *18*

I

Icecaps, polar: Mars, *36*
Ikeya-Seki (comet): path of, *59*
Impact sites: Hellas Basin, Mars, *38.* *See also* Craters
Inferior orbits: Mercury, *14, 22, 70-71;* vs. superior, *14;* Venus, *26, 72-73*
Infrared radiation: Jupiter, *43;* potential protogalaxy, *114;* Venus, *27*
Interplanetary magnetic field, *21*
Io (moon of Jupiter), *41, 133*
Iron meteorites, *62*
Irregular galaxies, *chart 112, 113;* Large Magellanic Cloud as, *107*
Ishtar Terra, Venus, *28*

J

Jets and lobes, radio, *117*
Johnson (comet), *chart 77*
Jupiter (planet), *40-43;* and asteroids, *61;* astrophotograph of, *133;* atmosphere, *42;* aurorae, *43;* data, *chart 17, 40;* interior, *43;* interplanetary magnetic field at, *21;* magnetosphere, *43;* moons, *41, 133;* moons' orbits, *40;* retrograde motion, *15, 76;* ring system, *41;* Saturn compared to, *46;* zodiacal path of, *76*

K

Kant, Immanuel, *104*
Kearns-Kwee (comet), *chart 77*
Kepler, Johannes: laws of planetary motion, *14*
Kirchhoff, Gustav, *81*
Kirkwood gaps, *61*
Kohoutek (comet): path of, *59*
Kopff (comet), *chart 77*
Krasnojarsk meteorite, *62*

L

Lacaille 9352 (star), *map 88, chart 89*
Lalande 21185 (star), *map 88, chart 89*
Large Magellanic Cloud (galaxy), *107;* location of, *106, 125*
Latitude: view of stars, effect on, *95*
Lavinia region, Venus, *28*
Leavitt, Henrietta, *104-105*
Lenticular galaxies, *113*
Leo (constellation), *66;* galaxy in, *112;* viewing, *69, 96, map 98*
Leonids (meteor shower), *chart 77*
Leverrier, Urbain, *52*
Libra (constellation), *67;* viewing, *69*
Light: Doppler shift, *84;* spectroscopic analysis of, *80-81, 84, 85;* telescopes' bending of, *126-127*
Light curves of stars, *86*
Line of nodes, *34*
Local Group of galaxies, *3, 106;* in

Local Supercluster, *2, 108;* members of, *4, 107, 112, 114*
Local Supercluster of galaxies, *2, 108*
Loop prominences, *19*
Lovas 1 (comet), *chart 77*
Luyten 726-8 A and B, 789-6, and 725-32 (stars), *map 88, chart 89*
Lyra (constellation): star in (Vega), *map 99*
Lyrids (meteor shower), *chart 77*

M

M, S, and C asteroids, *60*
M13 (globular cluster), *87*
M33 (galaxy), *map 106, 112*
M51 (galaxy), *104;* locating, *125*
M81 (galaxy): locating, *125*
M82 (galaxy), *113;* locating, *125*
M84 (galaxy), *109*
M86 (galaxy), *109, 112*
M87 (galaxy), *112*
Machholz (comet), *chart 77*
Magellan (probe): images by, *28-29*
Magellanic Clouds (galaxies), *107;* location of, *106, 125*
Magnetic fields and magnetospheres: Earth, *30;* interplanetary, *21;* Jupiter, *43;* Mercury, *25;* Neptune, *55;* Saturn, *47;* Sun, *19, 20-21;* Uranus, *50, 51*
Magnetotail: Jupiter, *43*
Magnitude of stars, *82-83, charts 89*
Main sequence of stars, *85*
Mantles: Earth, *33;* Mars, *39;* Mercury, *25;* Pluto, *57*
Maria: Moon, *35*
Mariner missions, revelations of: *Mariner 9, 39; Mariner 10, 24, 25*
Mars (planet), *36-39;* in astrophotograph, *133;* data, *chart 17, 36;* geology, *38-39;* interior, *39;* moons, *36, 37;* orbit, *14, 36, 74-75;* seasons, *36;* solar vs. sidereal day, *15;* visibility of, *14, 74-75*
Maximum elongation, *14;* Mercury, *14, 22, 70, 71;* Venus, *26, 72, 73*
Mensa (constellation): and Large Magellanic Cloud, *125*
Mercury (planet), *22-25;* anatomy, *25;* data, *chart 17, 22;* day, *15, 22, 23;* magnetosphere, *25;* orbit, *12, 14, 16, 22, 23, 70-71;* sunrise, double, *23;* surface features, *24, 25;* visibility of, *14, 22, 70-71*
Mesosphere, *30*
Messier, Charles, *104*
Metallic (M) asteroids, *60*
Metallic hydrogen: Jupiter, *43;* Saturn, *47*
Meteorites, *62;* impact site, *63*
Meteoroids and meteors: defined, *62*
Meteor showers, *63, chart 77;* locations, *63*

Methane: Neptune, *54;* Pluto, *57;* Uranus, *50, 51*
Microwave background radiation, *122*
Midocean ridge: Earth, *32*
Milky Way galaxy, *4, 80, 90-91;* astrophotograph, *133;* deviation from ecliptic, *93;* inner disk, *91;* in Local Group, *3, 106;* radio images of, *90, 91;* Solar System's place in, *4, 92;* viewing, *92, 96, maps 97-100*
Miranda (moon of Uranus), *48, 49*
Mizar (star): names for, *chart 82;* telescope viewing of, *129*
Moon, *34-35;* orbital mechanics, *34;* phases, *34;* photographing, *132, 133;* surface features, *35;* and tides, *35*
Moons: Jupiter, *40, 41, 133;* Mars, *36, 37;* Neptune, *52, 53;* number of, *chart 17;* Pluto, *56;* Saturn, *44, 45;* Uranus, *48, 49*
Morning apparition: Mercury, *71;* Venus, *73*
Mountains: Martian volcanoes, *38, 39;* midocean ridge, Earth, *32;* Venus, *29*

N

Nebulae: Crab, *87;* Dumbbell, *87;* galaxies as, *104, 105;* Gum, *90;* North America, *133;* Orion, *78-79, 87;* Tarantula, *107;* Trifid, *87*
Neptune (planet), *52-55;* atmosphere, *54, 55;* data, *chart 17, 52;* interior, *55;* magnetosphere, *55;* moons, *52, 53;* orbit, *52, 56;* rings, *52, 53;* zodiacal path of, *76*
Nereid (moon of Neptune): orbit, *52*
Neutrino, *18*
Neutrons in proton-proton reaction, *18*
Newton, Isaac, *80;* reflecting telescopes devised by, *126, 127*
NGC 175 (galaxy), *112*
NGC 891 (galaxy), *102*
NGC 2525 (galaxy), *112*
NGC 2811 (galaxy), *112*
NGC 3377 (galaxy), *112*
NGC 4622 (galaxy), *112*
NGC 5102 (galaxy), *113*
NGC 5128 (galaxy): radio source, *90*
NGC 5383 (galaxy), *112*
NGC 7252 (galaxy), *115*
NGC 7479 (galaxy), *103*
1989PB (binary asteroid), *60*
Nitrogen: Triton, *53*
North America nebula, *133*
Northern Claw (star): location, *67*
Northern Cross (constellation), *map 99*

North Polar Spur, Milky Way, *90*
Novae, 86; Nova Cygni 75, *86*
Nuclear reactions in Sun, *18*

O

Oberon (moon of Uranus), *49*
Oceans, Earth's: currents, *31;* ridge,
 32; tides, cause of, *35*
Octahedrite meteorite, *62*
Olympus Mons (volcano), Mars, *39*
Oort, Jan, 58
Oort cloud, *58*
Ophiuchus (constellation), 67
Opposition: vs. conjunction, 14; Mars
 at, 74, *75*
Orbital plane. *See* Ecliptic
Orbits, 12-13, *14-15, 16, chart* 17, 64;
 asteroids, *61;* comets, 14, *58, 59,
 chart* 77; distances, *16-17, chart*
 17; Jupiter's moons, *40;* Kepler's
 laws, *14;* Mars, 14, *36,* 74-75;
 Mars's moons, *37;* Mercury, 12, *14,
 16, 22, 23,* 70-71; Moon, *34;* Nep-
 tune, *52, 56;* Neptune's moons, *52;*
 Pluto, 16, *56;* retrograde illusion,
 12-13, *15,* 74-75, *76;* Saturn, *44;*
 Saturn's moons, *45;* and solar vs.
 sidereal day, *15;* star system, *86;*
 Uranus, *48;* Uranus's moons, *49;*
 Uranus's rings, *50;* Venus, 12, *26,*
 72-73
Orion (constellation), 63, *78-79;* position of, *95, 96, maps* 97-98, *101;*
 star in (Betelgeuse), *89*
Orionids (meteor shower), 63, *chart*
 77; location, *63*
Orion nebula, *78-79, 87*
Outer planets: retrograde motion,
 12-13, *15,* 76. *See also individual
 names*

P

Parallax shift, *83,* 104
Parker-Hartley (comet), *chart* 77
Parsons, William, 104
Peculiar galaxies, *115*
Pegasus (constellation): galaxy in,
 103; Great Square of, *100,* 125;
 viewing, *96, map* 100
Penzias, Arno, 122
Perihelion vs. aphelion: asteroids,
 61; comets, 14, *chart* 77; Mars, *36;*
 Mercury, 22, *23;* Pluto, *56*
Period-luminosity law for Cepheid
 variables, 105
Perseids (meteor shower), 63, *chart*
 77; location, *63*
Perseus (constellation), 63
Perseus cluster of galaxies, *111*
Peters-Hartley (comet), *chart* 77
Phases of Moon, *34*
Phobos (moon of Mars), *37*
Photon migration through Sun, *18*

Photosphere, *18, 19*
Pinwheel (galaxy; M33), *map* 106,
 112
Pioneer Venus Orbiter (spacecraft):
 topographic globe of Venus by, *28*
Pisces (constellation), *66;* viewing, *96*
Planetary motion. *See* Orbits
Planetary nebula, *87*
Planets, *17, chart* 17; minor (aster-
 oids), *16, 40,* 60-61; tenth, search
 for, *57. See also* Earth; Jupiter;
 Mars; Mercury; Neptune; Pluto;
 Saturn; Uranus; Venus
Plasma, solar, *19;* as solar wind, 20,
 21
Plasma sheet around Jupiter, *43*
Plasma tail of comet, *59*
Plate tectonics, *32, 33*
Pleiades (stars), *87, 133*
Pluto (planet), *56-57;* data, *chart* 17,
 56; interior, *57;* moon, *56;* orbit,
 16, *56;* surface features, *57*
Polar icecaps: Mars, *36*
Polaris (star): location, *94, 95, maps*
 97-100; stars circling, *101*
Pollux (star), *chart* 89; location, *66*
Positron, *18*
Precession, *35*
Procyon A and B (stars), *map* 88,
 chart 89
Prominences, solar, *19*
Protogalaxies, *114*
Proton-proton chain, *18*
Proxima Centauri (star), *map* 88,
 chart 89
Psyche (asteroid), *60*
Ptolemy (Greek astronomer), 12, *94*

Q

Quadrantids (meteor shower), 63,
 chart 77; location, *63*
Quasars, *116;* 3C273, locating, *125*

R

Radiative zone of Sun, *18*
Radio galaxy, *117*
Radio images of Milky Way, *90, 91*
Ra-Shalom (asteroid): orbit, *61*
Red giant star: spectrum, *85*
Redshift, *84*
Red supergiant star: Betelgeuse, *89*
Reflecting telescopes, 126, *127*
Refracting telescopes, *126*
Regular galaxies: lenticular, *113. See
 also* Elliptical galaxies; Spiral gal-
 axies
Regulus (star): location, *66, map* 98
Retrograde motion: Mars, *74-75;* out-
 er planets, 12-13, *15,* 76
Ridge, midocean: Earth, *32*
Rigel (star), *79, chart* 89
Right ascension, *92*
Rings: Jupiter, *41;* Neptune, 52, *53;*

Saturn, *44, 45;* Uranus, 48, 49, *50*
Ross 154, 248, and 128 (stars), *map*
 88, *chart* 89
Russell 3 (comet), *chart* 77

S

S, C, and M asteroids, *60*
Sagittarius (constellation), 67, *map*
 99; nebula in (Trifid), *87*
Sagittarius A (radio source), *91*
Sanguin (comet), *chart* 77
Saturn (planet), *44-47;* atmosphere,
 46; data, *chart* 17, 44; interior, *47;*
 magnetosphere, *47;* moons, 44, *45;*
 rings, *44, 45;* zodiacal path of, *76*
Schmidt, Maarten, 125
Schmidt-Cassegrain telescope, *127;*
 photography through, *133*
Scooter (cloud): Neptune, *54*
Scorpius (constellation), *67;* viewing,
 69, map 99
Seasonal changes, *13,* 68, 69; celes-
 tial sphere and, *10-11, 12-13,* 124;
 Mars, *36;* Milky Way, 92, *maps* 97-
 100; star maps, *97-100*
Seyfert, Carl, 117
Seyfert galaxies, *117*
Shoemaker-Holt 1 (comet), *chart* 77
Short-period comets, *chart* 77; paths
 of, *58, 59*
Sidereal days: Mercury, *22;* vs. solar
 day, *15*
Sif Mons (volcano), Venus, *29*
Silicaceous (S) asteroids, *60*
Sirius A and B (stars), *map* 88, *chart*
 89
61 Cygni A and B (stars), *map* 88,
 chart 89
Sky watching. *See* Earth-based ob-
 servations
Slipher, Vesto, 57
Small Dark Spot: Neptune, *54*
Small Magellanic Cloud (galaxy), *107;*
 location of, *106, 125*
Smirnova-Chernykh (comet), *chart* 77
Solar cycle, *20*
Solar days: Mercury, *23;* vs. sidereal
 day, *15*
Solar prominences, *19*
Solar System, *5, 16;* astro-
 photographs of, *132-133;* Milky
 Way, position in, *4,* 92. *See also*
 Comets; Planets; Sun
Solar wind, 20, *21. See also* Magnetic
 fields and magnetospheres
Solstices, *13,* 69
Southern Claw (star): location, 67
Southern Cross (constellation): posi-
 tion of, at different latitudes, *95*
Southern Hemisphere: views from,
 95, 101, 125
Spectra and spectroscopy, 80-81, *84,
 85*

Spica (star), *chart* 89; location, *67,* *map* 98
Spicules: Sun, *19*
Spiral galaxies, 90, 104, *112, chart* 112, 113; Andromeda, 105, *107;* barred, *103, 112;* density waves in, theory of, 90, *91;* Seyfert, *117. See also* Milky Way
Spring: equinox, *13, 69;* star map, *98*
Stargazing. *See* Earth-based observations
Starmaking material. *See* Nebulae
Stars, 78-89, *maps* 97-100, binary, *86;* brightest, *89, chart* 89; coordinates of, *92;* distances to, determining, 82, 83, 104-105; globular clusters, *87, 91,* 114; Hertzsprung-Russell diagram, 84, *85;* magnitude, *82-83, charts* 89; mass, judging, *86;* motion, components of, *84;* names for, *chart* 82; nearest, *4, 88, 89, chart* 89; Pleiades, *87, 133;* spectroscopic analysis, 80-81, *84, 85;* temperature, correlates of, *85;* variable, *86,* 105. *See also* Constellations; Galaxies; Sun
Stickney crater, Phobos, *37*
Stony and stony-iron meteorites, *62*
Stratosphere, *30*
Struve 2398 A and B (stars), *map* 88, *chart* 89
Sulfuric acid clouds: Venus, *27*
Summer: solstice, *13, 69;* star map, *99*
Summer Triangle of stars, *maps* 99-100
Sun, *18-21;* analemma, *132;* anatomy of, *18;* atmospheric layers of, *18, 19;* magnetism, 19, *20-21;* Mercury, effect on, *22;* and Moon, *34, 35;* and neighboring stars, *4, 88;* nuclear reactions in, *18;* seasonal shifts in, *13,* 68, *69;* zodiacal path of, *13, 66-67. See also* Orbits
Sun-grazing comet: path of, *59*
Sunrise, double: Mercury, *23*
Sunspots, *19;* cycle of, *20*
Superclusters of galaxies: chains of, *110-111;* Local Supercluster, *2,* 108
Supergranular cells: Sun, *19*
Superior orbits: vs. inferior, *14;* Mars, *14, 74-75*
Supermassive black holes, 116
Supernova remnants: Crab nebula, *87;* Gum nebula, *90*

Swift-Gehrels (comet), *chart* 77
Synchronous orbit distance: Mars, *37*

T
Tails of comets, *59*
Tarantula nebula, *107*
Tau Ceti (star), *map* 88, *chart* 89
Taurids (meteor shower), *chart* 77
Taurus (constellation), *66, 82;* Crab nebula in, *87;* Pleiades in, *87, 133;* viewing, *69, 96, map* 97, *map* 100, *101*
Tectonic plates, *32, 33*
Telescopes, *126-131;* aperture and focal length, *128;* binoculars, *131;* finder scopes, *129;* galaxy hunting with, *124-125;* mounts, *130;* photography through, *133;* tracking with, *131;* types, *126-127*
Tempel 2 (comet), *chart* 77
Thermonuclear reactions in Sun, *18*
Thermosphere, *30*
3C273 (quasar): locating, *125*
3C449 (galaxy), *117*
Tides: cause of, *35*
Titan (moon of Saturn), 44, *45*
Titania (moon of Uranus), 48, *49*
Tombaugh, Clyde, 56, 57
Trifid nebula, *87*
Triton (moon of Neptune), *53;* orbit, 52
Tritton (comet), *chart* 77
Trojans and Greeks (asteroids), *61*
Troposphere, *30*
Tucana (constellation): Small Magellanic Cloud in, *125*

U
Umbriel (moon of Uranus), *49*
Universe: expansion of, 105; galactic structure of, *118-121;* history and fate of, 122, *123*
Uranus (planet), *48-51;* data, *chart* 17, 48; interior, *51;* magnetic field, 50, *51;* moons, 48, *49;* orbit, *48;* rings, 48, 49, *50;* zodiacal path of, *76*
Ursa Major (constellation): as galactic guidepost, *124;* viewing, 96. *See also* Big Dipper
Ursa Minor (constellation): viewing, 96, *101*
Ursids (meteor shower), *chart* 77
UV Ceti (star; L726-8 B), *map* 88, *chart* 89

V
Valles Marineris (canyon complex), Mars, *39*
Van Biesbroeck (comet), *chart* 77
Variable stars, *86,* 105
Vega (star), *chart* 89, *map* 99
Vela supernova: remnants of, *90*
Venus (planet), *26-29;* clouds, 26, *27;* data, *chart* 17, 26; greenhouse effect, *27;* orbit, 12, 26, *72-73;* photographing, *132;* surface features, *28-29;* visibility of, *26, 72-73*
Vernal and autumnal equinoxes, *13, 69*
Viking missions to Mars, images by, *39; Viking 1, 37*
Vires-akka Chasma, Venus, *28*
Virgo (constellation), *67;* as quasar location, *124, 125;* star in (Spica), *67, map* 98
Virgo cluster: galaxies in, *109,* 112; in Local Supercluster, *2,* 108
Volcanoes: Mars, *38, 39;* Venus, *29*
Voyager missions: to Jupiter, *41, 43;* to Neptune, *52, 53, 54;* to Saturn, *45;* to Uranus, 48, *49,* 50
Voyager 1 spacecraft: Jovian aurorae, photo of, *43;* Jovian ring system detected by, *41;* Titan, photo of, *45*
Voyager 2 spacecraft, findings of: about Neptune, *52-55;* about Uranus, 48, *49, 50*
Vulpecula (constellation): planetary nebula in (Dumbbell), *87*

W
Waingaromia meteorite, *62*
Whirlpool (galaxy; M51), 104; locating, *125*
White dwarf stars: novae, *86*
Wild 2 (comet), *chart* 77
Wilson, Robert, 122
Winds: Earth, *31;* Uranus, 50
Winter: solstice, *13, 69;* star map, *97*
Wolf 359 (star), *map* 88, *chart* 89
Wolf-Harrington (comet), *chart* 77

Z
Zodiac, 13, *66-67;* on celestial sphere, *13, 64-65;* constellations outside, *94;* Mars's path through, *74-75;* Mercury's path through, *70-71;* outer planets' path through, *76;* seasonal shifts in, *69;* Venus's path through, *72-73*

ACKNOWLEDGMENTS

The editors wish to thank Kirk D. Borne, Space Telescope Science Institute, Baltimore, Md.; Robert A. Brown, Space Telescope Science Institute, Baltimore, Md.; Robert H. Brown, Jet Propulsion Laboratory, Pasadena, Calif.; Marc Buie, Space Telescope Science Institute, Baltimore, Md.; Marcia Bussey, NASA Department of Request Coordination and User Support, Greenbelt, Md.; Geoffrey R. Chester, National Air and Space Museum, Washington, D.C.; Dennis di Cicco, *Sky & Telescope,* Cambridge, Mass.; Gene Carl Feldman, NASA Goddard Space Flight Center, Greenbelt, Md.; Robert Fudali, National Museum of Natural History, Washington, D.C.; Margaret Geller, Smithsonian Astrophysical Observatory, Cambridge, Mass.; Kathy Hoyt, United States Geological Survey, Flagstaff, Ariz.; Andrew Ingersoll, California Institute of Technology, Pasadena, Calif.; William Kaula, University of California at Los Angeles, Calif.; T. D. Kinman, National Optical Astronomy Observatories, Tucson, Ariz.; Frank Lapore, National Oceanic and Atmospheric Administration, Suitland, Md.; William McKinnon, Washington University, St. Louis, Mo.; Alan MacRobert, *Sky & Telescope,* Cambridge, Mass.; Haig Morgan, United States Geological Survey, Flagstaff, Ariz.; Lisa Vasquez Morrison, Lyndon B. Johnson Space Center, Houston, Tex.; Jacques-Clair Noëns, Observatoire du Pic-du-Midi, France; Guy Ottewell, Furman University, Greenville, S.C.; Thomas N. Pyke, Jr., National Oceanic and Atmospheric Administration, Washington, D.C.; Christopher Russell, University of California at Los Angeles, Calif.; Fred Schaaf, Millville, N.J.; Rudolph E. Schild, Center for Astrophysics, Cambridge, Mass.; François Schweizer, Carnegie Institution of Washington, Washington, D.C.; Paul Spudis, National Air and Space Museum, Washington, D.C.; Marie Tharp, South Nyack, N.Y.; David Tholen, Institute for Astronomy, Honolulu, Hawaii; Ray Villard, Space Telescope Science Institute, Baltimore, Md.; Marie-Josée Vin, Observatoire de Haute-Provence, France.

PICTURE CREDITS

The sources for the illustrations in this book are listed below. Credits from left to right are separated by semicolons, from top to bottom by dashes.

Cover: Art by Stephen R. Wagner. Front and back endpapers: Art by Time-Life Books. 2-5: Art by Alfred T. Kamajian. 10, 11: Art by Stephen R. Wagner. 12, 13: Art by Time-Life Books—art by Stephen R. Wagner. 14, 15: Art by Damon Hertig (2); art by Fred Holz; art by Damon Hertig (2). 16, 17: Art by Time-Life Books (3); art by Damon Hertig. 18, 19: NASA; art by Stephen Bauer; Finley Holiday Film Corporation. 20, 21: Art by Stephen Bauer; art by Fred Devita. 22, 23: Art by Damon Hertig—art by Matt McMullen; art by Rob Wood of Stansbury, Ronsaville, Wood, Inc. Inset art by Damon Hertig. 24, 25: U.S. Geological Survey, Flagstaff, Ariz.—art by Rob Wood of Stansbury, Ronsaville, Wood, Inc.; art by Fred Holz (2); NASA/JPL (2); art by Rob Wood of Stansbury, Ronsaville, Wood, Inc.—art by Alfred T. Kamajian. 26, 27: NASA—art by Damon Hertig; NASA (4)—art by Rob Wood of Stansbury, Ronsaville, Wood, Inc.—art by Rob Wood and Yvonne Gensurowsky of Stansbury, Ronsaville, Wood, Inc. 28, 29: NASA. 30, 31: NASA courtesy National Space Data Center—John W. Warden/Superstock; art by Alfred T. Kamajian—art by Rob Wood of Stansbury, Ronsaville, Wood, Inc. (4). 32, 33: NASA—art by Alfred T. Kamajian—© 1977 Marie Tharp, New York; art by Fred Holz (3); art by Yvonne Gensurowsky of Stansbury, Ronsaville, Wood, Inc. 34, 35: NASA courtesy National Space Data Center—Lick Observatory (7)—art by Matt McMullen (3); art by Mark Robinson—NASA, Johnson Space Center, Houston, Tex.; Lick Observatory. 36, 37: Dr. Philip James/University of Toledo, NASA/ESA—art by Matt McMullen—NASA/JPL (2); Eric Thouvenot, Christian Buil, François Colas, and Jean Lecacheux; the image of Mars was taken from the Observatoire du Pic-du-Midi; NASA/U.S. Geological Survey, Flagstaff, Ariz.; art by Stephen R. Wagner, insets NASA/JPL. 38, 39: U.S. Geological Survey, Flagstaff, Ariz., except upper right, art by Matt McMullen. 40, 41: Finley Holiday Film Corporation—art by Matt McMullen—art by Stephen R. Wagner; NASA/U.S. Geological Survey, Flagstaff, Ariz.—NASA courtesy National Space Science Data Center; NASA/JPL (2). 42, 43: Art by Rob Wood of Stansbury, Ronsaville, Wood, Inc. (2); NASA/JPL (2); art by Stansbury, Ronsaville, Wood, Inc. (2). 44, 45: NASA, Space Telescope Science Institute—art by Matt McMullen (2); art by Fred Holz (2); NASA, courtesy National Space Science Data Center. 46, 47: NASA/JPL—NASA/Space Telescope (4); art by Matt McMullen—art by Alfred T. Kamajian. 48, 49: NASA/JPL—art by Matt McMullen; art by Fred Holz (2); NASA/JPL (4)—NASA/JPL courtesy National Space Data Center—NASA/JPL. 50, 51: NASA/JPL; art by Matt McMullen—art by Alfred T. Kamajian. 52, 53: NASA/JPL—art by Matt McMullen; art by Fred Holz; NASA/JPL (4). 54, 55: NASA/JPL (7); art by Alfred T. Kamajian (3)—art by Matt McMullen. 56, 57: NASA/ESA—art by Matt McMullen; NASA/JPL—art by Matt McMullen. 58, 59: Lowell Observatory, courtesy European Space Agency, Paris—art by Time-Life Books; art by Alfred T. Kamajian; art by Fred Holz. 60, 61: Steven Ostro/JPL; art by Andrew Chaikin; art by Stephen

R. Wagner—art by Fred Holz; art by Time-Life Books. 62, 63: Smithsonian Institution (4); art by Fred Holz (5)—David J. Roddy, Eugene M. Shoemaker, and Carolyn Shoemaker, U.S. Geological Survey, Flagstaff, Ariz. 64, 65: Art by Stephen R. Wagner. Inset art by Time-Life Books. 66-68: Art by Stephen R. Wagner. 69: Art by Stephen R. Wagner (4); art by Time-Life Books (4). 70-75: Art by Stephen R. Wagner—art by Time-Life Books. 76, 77: Art by Stephen R. Wagner—art by Time-Life Books (3); art by Fred Holz (5). 78, 79: David Malin and Anglo-Australian Observatory. 80, 81: Finley Holiday Film Corporation. 82, 83: Art by Fred Holz (2); art by Mark Robinson (2)—art by Fred Holz—art by Damon Hertig. 84, 85: Art by Fred Holz (2); art by William Hennessy; art by Nick Schrenk (2). Spectrum art by William Hennessy. 86, 87: Lick Observatory (2); art by Fred Holz (3); Finley Holiday Film Corporation; courtesy Royal Observatory, Edinburgh—Finley Holiday Film Corporation; National Optical Astronomy Observatories (3). 88, 89: Art by Alfred T. Kamajian; National Optical Astronomy Observatories (2). 90, 91: Justis Jonas courtesy *Astronomy Magazine;* art by Damon Hertig (2)—art by David Jonason/The Pushpin Group; National Radio Astronomy Observatory. 92, 93: Art by Stephen R. Wagner. Inset art by Time-Life Books. 94, 95: Art by Stephen R. Wagner. 96, 97: Art by Time-Life Books; art by Stephen R. Wagner. 98-100: Stephen R. Wagner. 101: Art by Time-Life Books. 102, 103: © 1987 Dr. James D. Wray, McDonald Observatory; Smithsonian Astrophysical Observatory, Cambridge, Mass. 104, 105: National Optical Astronomy Observatories. 106, 107: Art by Stephen R. Wagner; Smithsonian Astrophysical Observatory, Cambridge, Mass.—Anglo-Australian Observatory (2). 108, 109: Art by Alfred T. Kamajian; National Optical Astronomy Observatories. 110, 111: Art by Yvonne Gensurowsky; National Optical Astronomy Observatories (3). 112: National Optical Astronomy Observatories; *The Hubble Atlas of Galaxies* (2); Hale Observatories—Hale Observatories; National Optical Astronomy Observatories (2)—Hale Observatories; National Optical Astronomy Observatories; Hale Observatories. Insets National Optical Astronomy Observatories; *The Hubble Atlas of Galaxies* (2)—Hale Observatories; National Optical Astronomy Observatories (2)—Hale Observatories; National Optical Astronomy Observatories (2). 113: Anglo-Australian Observatory—Smithsonian Astrophysical Observatory. 114, 115: Richard Elston, George Riehe, and Marcia Riehe—Anglo-Australian Observatory; François Schweizer (2); sequence art by Matt McMullen. 116, 117: T. D. Kinman, Kitt Peak National Observatory—National Optical Astronomy Observatories; Lick Observatory—National Radio Astronomy Observatory/The Astronomical Society of the Pacific. 118, 119: Maddox, Sutherland, Efstathiou, and Loveday, Oxford Astrophysics, England; Changbom Park, Pasadena, Calif. 120, 121: Art by Yvonne Gensurowsky; Smithsonian Center for Astrophysics (2). 122, 123: NASA; art by Fred Holz (2). 124, 125: Art by Stephen R. Wagner; art by Fred Holz (4). 126, 127: Art by Stephen R. Wagner—art by Matt McMullen. 128-131: Art by Matt McMullen. 132, 133: William P. Sterne, Jr., Tulsa, Okla.; Dennis di Cicco; Christopher Galfo, Auberry, Calif.; Michael Stecker, Los Angeles, Calif.—Dennis di Cicco.

Time-Life Books is a division of Time Life Inc.,
a wholly owned subsidary of
THE TIME INC. BOOK COMPANY

TIME-LIFE BOOKS

PRESIDENT: Mary N. Davis

MANAGING EDITOR: Thomas H. Flaherty
Director of Editorial Resources:
Elise D. Ritter-Clough
Executive Art Director: Ellen Robling
Director of Photography and Research:
John Conrad Weiser
Editorial Board: Dale M. Brown, Roberta Conlan,
Laura Foreman, Lee Hassig, Jim Hicks, Blaine
Marshall, Rita Thievon Mullin, Henry Woodhead
*Assistant Director of Editorial Resources/
Training Manager:* Norma E. Shaw

PUBLISHER: Robert H. Smith

Associate Publisher: Trevor Lunn
Editorial Director: Donia Steele
Marketing Director: Regina Hall
Director of Production Services: Robert N. Carr
Production Manager: Marlene Zack
Supervisor of Quality Control: James King

Editorial Operations
Production: Celia Beattie
Library: Louise D. Forstall
Computer Composition: Deborah G. Tait
(Manager), Monika D. Thayer, Janet Barnes
Syring, Lillian Daniels
Interactive Media Specialist: Patti H. Cass

Correspondents: Elisabeth Kraemer-Singh (Bonn),
Christine Hinze (London), Christina Lieberman
(New York), Maria Vincenza Aloisi (Paris), Ann
Natanson (Rome). Valuable assistance was also
provided by Elizabeth Brown, Katheryn White
(New York), Judy Aspinall (London).

VOYAGE THROUGH THE UNIVERSE

SERIES EDITOR: Roberta Conlan
Series Administrator: Norma E. Shaw

Editorial Staff for *Atlas*
Art Directors: Robert Herndon, Cynthia T.
Richardson (principal), Barbara M. Sheppard
Picture Editor: Tina McDowell
Text Editor: Robert M. S. Somerville
Associate Editors/Research: Barbara Levitt,
Mary H. McCarthy
Assistant Editors/Research: Dan Kulpinski,
Patricia A. Mitchell, Quentin G. Story, Elizabeth
Thompson
Writers: Mark Galan, Darcie Conner Johnston
Assistant Art Directors: Bill McKenney, Brook
Mowrey
Editorial Assistant: Katie Mahaffey
Copy Coordinator: Juli Duncan
Picture Coordinator: David Beard

Special Contributors: George Constable (text);
Paul Edholm, Jocelyn Lindsay, Valerie May, Elizabeth Powell-James, Pamela Whitney (research);
John Drummond (design); Barbara L. Klein
(index).

CONSULTANTS

JOHN C. BRANDT is an astronomer at the University of Colorado at Boulder, where he studies
cometary plasma tails, focusing on their interaction
with the solar wind.

JOHN B. CARLSON teaches astronomy at the Uni-
versity of Maryland and serves as Director of the
Center for Archaeoastronomy in College Park,
Maryland.

GEOFFREY R. CHESTER, a member of the staff of
the Smithsonian Institution's Albert Einstein Plan-
etarium in Washington, D.C., lectures widely on all
aspects of astronomy. He is a noted astrophotog-
rapher, whose work appears in several astronomy
magazines.

MARGARET J. GELLER, a professor of astronomy
at Harvard University, works as an astrophysicist
at the Harvard-Smithsonian Center for Astrophysics and is a senior astronomer with the Smithsonian
Institution.

STEPHEN A. GREGORY is an astronomer affiliated
with the University of New Mexico's Department of
Physics and Astronomy. His area of interest is galaxy superclusters.

JOHN P. HUCHRA, an observational cosmologist, is
a professor of astronomy at Harvard University, the
associate director of the Harvard-Smithsonian Center for Astrophysics, and a senior astronomer with
the Smithsonian Institution.

JAMES B. KALER, an expert on spectroscopy, teaches stellar astronomy at the University of Illinois.

STEPHEN MARAN is a veteran astronomer with
extensive experience in the development and use of
both space and ground-based telescopes.

BRIAN MARSDEN, an astronomer specializing in
the orbital motions of comets and asteroids, is the
Associate Director for Planetary Sciences at the
Harvard-Smithsonian Center for Astrophysics in
Cambridge, Massachusetts.

ELLIS D. MINER, a Voyager assistant project scientist from 1978 through March 1990, is the science
manager for the Cassini mission to Saturn and Titan
and for the Comet Rendezvous and Asteroid Flyby
(CRAF) mission.

CHRISTOPHER RUSSELL is a professor of geophys-
ics and space physics in the Department of Earth
and Space Sciences at the University of California at
Los Angeles. His interests include Earth's magnetosphere, the planets, and interplanetary space.

PAUL D. SPUDIS is a senior staff scientist at the
Lunar and Planetary Institute, Houston, Texas. He
is a principal investigator in the NASA Planetary
Geology Program.

LAIRD A. THOMPSON is an astronomer at the University of Illinois. His areas of interest include cosmology and the study of galaxies.

**Library of Congress Cataloging in
Publication Data**
Atlas / by the editors of Time-Life Books.
p.   cm. (Voyage through the universe).
Bibliography: p.
Includes index.
ISBN 0-8094-6945-6
ISBN 0-8094-6946-4 (lib. bdg.).
1. Astronomy—Atlases.
I. Time-Life Books. II. Series.
QB65.A8 1991
520—dc20   90-47597 CIP

For information on and a full description of
any of the Time-Life Books series, please call
1-800-621-7026 or write:
Reader Information
Time-Life Customer Service
P.O. Box C-32068
Richmond, Virginia 23261-2068